a
casebook
in
group
therapy

with contributing authors

RAYMOND M. BERGER

JAY J. CAYNER

JEFF COURT

PHILLIPS KINDY, JR.

KEVIN MURPHY

LINDA PARICIO

PATRICIA M. PATTERSON

ALISON ROESSLE

STEVEN P. SCHINKE

AUDREY SISTLER

JAMES A. HALL

RON TOSELAND

LYN VEST

STANLEY L. WITKIN

STEPHEN E. WONG

TONI A. ZANDER

SHELDON D. ROSE

a
casebook
in
group
therapy

a behavioral-cognitive approach

PRENTICE-HALL, INC., Englewood Cliffs, New Jersey 07632

Library of Congress Cataloging in Publication Data

Main entry under title:

A Casebook in group therapy.

Bibliography: p.
Includes index.
1. Group psychotherapy—Case studies.   2. Cognitive
therapy—Case studies.   3. Behavior therapy—Case
studies.   I. Rose, Sheldon D.
RC488.C357 1979   616.8'915   79-15404
ISBN 0-13-117408-8

Printed in the United States of America

10   9   8   7   6   5   4   3   2   1

Editorial Production/Supervision by Penny Linskey and Barbara Kelly
Interior design by Amy Midgley
Cover design by A Good Thing, Inc.
Manufacturing buyer: Ray Keating

PRENTICE-HALL INTERNATIONAL, INC., *London*
PRENTICE-HALL OF AUSTRALIA PTY. LIMITED, *Sydney*
PRENTICE-HALL OF CANADA, LTD., *Toronto*
PRENTICE-HALL OF INDIA PRIVATE LIMITED, *New Delhi*
PRENTICE-HALL OF JAPAN, INC., *Tokyo*
PRENTICE-HALL OF SOUTHEAST ASIA PTE. LTD., *Singapore*
WHITEHALL BOOKS LIMITED, *Wellington, New Zealand*

this book is dedicated
to a Bouquet of Roses
Cindy, Leah, Wendy, and Alisa

contents

contributors

Raymond Berger is an assistant professor in Social Work at Florida International University. He received his Ph.D. in Social Welfare at the University of Wisconsin-Madison in 1976. His research interests and publications are centered on the aging and their adjustment patterns, social skill training, and mental health.

Jay Caynor received a master's degree in social work from the University of Wisconsin in 1976. He is now employed at the Pain Management Center of University Hospital, Madison, Wisconsin. His major interests are in developing coping strategies for pain management and working with patients and their families in developing communication skills.

Jeffrey Court received his master's degree in social work from the University of Wisconsin-Madison in 1976. Mr. Court is presently the coordinator of Children's Day Treatment Services for the Brown County Mental Health Center in Green Bay, Wisconsin. His current research interest is in developing a self-report questionnaire for parents and teachers who have referred children to the agency.

James Hall received his Ph.D. from the School of Social Work, University of Wisconsin-Madison in 1979. At present he is an assistant research professor at the School of Social Work, University of Washington in Seattle. His research and clinical interests include interview training, assertion training groups, leadership, single parents and adolescent social skills training.

Phillips Kindy, Jr. received his master's degree in 1975 from the School of Social Work of the University of Wisconsin-Madison. He is on the faculty of the Adult Medicine Clinic, School of Medicine, Madison, Wisconsin, and is a practicing group therapist in that clinic. His research interests include obesity and psychosomatic illness.

Kevin Murphy is currently working toward a bachelor's degree in social work at the University of Wisconsin-Madison.

Linda J. Paricio received her M.S.S.W. from the University of Wisconsin-Madison in 1976. She is currently the school social worker for the Milwaukee Center for Autistic Children (Milwaukee Public Schools). Her research and clinical interests lie in the area of autism and exceptional education, including work with families and within the community.

Patricia Miles Patterson received her M.S.S.W. from the University of Wisconsin School of Social Work in 1978. She is also certified by the American Association of Sex Educators, Counselors, and Therapists as a sex educator and therapist since 1976. She is currently employed at Midwest Sexual Counseling and Psychotherapy Center in Madison, Wisconsin. Her clinical and research interests include sexual functioning, psychosocial aspects of chronic diseases and mental and physical handicaps, depression, anxiety, and women's concerns.

Alison A. Roessle received her M.S.S.W. in 1978 from the University of Wisconsin-Madison. Presently she is employed by the Department of Family Medicine and Practice, University of Wisconsin, as an Academic Staff Specialist. Her responsibilities include family, individual, and group therapy, and education and supervision of resident physicians. One of her professional goals is to combine clinical work, research, and education in her practice.

Sheldon Rose received his Ph.D. from the University of Amsterdam (the Netherlands) in 1960. He is presently Professor of Social Work at the University of Wisconsin-Madison, where he teaches courses in group work and group therapy, interviewing, and behavior modification, and does outcome research on small groups. He is also director of the interpersonal skill training and research project and author of several earlier books on group therapy from a behavioral perspective.

Steven P. Schinke received his Ph.D. in social welfare from the University of Wisconsin-Madison in 1975. Currently, he is Director of Social Services, Child Development and Mental Retardation Center, and Associate Professor, School of Social Work, University of Washington. Dr. Schinke's interests and publications span areas of research with mentally retarded adults, adolescents, and young parents.

Audrey Sistler received her master's degree in social work from the University of Wisconsin-Madison in 1975. She is presently employed as a nursing home ombudsman specialist by the Louisiana Aging Services Bureau. Her major clinical interests are in programs to increase self-advocacy and self-sufficiency of older people.

Ronald Toseland received his Ph.D. in social work from the University of Wisconsin-Madison in 1977. He is presently assistant professor at San Diego State University where he teaches social work practice and research methods, concentrating in aging and adult development.

Lynn Vest, B.S. in Recreation Administration and M.S. in Therapeutic Recreation, is a therapist consultant and director of activity therapy, Mendota Mental Health Institute, Madison, Wisconsin. A registered, therapeutic specialist,

Ms. Vest was a recreational therapist in the deaf treatment center at the time her paper was written.

Stanley Witkin is an assistant professor at Florida State University, Tallahassee, Florida. He received his Ph.D. in social welfare from the University of Wisconsin-Madison in 1976. His interests include dyadic interaction, single-case research, and marital counseling.

Stephen E. Wong earned his M.S.W. at the University of Washington in 1977. A doctorial student in the Applied Behavior Analysis Program, Department of Psychology, Western Michigan University, Mr. Wong has published a number of articles on clinical social work research. His present interests are in developing methodologies appropriate for evaluating behavior change.

Toni Zander received her master's degree in 1975 from the School of Social Work, University of Wisconsin-Madison. She is currently a doctoral student in the Department of Counseling and Guidance at the same University, and a research assistant for the Guidance Institute for Talented Students (GIFTS). Her present research interests include cognitive-behavior modification and counselor training.

preface

In the past ten years there has been a dramatic increase in empirical research and clinical examples in the area of behavior modification. A more recent development in the area of cognitive therapy has also enriched the literature and broadened the possibilities open to the clinician.

In spite of the fact that almost half of the sample of praticing behavior and cognitive therapists belonging to the Association for The Advancement of Behavior Therapy indicated they worked with groups (Rose, O'Bryant, and Siemons, 1979), there has not been a corresponding development of the professional literature in this area. Only very recently several books on behavior group therapy (Rose, 1972, 1977; Harris, 1976; Upper and Ross 1979) have begun to fill this gap. Even with these and other books, the literature seemed to be acutely deficient in detailed, data based, case examples of group therapists using behavioral and cognitive theoretical perspectives.

It has become increasingly apparent that a casebook on groups is necessary to provide students of practice, practitioners, educators, and researchers with detailed examples of group therapists, group workers, or group counselors at work. Such a casebook would be limited to cases involving those group therapists who were oriented toward behavioral and cognitive change and who used a paradigm consistent with theory and data derived from behavioral-cognitive orientation.

This need was also registered by the many requests my colleagues and I have received for examples of the mimeographed cases which, until recently, were among the few available. As these cases have been revised and new cases were developed, the structure of a casebook evolved. The criteria for inclusion in the casebook were that a given case had to describe a unique population or deal with a unique common problem area; or it had to articulate an unusual or usual set of change strategies. The group in each case had to be more than the context of treatment or change. Group procedures had to be included. Cases were included only if data were to have been used for improvement of pactice or evaluation. Preference was also given to cases which described in detail the planning and implementation activities of the therapists.

By using these criteria this book could be oriented toward many audiences. First, it is oriented toward the behaviorist who works primarily with individuals or families and wishes to expand his or her practice to include groups. Secondly, it is oriented toward the experienced behavior group therapist who is in need of a basis of comparison. The question, "How do some other of my colleagues do it?" is hopefully answered. Third, it is oriented toward the group therapist from other orientations who seeks to explore another approach. Since this is a data-based approach, a fourth audience to whom the book is addressed is those researchers who examine systematically the processes in and effectiveness of group endeavors. For them as well as for the previously mentioned audiences, the strategies and techniques of systematic data collection are described in detail.

Because of the assumed training of most of these audiences, most of the technical terms in this book have not been defined in the context of the case. I have provided a glossary at the end in which the major concepts and procedures have been briefly defined and in some instances exemplified as they apply in the group context.

This book, like all edited books, is the result of the efforts of many people. First, this set of cases has evolved into a book because of the group experience of a number of young (average age, 29), practitioners and scholars of practice. Most are master's level practitioners. A few are Ph.D.s. These contributors not only were willing to experiment with a relatively new approach, but were willing to write up their experiences for others.

Not only am I indebted to these contributors but to the numerous colleagues, students, and other readers of the early drafts who provided encouragement and suggestions for their further development.

I am grateful to Martin Loeb and Anne Minahan, who were directors of the School of Social Work at the University of Wisconsin while this book was in progress. They made the facilities of the school available and helped to create an environment conducive to the development of this book.

I would also like to thank Carol Betts and those other members of the administrative staff who assisted in the typing and editing of the many drafts this manuscript required.

Finally, I would like to express special appreciation to Pat Ducey, my research assistant, who aided with editing, helped pull together index and glossary concepts, worked on the bibliographies, called the authors to get missing information, and performed a myriad of other administrative tasks to which an edited book so often falls prey.

REFERENCES

Harris, G. E., Ed. *The Group Treatment of Human Problems, A Social Learning Approach.* New York: Grune and Stratton, Inc., 1977.

Rose, S. D. *Treating Children in Groups.* San Francisco: Jossey-Bass, 1972.

_____, *Group Therapy: A Behavioral Approach.* Englewood Cliffs, New Jersey: Prentice-Hall, Inc., 1977.

_____, J. B. Siemon, and K. O'Bryant. *Use of Group in Therapy by Members of AABT.* Unpublished manuscript, University of Wisconsin, Madison, Wisconsin, 1979.

Upper, D., and S. M. Ross, Eds. *Behavioral Group Therapy, 1979: An Annual Review.* Champaign, Illinois: Research Press.

Sheldon D. Rose
Madison, Wisconsin
April, 1979

introduction

Group therapist (Jeanne):	Now that Vernon has described his bouts of anxiety and you've had the chance to discuss with him the situations which seem to be most conducive to these attacks, I wonder if we couldn't begin to propose some ideas to Vernon as to what he might do about it based on our own experiences and what has been learned thus far in the group.
Anita:	Well, the idea he has that he can't deal with people in authority needs to be looked at. I for one don't believe a word of it. Look at how he evaluated what was happening in the group and what you should be doing better, Jeanne.
Group members:	(Laughter and nods of agreement.)
Peter:	Another thing he might consider are these relaxation exercises we've been practicing in the group the last four weeks. I don't know about you, Vernon, but they sure help me when I get uptight.
Vernon:	How might I use them exactly?

Gordon:	Well, when you have to talk to your boss, like you said, which seems to scare the hell out of you, why don't you first sit down, take a deep breath, clear your mind, and then just practice the alternate tension and relaxation. You did it pretty well in the group. And after a couple of minutes then go in and see your boss.
Eileen:	And perhaps you might consider practicing with us what you might say to him in a number of different situations. And if you want, some of us might demonstrate to you, just as Jeanne modeled for Peter, some of the things you could say.
Peter:	And you could even do a kind of rehearsal in your head just before you talk to the boss. Remember, we worked on that technique last week?
Group therapist:	(After additional group discussion) Well, we've come up with some pretty good ideas. And Vernon, I could see that you were eager to discuss them. Why don't you take a crack at evaluating them in terms of their practicality for you? Let's begin with the notion that you *can't* deal with authority persons.

In this brief excerpt from a moment in the life of a group, we see a group therapist at work. With the help of the group, she had already assisted the client to clarify the manifestation of a problem and the conditions under which the problem seemed to occur. She was now involving the group in getting out various ideas as to what the client could do about the problem. These ideas, such as cognitive correction, relaxation, modeling, overt and covert rehearsal had been presented to the group at earlier group meetings and now the members had the opportunity to propose and work with them.

It should also be noted that though the group therapist attempted to involve the group members as much as possible in providing ideas and supportive feedback to Vernon, the ultimate decision based on his evaluation of his situation lay with him as to what strategies he might employ.

This is a book describing many such group therapists at work. It is a series of case examples focusing on the details of carrying out assessment, intervention, generalization, and evaluation procedures within the context and with the mediating effect of the small group. Group therapists have presented their own cases in a variety of settings with different populations. The targets of change include behaviors such as improving social skills, altering cognitions such as self-defeating thoughts, improving emotional states such as the reduction of anxiety, and modifying physical attributes such as attaining weight loss. The means of intervention include group dynamics exercises, social learning procedures, didactic techniques, and cognitive procedures.

PURPOSE OF CASE STUDIES

Several reasons existed for the development of this book. In the first place, a large percentage of practicing behavior therapists make use of groups as the context of treatment. In a recent survey (Rose, Siemon and O'Bryant, 1979) of a random sample of the membership of the Association for the Advancement of Behavior Therapy, it was discovered that of those persons practicing behavior therapy, 42 percent were currently working with therapy groups. The most common groups worked with by those who were surveyed were assertion training groups (60 percent); parenting skill training groups (60 percent); self-control groups (55 percent) with weight losers, cigarette smokers, and alcoholics; and group psychotherapy (46 percent). Other groups mentioned were children's social skills groups, self-help groups, and institutional groups. Examples of all these types of groups except group psychotherapy and self-help groups are described in this volume.

Considering the fact that so many behavior therapists work with groups and yet so little literature is available that deals with group therapy either in books or in the behavioral and cognitive journal literature, the need for additional material is all the more compelling. Those few books which do exist in the area of cognitive and behavior change through group as well as other interventions focus on explaining the underlying theories of assessment, evaluation, and intervention with the uses of only limited examples. This volume focuses on providing detailed examples to the person already familiar with the theory and basic concepts. These examples contain a step-by-step account of what the group therapist does in different phases of treatment and in different types of groups.

In focusing on case studies, we do not claim to validate a cognitive-behavioral group approach. Rather, as Ullman and Krasner (1966) have so clearly pointed out as reasonable purposes of case studies, we try to illustrate, to generate interest in, to develop hypotheses about, and to give instruction in the practice of group therapy from a cognitive, behavioral, and group perspective. Each case contains excerpts from actual practice, charts used in the groups, tips to the worker, samples of agenda for meetings, role play exercises, group problems and their resolutions, and instruments for data collection. These case studies have been designed to describe not only the specific procedures used, but also to capture the variety of ways in which these procedures are delivered and the give and take between group therapist and group member as these procedures are presented and carried out.

As a result each case selected for this book is too detailed to be accepted as a journal article and none has been previously published. It is in pursuit of this detail, usually omitted from journals and most books, that each chapter has been written. It is our assumption that in this very detail the proposed audience of this book—the student, the scholar, the practitioner, and the teacher of the group therapy, group counseling, and group work—will be most interested.

For these same reasons we have omitted most theoretical discussions and elaborate definitions of concepts which can be found elsewhere (see, for example, Rose, 1972; 1977). However, throughout, we have referred the reader to appropriate sources for theoretical or empirical justifications of the use of a given procedure or strategy.

THEORETICAL ORIENTATIONS

The orientation of the group therapists, in this volume, is multitheoretical. In the first place they are behaviorally oriented since the targets of change are usually social behaviors and the methods of intervention are derived, for the most part, from social learning theory, e.g., reinforcement, coaching, modeling, rehearsal, stimulus control, and discrimination training (see Bandura, 1969, for definitions). Most of the therapists are cognitively oriented as well since they also take as targets of intervention cognitions such as self-talk, self-descriptions, distorted perceptions of self and the world, and seek to alter these in more appropriate directions. Many also draw upon cognitive interventions such as cognitive restructuring, cognitive correction, thought stopping, cognitive rehearsal, and problem-solving training as means of bringing about cognitive and often emotional changes in the individual and/or to mediate overt behavioral changes (see Meichenbaum, 1977; Mahoney, 1974). Many of the principles of transfer and the maintenance of learning are also drawn from experiments on cognitive learning such as teaching the general concept once the behavior is learned and overlearning (Goldstein, Heller, and Sechrest, 1966).

Like all books on cognitive and behavior modification, this volume has a learning perspective. That is, it is assumed that all problematic behaviors, cognitions, and emotions have been learned and can be altered by learning. Although this process of alteration is called therapy, in fact, it is more an educational experience in which individuals are taught how to view their own learning process, to learn new ways of learning, and to try out these new ways of learning for their own behavioral, cognitive, and emotional change.

Didactic procedures which draw upon a number of different theories, educational practices, and assumptions about learning are also used. Brief lectures are used to present new materials. In many cases readings about principles are assigned between sessions and the activity of reading is often monitored at the following group meeting through quizzes or brief group discussion. Other homework assignments are also given, to which contingencies are usually attached in the early sessions. Case studies are discussed in some groups. Clients do exercises in subgroups as a means of learning through practice the various skills being taught.

These therapists also draw upon a theoretical conception of relationship best exemplified in the work of Truax and Carkhuff (1967). Although there is only limited empirical evidence, there is considerable anecdotal support for the notion that in groups as well as dyadic treatment the relationship of the therapist to the group should be characterized by warmth and empathic understanding to be effective.

Group therapists also draw upon small group theories to help them to ascertain relationships among group interaction, group attraction, group norms, and individual phenomena and to guide the practitioner in the selection of appropriate group intervention strategies. Many of the interventions have an experimental foundation in the group dynamics experimental literature (see, e.g., Cartwright and Zander, 1968).

The group in all cases is both the context as well as one set of means of change and not only as a source of feedback. Although the group therapists in this volume vary as to their emphasis on the group as a means of treatment, in addition to group feedback, most at least attend to increasing group attraction, broadening the distribution or participation, and keeping the interaction to a large degree on-task.

Subgroup projects are used in the group to increase interaction and opportunities for leadership; the buddy system is used outside the group for the same purposes and in addition as a means of transferring therapeutic activities to the outside world.

Group problems (dominance of several individuals, interpersonal conflict, low productivity) which impede progress are usually dealt with by a systematic problem-solving strategy (see Rose, 1977, pp. 132-151).

EMPIRICAL APPROACH

The foremost orientation of the therapists in this volume is empirical. The case studies in this book make use of a general paradigm and specific interventions which data have demonstrated (at least to some degree) to be effective with populations similar to the ones being treated by given group practitioners. In all of the cases data were collected before and after treatment and in some cases during treatment in order to evaluate whether change had occurred and for whom. In some of the cases data were collected at follow-up in order to ascertain how well changes were maintained. Ongoing process data, such as the rate of assignment completion, the distribution of participation, and member satisfaction, are usually collected as means of providing the leaders and members with feedback as to the ongoing effectiveness of the group and to signal group problems as soon as they occur.

Thus all groups in this volume can be considered, at least, small sample experiments with pre- and postmeasurement without a control group. Such quasi-experimental designs (Campbell and Stanley, 1963), in spite of their limitations, with replication begin to contribute to a general body of knowledge.

Some authors have reported on withdrawal designs within the ongoing treatment. Vest (chapter 7), for example, used contingency contracting as a way of increasing the productivity (percent of assignment completion) of her group members. The design included first a baseline in which contingency contracting was not used, followed by the use of contingency contracting for assignment completion, followed by a return to baseline, followed by a return to contingency contracting. Such a design carried out by a clinician adds to the findings of other studies demonstrating the usefulness of contingency contracting with adults in increasing group productivity.

STRATEGIES OF ASSESSMENT, INTERVENTION, AND GENERALIZATION

But adequate evaluation, like adequate intervention, depends on good preliminary and ongoing assessment which is a component of all of the groups in this volume. All the contributors have described how they have carried out the assessment process in such a way as to evaluate outcome and to determine appropriate strategies of intervention. Although general patterns of intervention (e.g., assertion training) are often determined by the reason the person comes to the group (e.g., difficulty in making refusal responses and speaking in groups), the choice of procedure to be used demands adequate inquiry into specific situations causing anxiety and inability to act, types of cognitions as well as emotional responses to these situations, effective as well as ineffective behaviors of the client used in dealing with other types of situations, and other factors which might impinge on a person's lack of assertive skill.

The effectiveness of a program is not only determined by changes which are observed at termination of treatment. All authors in this volume have been concerned with the transfer of those changes to nontherapy situations and the maintenance of those changes beyond the term of therapy (see Goldstein, Heller, and Sechrest, 1966 for a description of principles involved). Most of the contributors to this volume have discussed in detail their strategies for transferring and maintaining changes and for determining whether transfer and maintenance occurred.

VALUE ORIENTATION

In addition to a similar theoretical orientation, there are several values that all the case studies in this volume hold in common. First, in all cases, steps have been taken to show respect for the individual rights of group members and to protect and enhance their dignity. Although feedback from other group members is an important part of all group therapies, the client can and is protected from overzealous or anxiety-producing verbal attacks or ridicule. All feedback focuses on what others have observed and how they respond to what they have observed in the here-and-now, and those positive behavior characteristics of the target of feedback are always pointed out first. If negative feedback or criticism is called for, clients may terminate it at any time they find the comments are too uncomfortable to handle. Moreover, clients do not have to submit to negative feedback at all if they choose not to. In all of these groups observers have noted that positive responses far outweigh any type of implied or explicit criticism. In fact some members in some of the groups have asked for greater negative feedback from their peers.

Of greater importance, even in the institutional groups, is that clients may end their membership in the group at any time, even in the middle of a meeting. When deposits are used, the penalty is always sufficiently small as not to be financially distressful for the client.

Since data are collected and observers are used, clients are assured that such data and any events that happen in the group will be used solely for the use of the leader and members in improving the quality of the program. On those occasions that data are used as part of a larger study or as in the case examples published in this volume, anonymity of the members is guaranteed through the use of pseudonyms and the disguising of other recognizable features. Members of groups also enter into a contract with each other to hold the events of the meetings confidential.

Except for negative feedback no unusual or highly aversive procedures are used. In two of the groups, response cost programs (see chapters 5 and 7) were developed at the request of the members but even in these a higher ratio of positive reinforcement to response cost (taking away tokens) was used. However, even response cost is discouraged in most cases because of a tendency for it to become a "fining" program.

Where the clients are children, parents are told about the groups and their permission as well as that of the children is required before participation in the group is accepted by the therapist. Prior to treatment contracts are established which set out rights and mutual responsibility of the sponsor organization, the group therapist, and group members.

Clients are also protected from inadequate or poorly trained leaders, a danger in all groups, by the careful data monitoring system and the training all leaders must undergo, and skills they must demonstrate before being permitted to lead a group on their own. This training is described below.

The reader will be struck by the fact that all these groups are initially highly structured. In most groups agendas are used at every meeting. This structure is determined at first by the therapist. As the group evolves, members increase their contribution to the structure of the group. In many groups (even the children's groups) members assume major leadership responsibilities in the later sessions (see especially chapter 1).

The delegation of responsibility and teaching of leadership skills is an integral part of involving members in their own therapy and that of their peers. The assumption is that if a person can operate to help himself and others independent of the therapist in the group, he or she will better be able to operate independently once the group has terminated. Moreover, leadership skills are important social skills in all social situations; their achievement should facilitate both work and social relationships.

Not only are members taught leadership skills but they are also taught a systematic problem-solving paradigm. In the initial example the members went through problem clarification and brainstormed ideas how to deal with that problem. The next step would have been for the client to evaluate and select a strategy to deal with his problem and try it out. This paradigm is repeated for all problems that members bring to treatment until it too becomes a part of their cognitive repertoire.

Thus, members are not only trained in the specific behaviors for which they are referred to the group, but are also given practice in leadership and problem solving as means of maintaining their specific behavioral achievements and involving them effectively with their peers. Such skills are essential requisites of self-determination, a basic principle of the helping professions.

ORGANIZATIONAL AUSPICES

Of course no group is organized in a vacuum. All the groups reported in this volume were organized within some agency or context which contributed to the structure of and expectations for the program. Most of the groups were organized under the auspices of the Interpersonal Skill Training and Research Project (formerly the Group Therapy and Research Project) of the School of Social Work of the University of Wisconsin-Madison. Established in 1973, this project was designed primarily to evolve and test the efficacy of commonly used behavioral group therapy models. These included parenting skill training groups; assertion training groups; social skill training for the elderly, single parents, and children; self-control training groups; communication skills workshops for couples; problem-solving skill training groups for the elderly; and social interviewing skill training for students. Of equal importance was the goal of training group therapists, group observers, and researchers in the area of clinical group practice.

Such a project could not have been established if it did not fulfill an essential need in the community for such groups. Various county departments of social services, mental health clinics, organizations for single parents, Madison public and parochial schools, organizations for the elderly, institutions, the university counseling center, and the school of social work have cooperated with the ISTR project in organizing groups, and in providing publicity, space, and video and audio equipment, babysitting, transportation, and sometimes financial support for clients. There has also been a dramatic interest from the community at large.

Only one of the groups described in this book was developed after the group therapist had left the Interpersonal Skill Training and Research Project and hence organized under different auspices (chapter 10). In each chapter the cooperating agency under which the group was set up and its contribution to and restraint on treatment is described.

TRAINING OF GROUP THERAPISTS

Although not all of the therapists organized their groups under the auspices of the Interpersonal Skill Training and Research Project, all but one was trained in the Project. Since this training (as it has evolved since 1973) is not described in any of the case studies and since training is an important variable in effectively carrying out the process and achieving the outcomes of any group, a brief account of that training is presented here.

The training consisted of two parts: The theoretical course work and required readings overlapped with the fieldwork or practical applications. The course work involved training in behavior modification and in cognitive and small group theories. The trainees were assigned readings in each area which were monitored weekly. They were also expected to write weekly small papers on various aspects of treatment as applied to the groups that trainees were coleading. In the course, the trainees presented their groups, the procedures they used, the problems they encountered, their data as it was obtained, and their judgment as to the ongoing effectiveness of the group. Classmates, on the basis of their own experience and the readings, discussed the merits of each method and alternative ways of approaching the various situations being presented.

The field training component was designed to provide the trainees with gradually increasing skills in group leadership and gradually increasing responsibility while at the same time provide the clients with the best possible service. In the first month trainees underwent a simulated assertion training program of six two-hour sessions under the leadership of an experienced student or the instructor. After each session the content of the meeting was discussed in terms of its requirements for leadership behaviors. Even in the simulated groups, trainees were gradually delegated leadership roles and eventually some took over the leadership of the group.

In the second month trainees received their first group—usually assertion training group for adults—in the role of coleaders. The senior leaders were either advanced students or paid parttime professionals. The senior leaders faded their leadership on the basis of demonstrated skills of the coleader. In the final sessions the senior leaders would go behind a one-way mirror and observe; later they would pass on their observations to the leader.

Usually in the third month those trainees who had demonstrated independent group leadership skills participated in giving a two-day workshop to agency workers or organizations requesting a program on assertion training. At that time the trainees would lead a small group alone. A senior staff member would rotate among the groups to offer help if necessary and later to offer feedback to the group leader.

Usually in the fifth month trainees would lead new groups as either the only leader or as senior leaders with supervisory responsibility for a junior leader to whom they in turn gradually delegated responsibilities of leadership.

During the first four months there was also group supervision in which each treatment session was planned and discussed and new exercises were practiced. During this period most of the trainees were also working on specific sets of professional skills and would role play these in varous training sessions. They worked on such behaviors as setting time limits when appropriate, increasing praise responses, increasing the latency between the questions of members and their answers so as to increase group participation, decrease interruptions on their part. At these sessions the satisfaction, productivity, and participation data were also examined and discussed for their implications for leadership. Deviations from the norms were especially noted and discussed. Trainees were encouraged to give increasing responsibility to their members as the group progressed. During these sessions problems which arose in the group were also presented and discussed. Often the trainees would make use of the systematic problem-solving process to find solutions to these problems.

At every group session one or two observers were present. Observers, depending on their level of training, collected one of two kinds of data—participation of each group participant, or various categories of participation (see chapter 1 for details). Both systems provided, at least, the distribution of participation among members and leaders as indicated by a standard deviation per meeting, the distribution between the leaders, and the distribution between members and leaders. In addition, data were collected on the degree of satisfaction of each individual per session, the percentage of assignments completed (productivity) per session, and the attendance. An analysis of these data provided weekly feedback to the leaders about their ongoing effectiveness and cues as to emerging group problems. Furthermore data were collected from a role play test and the Assertion Training Inventory (Gambrill and Richey, 1975) before and after treatment so that each trainee could see how his or her process of leading was related to outcome. (See chapter 1 for more details on how these data were collected and used.)

As an additional part of their program, group therapist trainees would observe other groups. Using a leadership checklist each observer (therapist trainee) provided his or her observations to the coleaders about their leadership activities. (This checklist is available from the author on request.) This gave each trainee an opportunity to view many other styles of leadership and provided each therapist trainee with multiple sources of feedback.

During the fourth and fifth month of training, most trainees also led a social skills group for children. These groups were organized in the public or parochial school system at the request of teachers or social workers at the given school. A separate weekly supervisory training session was organized for the leaders of the children's groups. In addition, two all-day game and craft workshops were organized to provide the trainees with survival skills in dealing with groups of children.

These groups usually met twice a week for 10 to 16 weeks (see chapters 6 and 7). At each 40-minute session, at least one game was played, one situation was practiced by each member, and one contingency contract was designed for each member, the completion of which would add points to a group project.

At least one of these sessions was videotaped (with permission of the children, parents, and school). This videotaped session was used to provide feedback to the leaders; it also served as group project for the children who could use tokens earned for good behavior to make such a tape, and allowed parents and teachers to see how the children were performing in the group.

The children in the groups were observed in the classroom prior to, during, and following treatment. Occasionally, participation was also observed during the group sessions. For the younger children, satisfaction data were always so high that they failed to discriminate between meetings or members and were therefore discontinued. Productivity data were kept since completion of assignments was a difficult activity for children to maintain. Attendance data were also kept. In addition, behavioral checklists (Walker, 1970) by both parents and teachers were kept as a way of ascertaining change of the children during treatment along with the observation of problem behavior.

During the last half of the training year, trainees would also organize and lead other groups such as parent skill training, weight loss, or institutional transition groups with as much independence as the quality of their previous experience permitted. However, all trainees would continue to bring their ongoing data, problems, etc. to group supervisory sessions.

Let us now look briefly at what these leaders did with all this training.

SUMMARY OF CHAPTERS

In chapter 1, Hall and Rose describe a typical assertion training group in the Interpersonal Training and Research Project. They describe how the members were recruited and the group was organized. They elaborate on the types of individual data, an assertion inventory and a role play test, and the types of group data (satisfaction, productivity, attendance, promptness, distribution of participation) collected and how these were used to facilitate treatment and to evaluate the effectiveness of the program. In a session-by-session description of the group, the authors illustrate how members were introduced to one another and how they were involved in the group programs. Of particular interest is the way in which members were trained in the use of the various procedures in the treatment package: modeling, rehearsal, group feedback, and contingency contracting, and how the leaders dealt with the members' questions and concerns about these procedures. The authors also recount in detail how members were trained in group procedure such as the buddy system, the use of group feedback, small group exercises, and leadership training. Of particular importance are the strategies employed by the leaders in dealing with group problems such as the uneven distribution of participation, the discrepancy between the activity of the leaders, and the persistent off-task behavior of one of the members. Finally, the leaders describe briefly how they planned and prepared the clients for termination of the group and the transfer of change to the real world. The authors also present the data accumulated on each person and on the group and show how these were used to evaluate outcome and to facilitate the treatment process.

It should be noted that assertion training as presented in this chapter is a multitheoretical and empirical approach. It draws upon operant procedures such as contingency contracting to promote transfer of change and frequent verbal reinforcement to shape participation in the group; it draws upon modeling theory to use role-played modeling and behavior rehearsal under prescribed learning conditions; it draws upon cognitive theory in its use of such procedures as cognitive rehearsal, problem solving, and training in positive self-statements. It draws upon small group theory in its use of the introduction exercises and the buddy system and other subgrouping procedures. But in the final analysis it is an empirical approach in that data were collected continuously as an integral part of carrying out the program, and outcome and process were evaluated.

In chapter 2, Toseland describes a more consistent cognitive approach which, though having the same aims as the assertion training group, used primarily, though not exclusively, problem-solving procedures to teach assertive behaviors to the elderly. Though less typical in its emphasis of the approaches used in the Interpersonal Skill Training and Research Project, this chapter has been included because it demonstrates how problem solving can be taught and carried out in treatment groups. Although many authors in this book refer to problem solving, this is the only chapter in which the author has described the many subtle elements of its application and provided varied examples of how each of the steps were carried out. Toseland describes how elderly persons were recruited to the group, how his data were collected; how the group was begun; how the problem-solving process was divided into its component parts and taught to the members; how these procedures were enriched with the use of modeling, rehearsal, and homework; how members were taught to keep and use a log for monitoring their own behaviors. He also provides one detailed process example of one session in which the entire problem-solving process is exemplified.

Not to be overlooked is the author's description of how leadership was delegated to the group members as a means of training them in using the problem-solving process themselves. Also of importance was the description of the use of cognitive restructuring of the clients' statements about themselves and their expectancies as part of the problem-solving process. Finally, it should be mentioned that this was one of only two chapters in the book specifically oriented to group work with the elderly. The author describes in particular how the method was tailored to their unique needs and wishes.

The author also describes the development of a role-play test for the elderly; how items were collected, evaluated, selected; and how the coding for responses was developed. Not only does the author describe the results of the members of this group on the role-play test, he reports the results of the larger project (of which this was a part) in which problem-solving and assertion training groups did about equally well and better than a discussion control group.

In chapter 3, Zander and Kindy describe a child management group for parents. In this group parents are taught general parenting skills and are helped to deal with specific problems that were annoying them at the time the group took place. The population consisted of parents on welfare, most of whom had limited educational background. In this chapter the authors describe in detail how the group was organized, the procedures used to recruit the parents and keep them coming, and the individual and group data collection procedures and how they were integrated into the general group format. In a session-by-session description of the eight-week, two-hour a week program, the authors laid out the agenda for each meeting and the specific details of how the agenda items were promoted into program. In particular they tell about the reading assignments they gave and how these were discussed and monitored, what and how new concepts were taught, the specific modeling and rehearsed situations used each week, and how assignments were developed and prepared for. The authors demonstrate in particular detail, preparation for and the use of the buddy system, use of subgroup exercises, and the use of weekly evaluations. This group is also one of the few in which home observation, described in detail, was used to facilitate assessment.

Specifically, the authors describe how programs were evolved for the five parents in the group for treatment of such problems as enuresis, excessive crying, performance of household chores, and compliance. Zander and Kindy go on to show how in teaching parents to deal with these behaviors, the parents learned the general child management skills of social reinforcement, time out from reinforcement, cueing, extinction, and contingency contracting. Finally after reviewing their results, the authors make some important suggestions which practitioners dealing with all groups might consider.

In chapter 4, Kindy and Patterson describe a comprehensive group training program designed for patients 15 to 20 percent overweight as a means of preventing eventual obesity. This program was implemented in an adult primary care medical setting. The program articulated by the authors provided the patients with a cognitive and behavioral learning framework; it trained them in self-management skills such as self-monitoring, goal setting, self-reinforcement, cognitive restructuring, stimulus control, use of the social environment, control of consequences, and relaxation. The patients were also taught autonomous problem solving skills so that they could continue to work on their own problematic behavior after the group had terminated. In teaching self-control in eight weekly sessions of two hours each, the group therapists made use of the procedures described in the assertion training chapter, the problem-solving procedures described in the problem-solving chapter, and extensive cognitive training procedures designed to replace self-defeating thought patterns and unrealistic performance standards with more appropriate thought patterns and standards.

In addition patients were provided basic information on nutrition and were helped to develop more appropriate long-term eating patterns. They were also given instruction in exercise management and diet control.

The therapists made use of group procedures described earlier such as group feedback, the buddy system, subgroup exercises, and leadership training for the participants. The therapists also kept data on assignment completion, attendance, promptness, and satisfaction as well as ongoing estimates of their motivation to lose weight. As outcome measures, actual weight loss, a weight reduction index, and behavior change in related areas were used to estimate the effectiveness of the program. At the end of treatment all but one member lost between 6.75 and 21.5 pounds. The remaining member gained weight.

In chapter 5, Court and Rose describe two groups of first-, second-, and third-grade children who were referred by their teacher from one open primary classroom. These groups met for one hour twice a week for 12 weeks. They focused on the development of appropriate classroom behaviors and social skills. Intervention in these groups differed from intervention the groups reported on earlier in their use of a token system which was integrated into exercises, group games, and other activities. Tokens were distributed for desirable classroom behavior on fixed and variable intervals throughout the early group sessions. Tokens were also awarded for the completion of out-of-group assignments which were monitored by the teachers and/or the parents. The chapter describes typical early, middle, and late sessions and how the token system was developed and faded. The authors also describe in detail their use of simulated art and music classroom activities as a means of facilitating the transfer of change. Other transfer of change procedures such as teaching self-reinforcement, fading the activity of the leaders, and greater involvement of the children are also described. Data collected by observers in regular classroom settings over the course of the group program revealed an overall increase in the frequency of the children's attending behavior and an overall decrease in the frequency of the children's nonattending and disruptive behaviors. Teacher reports were also favorable.

In chapter 6, Rose and Roessle describe a group of five boys, aged 9 to 11 (grades four and five) who were referred by their classroom teachers for exhibiting acting out or withdrawal behavior. The group met for 19 half-hour sessions over a nine-week period.

The treatment package consisted of various interventions such as behavioral rehearsal, shaping, behavioral assignments, modeling, problem-solving skills, group discussion, observation techniques, games, and trips. As in chapter 5, a token economy and verbal reinforcing statements were employed to increase the frequency of individual prosocial behaviors and to modify two group interactional patterns—the distribution of verbal responses and the frequency of positive praise statements.

Pre- and postdata were collected by means of the Walker Problem Behavior Identification Checklist, and progress was evaluated throughout the program with systematic classroom observations and weekly teacher reports on two specific behavioral achievements for each child. Data were also collected at the sessions on productivity, attendance, frequency of verbalizations and positive praise statements.

Intermittent contact was made with the teachers and parents throughout the program via phone contacts, meetings, and newsletters. As a special group project a videotape of one session was made which was shown to both the parents and teachers as a means of illustrating the actual processes of that group.

The results indicated that the token economy and verbal reinforcements served to equalize the distribution of verbalizations within the group, and increase the frequency of praise statements. But more important the treatment package served to effect a change in the individual target behaviors of four out of five boys.

In chapter 7, Vest describes a transitional activity group involving deaf individuals from a deaf treatment center who sought involvement in community activities away from the hospital and sheltered situations. The group met once a week for one hour for a total of 11 weeks. The purpose of the group was to increase each member's knowledge of activities in the community and of procedures for getting into the activities, in order to become involved in at least one ongoing community activity.

Individual goals and group goals were broken down into 14 specific behavior assignments progressing toward completion of the goals. Reinforcement was both individual (as specified in each contingency contract) and group administered.

Treatment consisted of contingency contracting, modeling; and behavior rehearsal. This type of treatment and all procedures provided sufficient visual cues to be readily understood without hearing. Data collection was through unit charts, questionnaires, systematic observation, and group members' evidence of completing assignments.

Analysis of treatment results indicated that all members increased their knowledge of community activities and of procedures leading to involvement in community activities. All members of the group completed all behavior assignments and brought in information on the groups they would join. Actual involvement in activities on an ongoing basis was not achieved for all members due to the timing of these activities in town. The major contribution of this chapter is its discussion of the unique problems of working with the deaf in groups, and the strategies employed by the leader for dealing with these problems.

In chapter 8, Sistler and Berger describe a group of five male nursing home patients who participated in eight one-hour group treatment sessions. The patients ranged in age from 63 to 91 years. For each member of the group the treatment goal was to increase social interaction and participation in nursing home activities. Group members were selected by nursing home staff on the basis of three criteria: The resident (1) seldom interacted with others, (2) rarely attended regularly scheduled nursing home activities, and (3) spent most of the time in his own room.

Group treatment techniques included social reinforcement, shaping, direct instruction in interpersonal tasks, modeling, behavioral rehearsal, feedback on performance. Homework assignments included preparing a list of reinforcers, preparing and giving a group presentation, initiating a conversation with one group member and one nonmember, and monitoring frequency of interactions with residents. Paper and pencil evaluations were completed by each member at the end of each session. These evaluations as well as data on frequency of member participation were fed back to group members at subsequent sessions. To facilitate transfer of change, group members planned and attended a social activity which was included in the regular nursing home recreational program. Evaluation of the treatment program indicated that the frequency of member-member group interaction and attendance at other nursing home activities increased substantially by the end of the group.

In chapter 9, Witkin and Cayner describe a communication skills workshop (CSW). This program is a behavioral-cognitive-communication skill training group for couples. Based on the assumption that marital discord can be reduced or avoided by teaching couples skills that increase their communication effectiveness in difficult or critical situations, couples are initially taught skills which increase the ratio of positive messages (qualify); the ability to understand partner's positions (accuracy); and how to provide or generate feedback useful in behavioral change (openness). How these concepts are taught is described and illustrated in detail.

Once these skills were mastered, the authors describe how the emphasis shifted to using these skills to deal with ongoing problems. The last half of the workshop required the introduction of "real-life" situations that were examined and worked on using a problem-solving format.

In this chapter, the authors describe intervention procedures such as modeling, rehearsal, instruction, and group feedback as they applied to the unique problems of couple communication. The assessment instruments used in the evaluation of this group were the Locke-Wallace Marital Adjustment Questionnaire, the Marital Communication Inventory, and behavioral data obtained by using the Marital Interaction Coding System of role-played problem-solving behavior of each of the couples.

The authors report that four of the five couples showed changes in the desired direction of the Marital Interaction Coding System and three of the five couples on the marital inventories.

In chapter 10, Schinke and Wong describe a group training program for the staffs in two group homes for the mentally retarded. The staff participated in eight 90-minute instructional sessions in behavior modification. Two social work graduate students led on-site group training sessions in each home. An operant model of family interaction served as the instructional curriculum. This curriculum was delivered through behavioral training methods of role play, feedback with social reinforcement, cueing, and contracting. Efficacy of the groups was evaluated by process measures of staff responses on weekly evaluation forms, proportion of homework assignments completed, and results of resident behavior-change projects conducted in the home.

The authors also describe the types of group problems which arose and how they were dealt with. Process results from both homes showed a mean of 83 percent of staff evaluative responses as positive, a mean of 83 percent of assignments satisfactorily completed, and two of the three resident behavior-change projects as successful. Outcome results, consistent across both homes, indicated knowledge increases, declines in job satisfaction, improved attitudes toward residents, and increased frequency of contingent staff positive reinforcement. Results suggest this format is an effective mode for in-service group training of staff in group homes for the mentally retarded.

Now that the reader has an overview of all the chapters in this book, let us look in more detail at the type of group most commonly led by behavior and cognitive group therapists (Rose, Siemon, and O'Bryant, 1979) the assertion training group.

REFERENCES

Bandura, A. *Principles of behavior modification*. New York: Holt, Rinehart and Winston, 1969.

Campbell, D. T. and J. C. Stanley. *Experimental and quasi-experimental designs for research*. Chicago: Rand McNally, 1963.

Cartwright, D. and A. Zander (eds.). *Group dynamics: Research and theory*. New York: Harper & Row, 1968.

Gambrill, E. D. and C. A. Richey. An assertion inventory for use in assessing competence. *Behavior therapy*, 1975, *6*, 550-61.

Goldstein, A. P., K. Heller and L. B. Sechrest. *Psychotherapy and the psychology of behavior change*. New York: John Wiley & Sons, Inc., 1966.

Mahoney, M. J. *Cognition and behavior modification*. Cambridge, Mass.: Ballinger Publishing Co., 1974.

Meichenbaum, D. *Cognitive-behavior modification: An integrative approach*. New York: Plenum Press, 1977.

Rose, S. D. *Treating children in groups*. San Francisco: Jossey-Bass, 1972.

———— *Group therapy: A behavioral approach*. Englewood Cliffs, N.J.: Prentice-Hall, 1977.

———— and J. Hall. Observation of leadership in groups, categories and definition. School of Social Work, University of Wisconsin-Madison, 1978.

————, J. B. Siemon, and K. O'Bryant. Use of group therapy training by members of the Association for the Advancement of Behavior Therapy, *Behavior Therapist*, 1979, in press.

Truax, C. B. and R. R. Carkhuff. *Toward effective counseling and psychotherapy: Training and practice*. Chicago: Aldine-Atherton, 1967.

Ullmann, L. P. and L. Krasner, *Case studies in behavior modification*. New York: Holt, Rinehart and Winston, Inc., 1966.

Walker, H. M. *Walker problem behavior identification checklist*. Los Angeles: Western Psychological Services, 1970.

JAMES A. HALL and SHELDON D. ROSE

1

assertion training
in a group

INTRODUCTION

Social anxiety and difficulty in relating effectively to others is a problem shared by a large part of the population. Many clients that come to private practicers or social agencies for help are highly anxious in some social situations and lack the social skills necessary to express their desires effectively. These problems are often linked with other problems such as delinquency, school and work absenteeism, alcoholism, depression, and loneliness. In order to improve social relational and verbal skills, a program has been developed to work on them directly. In this program, clients are taught such sets of skills as meeting people and making new friends, conversing and interviewing, and expressing their feelings when appropriate. There is evidence that as a person learns such skills, the intensity of social anxiety is often reduced (Wolpe, 1973; Percell, Berwick, and Beigel, 1974; Percell, 1977; and Rathus, 1972) and that self-esteem is increased (Percell, 1977).

This approach to treatment is called assertiveness or assertion training and refers to a general paradigm and to a set of procedures by which clients are trained in social and verbal skills. These procedures primarily include modeling, coaching, and behavior rehearsal and therapist feedback, although other procedures are often added. Not only is there considerable anecdotal evidence for this approach, but, in recent years, many experiments have demonstrated the efficacy of various procedures within this approach in modifying specific behaviors related to social anxiety and unassertiveness. (See for example, Eisler, Hersen, and Miller, 1973; Galassi, Kostka, and Galassi, 1975; Hersen, Eisler, Miller, Johnson, and Pinkston, 1973; Hersen, Eisler, and Miller, 1974; Mac-Donald, Lindquist, Kramer, McGrath and Rhyne, 1975; McFall and Lillesand, 1971; McFall and Marston, 1970; McFall and Twentyman, 1973.)

Although most of the above experiments were conducted with individual subjects, it would seem that social skill deficits could be most effectively treated in social situations involving more than one client. The group can serve as a protected laboratory to practice skills which must be eventually carried out in the community. The group provides clients with a variety of social situations to which each must respond. Moreover, in role-played modeling and rehearsal, the clients provide each other with an assortment of different types of roles—e.g., discussion leader, therapeutic partner, and consultant to one's fellow clients. Several studies have made use of the group context for assertion training experiments. (See for example, Shoemaker and Paulson, 1976; Rathus, 1972; Lomont, Gilner, Spector, and Skinner, 1969; Rimm, Hill, Brown, and Stuart, 1974; Hedquist and Weinhold, 1970; Rimm, Keyson, and Hunziker, 1971; Thorpe, 1975; Percell, Berwick, and Beigel, 1974; Galassi, Galassi, and Litz, 1974; and Eisler, Hersen, and Miller, 1973.) However, in none of these experiments was explicit use of the group made. The group was described merely as a context for treatment.

To make use of the group, the therapist must initially strive to make the group attractive to its members; create group situations requiring social competency on the part of the members; create a variety of functional group roles which members can learn to play; delegate gradually the responsibilities of leadership; present situations in which members function as consultants and partners in the therapeutic endeavor; control excessive group conflict; and maximally involve all members in the interaction of the group.

This chapter describes a particular program that has incorporated group methods and has been used in the Interpersonal Skills Training and Research Project (ISTRP) (Rose, 1977; Schinke and Rose, 1976; and Rose and Schinke, 1978). Generally, this package consists of several overlapping phases of treatment, conceptual structuring of therapy, assessment, intervention, and the transfer and maintenance of behavior change. We shall discuss each of these topics as they occurred in a recent assertion training group which was typical of most of the groups sponsored by the ISTRP. We shall tell the story as it happened, beginning with the recruitment of members.

ORGANIZING THE GROUP

Recruitment

Group members were recruited for the group described in this paper and for three other groups at the same time by advertising in city and university newspapers; by posting signs at churches, factories, and the university; by announcements over radio and television; and by referral from former group members. Since the target population was the general public, the most effective means of recruiting group members appeared to be the newspaper which carried advertisements at no cost as a public service (since the groups were nonprofit and sponsored by a university affiliated organization).

As persons called in, they were given basic information about the program and about the group leaders. A written description of the group, along with an application were mailed to those interested. The group was filled on a "first come, first served" basis (i.e., the first eight persons who got their applications to the group staff became the members), and any others were placed in one of the other groups not yet filled, referred elsewhere, or put on our waiting list. A fee and deposit were required along with the application. The only occurrence of dropouts between recruitment and the first session was when applications were accepted without a check. The fee was minimal to cover some administrative costs of the group, while the deposit was returned to the members for attendance. The criteria for the return of the deposit were written, so that potential members could decide whether or not they wanted to take part in the groups.

We conducted our program in a university setting at a school of social work. The ISTR project incorporated the training of new leaders in the groups by pairing a trained, experienced leader with an inexperienced leader in training.

Pregroup Interview

When the group was filled, the group trainers called each member to arrange individual, pregroup interviews which were designed to familiarize the client wth the role play approach to assertion training, to assess levels of anxiety and assertiveness, to discuss the expectations of the group member concerning the group program, and to help the client become confident and comfortable with at least one trainer before the first group session. The trainers conducted the pregroup interviews on the same evening as the group session, and scheduled each client for a total of 45 minutes. Each trainer conducted four interviews. After their interviews, group members were introduced to the other trainer and to other members who were there.

The agenda for the pregroup interview was as follows:

1. Introduction and overview of the pregroup interview
2. Completion of assessment forms
   a. Pregroup Information Sheet
   b. Gambrill-Richey Assertion Inventory
   c. Situation selection for role play test
3. Completion of brief reading assignment: the group contract
4. Role play test
5. Discussion of group contract (group format)
6. Assignments given for first group session
   a. Reading from text (Alberti and Emmons, 1975, pp. 1-97)
   b. Recording of one nonassertive situation in diary
7. Review of interview/feedback concerning member expectations and appropriateness of group for member needs.

Each client had been informed briefly over the phone about the purpose and content of this interview. However, the trainer began the interview by giving each member a review of what was going to happen in order to remind the client about specific agenda items.

The Pregroup Information Sheet requested basic demographic and self-assessment information. Only that information which has in the past been of use to help the member in the group or which helped to evaluate the program was included. Besides basic descriptive data (i.e., age, sex, family, etc.), the questions included client specification of goals for the group, description of situations that were and were not problematic for them, and a self-assessment of assertiveness.

After completing the Pregroup Information Sheet, the group trainer asked the client to complete the Gambrill-Richey Assertion Inventory (Gambrill and Richey, 1975). This is a 40-item inventory that gives two representative outcome scores for the client—one for discomfort (anxiety) in certain situations and the second for the probability that the client will act assertively.

The client was then asked to read over lists of role play situations. The first was a list of 10 standard role play situations which would be later presented during the role play test. The client was asked to rate each of these situations according to difficulty (how uncomfortable is the client in this situation?) and frequency of occurrence (how often does the client confront this situation in real life?). The other list consisted of 20 optional role play situations which had been previously designated as difficult by group members from similar backgrounds. The client was asked to select 5 of these situations as those that were most important to him or her (i.e., most relevant). The 10 standard situations and the 5 optional situations were used later in the role play test (RPT). The situations were originally selected by a process described by Goldfried and D'Zurilla (1969), and revised on a continuing basis from feedback of trainers and members. (See Rose, 1977, pp. 58-59, 194-199, for details about development of the role play test.)

The next step was conducted in the group meeting room. The client read over the group contract (see Hall and Rose, 1978, for further description) which describes the format and the "rules" of the group. When the client finished with the contract, the role play test (RPT) was administered. After first demonstrating one or two "neutral" situations, the trainer read each of the situations to the member whose responses were recorded on an audio tape recorder for later evaluation.

The client responses to the situations were evaluated at the conclusion of the group as an additional means of evaluating the effectiveness of our program. Two independent raters scored each response according to specific predetermined assertion criteria (see Hall, Lodish-Hall and Rose, 1978).

After the role play test had been administered, the leader discussed in detail the group contract. This contract continued the conceptual structuring that had been taking place in the interview. Through the RPT and by means of discussion at this time, the member had been introduced to "learning by practice" to be employed in the group. The trainer then sought the client expectations concerning the group by reviewing the Pregroup Information Sheet questions about client goals and problematic situations.

Finally, the interview was completed by the group leader giving the client two assignments to be completed before the first group session. The first was to read the first 97 pages of *Stand Up, Speak Out, Talk Back!* by Alberti and Emmons (1975). This book is a general introduction to assertion training and, again, aids in the process of conceptual structuring with group members (i.e., helping them to think of "problems" in a situational context rather than as global personality deficiencies). The second assignment requested the client to record one situation that had occurred before the first session in which he or she wanted to be more assertive. The early description of such situations helps the client to begin analyzing his or her problems in the specific approach mentioned above. (See Rose, 1977, pp. 37-38, for more information about the use of diaries.)

Group Description

In the given group, five said they were recruited by the newspaper ad, two by a poster on campus, and one by referral from a former member. Seven members were female and one male. The mean age was 35.4 with the youngest member 22 years old and the oldest member 51 years old. Four were married, two separated, one single, and one listed "coupled." Four indicated employment outside of the home (although one of these was part-time), two listed an occupation as housewife, and two listed student (although one of these was employed half-time).

The reasons for taking the assertion training course were varied and included the following:

1. I read a book and realized how being nonassertive was influencing my life in many negative ways; realized the class was the best way to go about being more assertive.
2. Help get over any shyness and to not feel guilty when I do the things I feel I want to when someone else is involved.
3. I am interested in these skills. I had a short T.A. course, and sought to learn about assertiveness training.
4. Learn more about assertiveness—use in my employment.
5. I thought it might lead to better relationships in work and peer group situations. Thus, I should feel better about myself and others. Would get more out of relationships too.
6. I feel the need to be more assertive in certain situations, i.e., work, social situations.
7. To increase my ability to constructively express my desires and to increase my self-confidence.
8. It was suggested to me that I was unassertive on job.
9. I feel uncomfortable in various social situations.
10. To learn to feel more comfortable in group situations, both formal (seminar giving) and informal.
11. I have been saying too long that I am going to take a course at the U so when this one was announced, I decided it would be when I began.
12. So I can better express my feelings. It can help me be a better person in my eyes.

Since two members (who, by the way, had not paid their fee or deposit) dropped out of the group following the pregroup interview, the group was ultimately composed of six members and two trainers. The senior trainer had previously led three assertion training groups in this program and had other group leadership training and experience. The junior leader had no previous assertion training group leadership but had observed three such groups. The members[1] were

Debi: 28-year-old female, separated from her husband, part-time student, part-time lab technician, lived in a house with three other roommates.

Andrea: 22-year-old female, single, works as a custodian full time, lives with one roommate in apartment.

[1] Names and identifying information have been disguised in this and all subsequent cases in this book in order to maintain confidentiality.

Ruth: 49-year-old female, married with three children (one at home), housewife, writer, secretary.

Phyllis: 51-year-old female, married with two children (none at home), part-time administrator at a social service agency, homemaker.

Tom: 29-year-old male, coupled, living in a house with two other roommates, student, and part-time editor of community newspaper.

Susan: 26-year-old female, married, working as an audit clerk for the state government.

Each of the six group sessions will now be reviewed in order to demonstrate techniques used by the trainers and to describe problems encountered.

SESSION ONE

Session One is the first opportunity for all group members and leaders to meet together at one time. The agenda for Session One:

1. dyad introductions of group members and leaders;
2. review of goals and agenda;
3. review of group format;
4. review assignments;
5. introduction to behavioral rehearsal;
6. new assignments;
7. session evaluations.

The trainers began the meeting promptly at 7:00 P.M. even though three of the members were not present. It was later found out that two of these members had dropped out while the third, Ruth, had a family emergency that evening and could not attend for that reason. The trainers did meet with her later in the week for a makeup session.

After the trainers welcomed the group members, they read over the goals and agenda, and the trainers described the main activities of the session. Group members were then paired off and asked to "interview" each other. Although the trainers suggested that introductory information be obtained (i.e., name, area of residence, interests, reason for joining the group, etc.), the clients needed to find out information about their dyad partner in order to introduce him/her to the group. This exercise continued for about 15 minutes in this group, but has been varied to accommodate group differences.

Next, the trainers briefly reviewed the group contract and session agenda. Members were encouraged to ask questions at this time and at other times during this first session. However, they indicated that they adequately understood the contract and agenda, so the trainers went to the next agenda item.

Barb, the junior leader, reviewed the assignments which were to have been completed by this session (reading several chapters and writing a diary entry). She did this by asking group members to fill out a special form, the assignment checklist, which is usually completed before the group begins. For the first session only, members filled this out during the meeting time. Each member reported that both assignments had been completed.

> *Barb:* Great! Our group gets a 100 percent for productivity this week. Keep up the good work. I think it would be helpful to hear about some of the diary situations that you wrote up. What kinds of situations did you record?
>
> *Tom:* Well, I wrote on a situation that happened to me with my roommates. I don't know if it's what you're looking for. (Pause)
>
> *Barb:* If it's important to you, it's what we're looking for. Why don't you go ahead, Tom?
>
> *Tom:* OK, I live with two others in a house over on the east side. And we have this arrangement where one of us is responsible for the kitchen each week. Anyway, Bill was in charge this week but he was leaving dishes all over and the floor was a mess. So, I'm trying to figure out a way of saying something to him. I tried the other night but he said he had been busy and would get things cleaned up the next day. But nothing happened.
>
> *Barb:* That's a good situation to bring in to role play. I think we will be able to come up with some good, assertive alternatives when we get to role playing. Anyone else?

The trainer assisted two others in telling their situations. Susan told about a situation in which she had to tell someone at work that she didn't want to work on a committee anymore and really felt uncomfortable about doing so. Phyllis described a recent situation in which she had to turn down a door-to-door salesperson and also was very uncomfortable in telling him that she wasn't interested. They were told they would be able to go into more detail later in the meeting, but that the description of appropriate situations for role playing was a prerequisite for rehearsal. Although some members were readily able to do this when they first came to the group, others had difficulty. For example, Debi had difficulty initially describing her situation in the "first person" and in being specific.

After the brief review of the situations, the leader asked for questions about the reading and then reviewed the basic distinction between unassertive, assertive, and aggressive responses (see Alberti and Emmons, 1975).

The review of assignments was continued by demonstrating the differences between nonassertive, aggressive, and assertive responses to one situation. The "criteria of assertiveness" list was first handed out to all members (Hall and Rose, 1978). This information sheet lists several verbal and several nonverbal components of an assertive response and explains a self-rating system relating to these critiera. This list includes:

   A. Nonverbal criteria (use based on personal style and situation)
1. eye contact
2. degree of relaxation
3. gestures
4. facial expressions
5. volume of voice
6. fluency of spoken words
7. response latency
8. interpersonal distance

   B. Verbal criteria (used if appropriate to the situation and the relationship)
1. refusal
2. reason
3. empathy
4. description of the problem
5. request
6. information seeking
7. personal expressions
8. receiving expressions
9. appropriate humor

These criteria which are also used to evaluate the member role plays, were adapted from Alberti and Emmons (1975), Serber (1977), and from our experience in the groups. Rather than have members give each other feedback that is general (e.g., "You were really assertive that time," or "That was a real good role play"), we encouraged specific feedback initially based on these critiera. As members became more knowledgeable about these criteria, the trainers asked them to explain what the role player did that demonstrated the specific, assertive criterion (e.g., "You had good eye contact *because* you kept your eyes directed at him in a very natural, but forceful way").

After the members had briefly looked over the critiera, the leaders modeled. the three types of responses to one situation. Members commented about why they thought a particular response was assertive or aggressive. Then, the members were paired off again and asked to come up with their own situation in which they could demonstrate the three types of responses. The members came up with the following situations—borrowing an article of clothing, sending back a steak that was burned, and telling a friend that they didn't want to go to a party. The dyads were used to maximize the participation of each member by directly involving them in a creative but structured role play without the focus of the entire group upon them. Both leaders circulated among the dyads to answer questions and to insure that each pair was setting up appropriate situations.

The preparation in dyads took about five minutes and was immediately followed by the demonstrations with the entire group. Each demonstration was followed by a brief, leader-led discussion about the differences between the aggressive, nonassertive, and assertive responses. The members used the criteria for assertiveness list to give feedback.

Next, the technique of role playing was reviewed. Leaders handed out the ISTR project format for role playing called the "Steps of Behavioral Rehearsal." These steps included:

1. Description of the "problem" situation
2. Identification of an assertive goal for the response by the role player
3. Suggestion of alternative responses by other group members and the leaders
4. Demonstration of one of these responses by one of the group members for the role player (modeling)
5. Selection of an appropriate response by the role player based on goal (number 2) and the suggestions/demonstration by others
6. Covert practice by the role player in preparation of the role play
7. Rehearsal of an assertive response by the role player (role play)
8. Assessment of the effectiveness of the response
    a. by the role player based on level of anxiety present and how effective he or she felt their response was
    b. by other group members/leaders, based on the criteria of assertiveness
9. Suggestion of alternative ways to respond by other members/leaders
10. Re-rehearsal of the same, modified or new assertive response by the role player (second role play)
11. Brief assessment by group members and leaders.

After the members read through this format, the leaders modeled how to use the "steps" to present a role play situation. Barb presented a situation which had happened the previous week at work. (The trainers had rehearsed and reviewed this situation in preparation of this session in order to insure that it did indeed demonstrate the "steps" in a nonconfusing manner.)

Rick: Now that all of you have had a chance to look over the "Steps in Behavioral Rehearsal: Training Format," Barb and I will demonstrate how to use them. If you have questions as we go along, could you write them down on your sheet and we'll handle them at the end of the demonstration. OK, Barb, would you describe your situation for us?

Barb: Well, I work as a waitress at a restaurant on County Street. This week my boss changed my work schedule at the last minute so I'd have to work on Saturday. I was really mad so I went to her and asked if there was a mistake in the schedule. She said there wasn't and that Mary had asked to switch so the schedule was changed. I said that I had already made plans and couldn't change them, but she just said that the schedule was final and couldn't be changed. (Pause) So anyway, I'm not sure how to handle this. This is the third or fourth time this has happened. I think she knows she can get away with this with me, so she keeps doing it.

In order to get a better idea of how Barb's supervisor would react, Rick had Barb play her supervisor in an "assessment rehearsal" (included as a part of the description of the situation, step 1). Rick played the role of Barb as Barb had described it.

Rick: OK, does everyone have a clear picture of Barb's situation and how her supervisor will act? (Everyone agrees that they do.) Before we think about what kinds of things you could say, Barb, let's think about your goal in this situation. What would you like to accomplish in this situation?

Barb: I'd like her to change the schedule and I'd like to tell her that she doesn't respect me. I'd really like to tell her off.

Rick: Tell her off?

Barb: Oh, would that be too insulting? Maybe I should just tell her what I think about the schedule change.

Rick: OK, that sounds good. Remember, when we talked about setting an *assertive* goal, we talked about specifying what you want to do or say, rather than what you want the other person to do.

Barb: OK, I can see your point. I guess a more assertive goal for this situation would be to tell her that I've already made plans for the weekend, that I really get mad when she makes these quick changes in the schedule, and that I just can't work this Saturday.

Rick: Good. I think you have the idea now. Of course there are some risks and you have to think about those too. Are there any?

Barb: Well, if I come across too aggressive, I might get fired, but I don't think that's too likely. The owner really likes me, and I can't really get that angry in the real situation anyway.

Rick: OK, let's move on. Are the goals clear to the rest of you? (Everyone nods agreement.)

In our earlier groups, members had difficulty in the setting of assertive goals for themselves rather than goals which included what they wanted the other person to do or say. Thus, appropriate goal setting was stressed prior to the rehearsal of an assertive response.

Rick: Keeping these goals in mind, let's provide some examples of things that Barb could say. (Pause) Remember, the idea is to come up with different ways Barb could respond to this situation. Don't worry how good or accurate they are, there really aren't perfect statements for any situation. Each of us feel comfortable saying things in different ways—being assertive or making assertive statements is no different.

Andrea: You could tell her that you are really upset and feel that she is continually taking advantage of you.

Rick: OK, that's a good alternative. How about another?

Susan: Another way might be (pause), I don't know if you'll like this one, but, you could say, "I wish you would have told me sooner about the change in the schedule. I've made plans for Saturday and there's no way that I can change them now."

Rick: OK, another possibility, Susan. By the way, you just demonstrated another way of giving a suggestion, that is by giving an actual statement. We call this "modeling." OK, Barb, you've got a couple examples here. Would you like other suggestions?

Barb: I guess a couple other suggestions wouldn't hurt.

Tom: I was thinking that you might want to call your supervisor aside, away from any crowd and let her know what you're feeling. Sometimes people feel better about being criticized if they don't have to have everyone listen in.

Phyllis: Another way that I was thinking about from a supervisor's view point, is that you could make a suggestion that the schedule be posted at least one week in advance or that you would help her develop a way of writing up the schedule in advance. That's a lot of work but I know that I'd be open to suggestions.

Rick: Both of those are different ways of handling this situation. Barb, let's evaluate each of these suggestions.

Barb then selected a response by combining her goals and the suggestions of the members.

Rick: Now that you know what you're going to say, what I want you to do is to practice saying it to yourself. We call this "covert practice" which we have found to be very helpful to prepare for the role play. The rest of you might imagine the situation at the same time and what you would do. So, let's take a few seconds and imagine yourself in the situation at the restaurant. You're about to talk with your supervisor just after she has changed the schedule. Then, you say . . . (pause). You might want to close your eyes to help visualize the scene. (Pause) Practice a couple times if you'd like. (Pause) OK, when you're ready, I'll play your supervisor and you say just what you practiced.

After she covertly rehearsed what she wanted to say, the role play began. Rick played the supervisor and Barb played herself.

Barb: Excuse me, Mary, but I just noticed the schedule had been changed so that I'm working on Saturday.

Rick (as Mary):   Right, I had to make some adjustments. Sally just quit and a couple of others couldn't come in on time.

Barb:	Wow, I can see why you had to make the adjustments. But, I've got to let you know that I've already made some unchangeable plans for Saturday so I won't be able to come in either. I wish I could help you out, but I can't.
Rick:	OK, that was good! (enthusiastically) Was that an effective response for this situation for you?
Barb:	Yeh, it sure felt better than when I really said it at work. I think it was effective, I let her know that I couldn't come in. Oh no! I forgot to tell her that I was really mad about her changing the schedule. Will that make a difference?
Rick:	What do the rest of you think?
Phyllis:	I don't think it would help to tell her that you're mad. I know that as a supervisor I don't want a lot of that dumped on me in a hectic day.
Rick:	OK, we'll come back to that. Thanks Phyllis. I'd like you to take out your criteria of assertiveness again and under the column marked role play #1, rate how Barb responded. Take a minute to write down the plus marks for what she did effectively, minuses for areas to improve and N.A. if it's not applicable. (Pause as members write down feedback.)
Rick:	OK, let's give Barb some feedback about her response. First let's go over the pluses.
Phyllis:	Well, I thought you had good eye contact. You never looked away but you didn't stare either.
Rick:	Good comment, I see others are nodding in agreement.
Susan:	I thought you had good voice tone. I could hear you easily and you seemed relaxed, yet you seem to be firm.
Rick:	Another good observation. Any others?
Debi:	Well, I thought you did a good job. I mean you were really assertive.
Rick:	What exactly did she do that you thought was good, Debi?
Debi:	Well, I think she reached her goal. She got across the main part of her goal when she said she couldn't come in at such a quick change in the schedule. I guess what she said just sounded right.
Rick:	Good point. Besides the nonverbal criteria, the content of what Barb said was assertively presented. What you're saying, then, Debi, is that Barb was effective because she reached her goal of assertively refusing to come in on such short notice.
Debi:	Yeh, that's what I mean.

Rick: OK, you've mentioned some good points about Barb's response. Is there any other way that you can think of that Barb could have acted in this situation? This doesn't mean better, just different.

As in previous groups, during the first couple sessions, the members were not able to come up with alternatives (constructive criticism) for this situation. After pausing, Rick made a couple of suggestions.

Rick: Well, Barb, you've heard a couple other alternative responses and you've heard the feedback about your response. Now I'd like you to go through the role play again. We've found that it helps a lot to practice a response a second time. If you want, you can use exactly what you said last time, or you can change it based on what you've heard. So any time you're ready, why don't you begin the role play? Do you want me to act differently as your supervisor?

At this point, Barb re-rehearsed her response and briefly received feedback from the group. Rick said he would limit the role play to 10 minutes and had one of the members act as timekeeper to help stay within this limit.

After the demonstration of the steps of behavior rehearsal, each member was given a chance to role play his/her diary situation or a situation from the "Optional Role Play Situations" list. The group took a 10-minute coffee break about halfway through the session. The trainers brought refreshments for the first session (a job to be carried out by members in the later sessions).

After the break, all five members role played one situation. Each member drew upon one situation recorded in his or her diary during the week. The trainers collected the diaries at the end of the session, and, at the following session, handed them back with comments about how they were written and about the appropriateness of the situation for role playing. Tom role played first and practiced making an assertive request to his roommate to clean up the kitchen. Phyllis used the situation which she had described earlier to practice assertively refusing (saying she wasn't interested) a door-to-door salesperson. Susan rehearsed talking with a coworker and informing this person that she could no longer work on a departmental committee. Andrea then role played a situation that she had written about by asking her roommate to pay for some damages to their apartment (which the roommate was responsible for). And finally, Debi practiced expressing her opinion in a class she was taking.

New assignments were made after the role plays had been completed. These included reading chapter 14 in the Alberti and Emmons book, reviewing the reading from last week (pages 1-97), filling in an information sheet concerning assertive refusal, reading an information sheet about the buddy system, and recording one problem situation on a diary entry sheet.

The trainers then handed out session evaluation sheets which included questions about which of the procedures or techniques were useful and which were not useful. Members also were asked to point out concepts that needed to be clarified as well as to rate their satisfaction with this session on a six-point scale.

Discussion of Session One

The mean satisfaction level for this session was 5.4, with six representing very satisfied. This followed the pattern in most of our previous groups which had fairly high satisfaction ratings for the first session. As mentioned previously, the productivity percentage (the number of completed assignments divided by the total number of assignments given) was 100 percent for the five members who were present. Ruth came to a makeup session just before the second session and had completed all assignments except the recording of a diary situation. Therefore the overall productivity percentage for all members for Session One was 94.4 percent. During the week, the trainers found out the two other members (who had not paid their fee or deposit) had decided not to continue with the group after they had been pretested.

There were two observers present in the meeting room who recorded who was saying what to whom (see Hall, Lodish-Hall and Rose, 1978, for description of observation code). The trainers here were mainly interested in the distribution of participation so percentages were computed and are shown in Table 1-1.

TABLE 1-1   Session One Participation Percentages

Barb	25.5%	Leaders	70.0%
Rick	44.5	Members	30.0
Phyllis	5.5		100.0%
Andrea	8.1		
Tom	3.2	Mean Percentages	
Debi	7.4	Overall	14.29%
Susan	5.8	Members	6.00%
	100.0%	Standard Deviations	
		Overall	15.26
		Members	1.90

From this data the leaders became concerned about the distribution of participation. More specifically, they noted that the leaders had a combined percentage far greater than for all members combined. Second, they noted that Rick, the senior leader, spoke almost twice as much as Barb, the junior leader. And third, they noted that Tom talked very little. Although Session One is rather atypical in that the leaders present more information than at other sessions and in that the more "passive" members will not talk as much as at other sessions, the leaders decided that they needed to make some changes.

In order to equalize the leader percentages, it was decided that Barb would take the longer agenda items for Session Two and that Rick would not break in unless there was an "extremely crucial" point to be made. We also decided to wait until we had Session Two data in order to see if member percentages would increase.

The trainers decided that the points of confusion listed on the session evaluations would be covered adequately by the Session Two agenda. They divided up the agenda items, practiced how they would present the items and then discussed each member. A brief assessment of each member was written:

Phyllis: was fairly quiet during session one. She listed three types of situations on which she wanted to work in the group. These were situations with (1) tenants, (2) employees, and (3) her family. Her Assertion Inventory scores were 133 for "Degree of Discomfort" (which is somewhat above the norms from our groups), and 123 for "Response Probability" (which is at the upper limit of the norm for our groups). These scores would predict that, although fairly anxious in some situations, she did have good assertive skills overall.

Andrea: was the most shy person in the group. She did not do a lot of talking either at the pregroup interview or during Session One. She did, however, spend more time describing her problem situation in Session One than did the others. Thus, her higher percentage of talking. Her three goal areas were (1) accepting criticism, (2) accepting a compliment, and (3) "hopefully offering suggestions when I want to do what I feel when other people are involved." She scored 107 for "Degree of Discomfort" (which is in the middle of the normal range for our groups), and 115 for "Response Probability" (which again is within the normal range for our group members).

Tom: seemed to be somewhat anxious when he spoke both at the pregroup interview and during Session One. However, both leaders noted that he seemed to understand the concepts about assertiveness more quickly than the other group members. He listed three goal areas which were: (1) relationships with close friends, (2) work relationships, and (3) family relationships. He scored 128 for "Degree of Discomfort" on the Assertion Inventory (which is somewhat above the norm), and 123 for "Response Probability" (which is just slightly above the norm). He did report that he felt very anxious in most interpersonal interactions and that he had a difficult time responding in a satisfactory manner.

Debi: had read Smith's book, *When I Say No, I Feel Guilty*, before she took our course, so had more information about assertiveness than the other members. She made several good suggestions during Session One. She scored, however, 159 on the Assertion Inventory for "Degree of Discomfort" (which is way above normal), and 132 for "Response Probability" (which again is above normal). According to these scores and her diary situations she appeared to be highly anxious and needed a great deal of work on developing assertive responses. Her goal areas focused on her work situation, her living situation, and expressing her feelings with her friends.

Susan: became very anxious when initially called upon in the group. Her blushing was very noticeable because of her very fair complexion. She wanted to work on how to feel comfortable in job interviews, how to interact appropriately at work and how to converse in social situations, such as at parties where she might not know anyone. Susan scored 95 for "Degree of Discomfort" (well within the normal range), and 101 for "Response Probability" (also within the normal range).

Ruth: missed the first session so that we did not have participation data for her. She did appear highly anxious during the pregroup interview and had difficulty role playing in the first person. She indicated that she wanted to work on receiving criticism, expressing personal feelings, and handling anger. She scored 74 for "Degree of Discomfort" (which is slightly below normal for our groups) and 115 for "Response Probability" (which is in the normal range for our groups). However, from the observation of the leaders, Ruth seemed highly anxious most of the time and was very concerned with whether or not she was doing the proper thing.

SESSION TWO

The goals for Session Two were to have each group member practice one situation taken from his/her diary, to review the criteria of assertiveness, to practice assertive refusal, and to set up the buddy system. The agenda was:

1. Review goals and agenda
2. Review last session's evaluations
3. Review criteria of assertiveness
4. Review assignments
5. Group exercise: assertive refusal
6. Behavior rehearsals (role plays)
7. Buddy selection
8. New assignments
9. Session evaluation.

All six members attended the second session and were in the meeting room before seven o'clock. Both leaders were present as well as the two observers.

After reviewing the goals and agenda for Session Two, Barb reviewed the evaluations from Session One.

> *Barb:*   At the end of last session, each of you filled out an evaluation form. We feel that these are very important to our planning for the group. Overall, your comments were very helpful. The average satisfaction rating was 5.4, which is extremely good. In addition to a lot of positive comments, you also listed a couple things that need clarification such as the general definition of an assertive response. This one should be clarified in the exercise on the criteria of assertiveness. A couple of you also mentioned dissatisfaction with your role playing ability or with your situation. Hopefully, we should be able to give each of you an opportunity to role play at least once tonight and longer than last week. Please bring up any questions you have as we go along tonight. Are there any questions or comments left over from last week?

Since there was no response the trainers went on to the group exercise on the criteria of assertiveness.

The goal of this exercise was to demonstrate how assertive behavior could be broken down into verbal and nonverbal components. This exercise also gave each member a chance to plan a series of simple role plays in dyads and then present them to the total group. First, the trainers modeled the kind of situations and criteria to use. Then the members were paired off into three groups of two and assigned two criteria to demonstrate. They were given one nonverbal and one verbal criteria from the total list. After five minutes of preparation, the dyads presented a situation in which the response was not assertive, and then the same situation in which the response was assertive. Discussion followed each role play concerning the differences between the two responses and concerning the appropriateness of the criteria in certain situations.

After the exercise, Rick reviewed the completed assignments with the group. The assignment completion checklist had been filled in by all members before the group began and the productivity score had been computed. Rick announced the completion rate to the group (92 percent) and then asked if there were any questions from the assignments. When there were no questions or comments, Rick paired off the members again and asked them to summarize one of the assignments. After two or three minutes, the dyads gave brief summaries. Debi and Andrea discussed the buddy system. Tom and Phyllis summarized the reading, and Ruth and Susan talked about assertive refusal.

This led to the next exercise concerning assertive refusal (Hall and Rose, 1978). Each member had read an information sheet and completed a written exercise as an assignment for the session. Ruth and Susan's discussion mentioned above also helped members understand this concept and technique.

> *Rick:*   Barb and I have worked out another brief role play to show you how to make an assertive refusal. This scene takes place at the

West Towne Shopping Center and Barb, alias "collection agent," approaches me to donate to the Verona Hockey Club. I'm not interested in giving.

Barb: Hello, I'm Barb, and I'm working with the Verona Hockey Youth Club. We're out asking the good people around the area here for donations to help buy equipment for our new girl's team. Could you donate any amount of money? Anything would help.

Rick: I'm sure that it's a worthy cause, but I won't be able to give anything.

Rick (as leader): OK, notice that no reasons were given, although I did express some understanding of the situation. Does everyone have the idea? (Pause)

The group then broke into two groups of three members and one trainer to practice assertive refusal. After five minutes, when the group returned members commented on the usefulness of the exercise as well as the appropriateness of assertive refusal for specific types of situations (e.g., with friends, with family, etc.). In this exercise, situations in which the members had to make a refusal were presented and the member responded accordingly. The main discussion took place in the large group.

After the exercise, the trainers asked for one of the group members to describe his/her situation from the diary. Susan volunteered first and described a situation in which she was bothered by a coworker who chewed gum very loudly at the desk next to hers. Although she did not have a planned response, Susan got several ideas from the group and then practiced saying, "Excuse me, Betty, that gum sounds delicious, but I'm having a difficult time concentrating on my work here. Every little thing seems to disturb me. I've got to get this out by 4:30. Could you chew in "low gear" for awhile? Thanks."

Tom role played before the break also. He did not have a diary situation written but was able to briefly describe a situation with his roommates concerned with the expenditure of money for food. Although Tom was not a vegetarian, he did not want to buy a lot of expensive meat. His roommates had been buying meat for almost every evening meal, and Tom wanted to express his feeling that he did not like to spend so much money. He practiced bringing up the topic with his roommates and even suggested in the role play that they go ahead and buy meat but that they have separate meals on some evenings. He was very satisfied with his response and received broad support from the group.

Immediately after the coffee break, members were divided again into pairs or "buddies." Each member had read an information sheet concerning the buddy system before this session, so had the basic knowledge about why it is used in the group (see Rose, 1977, p. 189, for details on buddy system). The buddies were given five minutes to set up a time to meet during the week. Phyllis was paired with Ruth, Tom with Debi, and Susan with Andrea. After five minutes of planning, the teams briefly reported when and where their contact would be. The trainers also assigned the teams to talk about various role playable situations from their immediate past and then role play an assertive response to one they thought to be most relevant to them. During the review of assignments at Session Three, the dyads would be able to report on the kinds of situations role played.

After the buddy planning, Andrea volunteered to describe a recent situation at a local service station. She brought her car in for a tuneup and had asked the attendant to save the old parts. When she returned to pick up the car, the old parts were nowhere to be found and she hadn't been able to respond assertively in this situation. She practiced expressing her feelings of being "ripped off" and that she wanted to talk with the manager. On the re-rehearsal, she practiced talking with the manager to register a complaint. Although the group gave her encouraging feedback, Andrea felt her response was somewhat aggressive so wanted to practice this again with her buddy later.

Phyllis next described a situation that occurred at work. Two of the employees at her agency were having an argument and Phyllis wanted to say something to stop it. She decided it would be her place as the supervisor to at least move the quarrel to an office where they wouldn't disturb the other workers. So she practiced breaking in to the argument, suggesting the move to a new location, and even began to clarify what the argument was about. She had just let the argument continue during the week and hadn't said a thing. She was very pleased with her practiced response.

Debi did not have a diary situation and asked to wait until next week. She did participate in two of the role plays by the others, however.

Ruth presented last and described an old situation from work in which she felt put down by a coworker and wanted to tell this person off. She spent an enormous amount of time describing the dynamics of the office and why she thought she felt "one down." She was not able to specify a goal for herself before the end of the session, and thus was not able to role play a response.

The new assignments were outlined by Barb. These assignments included writing two diary entries instead of one. Of these two one was to be a stressful situation to which the client responded at least partially successfully, and the other, a problem situation, as the previous ones. She also reminded the buddy teams to meet at least once during the week to discuss the group and to practice one response each. The reading assignment was to read chapters 11, 12, and 13 from Alberti and Emmons, and to complete an information sheet concerning assertive requests (the technique to be practiced at Session Three). There were information sheets to read about "contingency contracts" and the "survey of reinforcers;" finally, members were asked to fill out the "survey of reinforcers." (See Rose, 1977; pp. 94-95, 188-189, concerning contingency contracts; pp. 96-97, concerning the survey of reinforcers.)

After the presentation of the new assignments and subsequent discussion, the members filled out session evaluations. The trainers were able to complete the meeting within five minutes of the designated two hour limit, even though Ruth had taken nearly 20 minutes to describe her situation.

Discussion of Session Two

The average satisfaction rating on the member evaluations was 4.8 for Session Two. This was down from 5.4 for Session One and may have reflected the discomfort raised by Ruth's complex description.

Comments on the evaluations were mainly positive, however, as four persons commented that they felt that their role played response was very useful. Three persons mentioned that they liked how freely the members spoke in the group and how comfortable they were feeling now. One person commented that she liked the structured approach to role playing: "It makes it a lot easier." The "negative" comments had to do with questions about role playing and about assertiveness in general ("Can I always expect to be assertive?").

The participation percentages for Session Two are shown in Table 1-2.

TABLE 1-2 Session Two Participation Percentages

Barb	18.8%	Leaders	57%
Rick	38.2	Members	43%
Phyllis	8.1		100%
Andrea	4.2		
Tom	5.2	Standard Deviations	
Debi	5.2	Overall	11.41
Susan	8.4	Members	2.91
Ruth	12.0		
	100.1%	Mean Percentages	
		Overall	12.51
		Members	7.81

We were pleased to see that the leader percentages (the amount of time the leaders were speaking) decreased from Session One, but there was still a two-to-one ratio between Rick and Barb. The members' percentages were generally increased with the mean percentage going from 6.00 percent for Session One to 7.18 percent for Session Two. The overall standard deviation remained high indicating that there was a large imbalance between some of the participation percentages. The standard deviation for the percentages of member participation only increased from 1.90 to 2.91 percent. This also indicated a larger spread in the member percentages from Session One to Session Two.

These changes were consistent with our previous experience with assertiveness training groups. Generally, after the first session, leader participation decreases until the sixth session when there is a slight increase.

Ruth's high percentage of participation (12.0 percent) represents primarily her description of her problem situation. Although she had written one diary entry for this session, she decided to describe another situation and analyzed the situation rather than briefly describing it. The leaders failed to limit her quickly enough and felt as a result that the other group members were bored at this time. A couple of the members stared at the floor and there was little participation while Ruth described her situation. After discussing this situation in supervision and at the weekly staff meeting, the trainers decided that the situation, as described, was inappropriate for our group. It dealt more with an overall state of feeling and a self-assessed personality characteristic (Ruth stated that she had always had an inferiority complex and got "put down" a lot). Their supervisor suggested that if this happened again to cut off the description by questioning its appropriateness and ask for another situation. Also, it was suggested that Ruth may need additional help in situation description as she had missed the first session and had not done her diary homework for the first two weeks. The trainers planned to talk with Ruth immediately before the next session to discuss her new diary situation, and thus help focus her comments before she went into the group.

The only other "problem" with this session was that Debi did not role play a situation. She did not write a diary situation but did state that she would role play first at Session Three. Her evaluation was very positive and stated that she had been very tired during the session. No plans were made concerning Debi other than to offer her the opportunity to role play first at the next session.

The assignment completion percentage was 92 percent with the only two assignments not completed being diary entries (Tom and Debi). All members were on time and stayed for the entire meeting. Although some of the participation percentages decreased (Andrea and Debi), the others increased, and, with the addition of Ruth to these statistics, the trainers planned to wait until the Session Three data was in to make any judgments about members who talked too much or too little (in relation to the group).

SESSION THREE

The goals for Session Three were to continue role playing situations from member diaries, to practice writing contingency contracts, and to practice the technique of assertive requests. The agenda followed the same format as for Sessions One and Two.

All six members attended the third session. Barb reviewed the nine assignments given for this session and found the completion rate to be 75.0 percent. Tom did not record either diary entry, Phyllis recorded only one, as did Ruth. Ruth also did not complete any of her reading assignments stating that she had a very difficult week at home.

The remainder of the assignments were again reviewed by dividing into pairs and having each dyad summarize the main points of two assignments. During the subsequent discussion, the trainers found that only one team actually got together for buddy contact. Andrea and Susan said they couldn't find the time. Tom questioned the purpose of the buddy contact and felt like it was an infringement on his private life. Ruth and Phyllis were the only two to actually meet, but they discussed only a couple of situations and did not role play.

The trainers then briefly reviewed why the buddy contact was used and suggested that, though it was not required, the members try it again during the coming week. After a short discussion, the members did agree to try it again.

Next, the trainers introduced the exercise on assertive requests (Hall and Rose, 1978). Members had prepared for this exercise by reading an information sheet and by completing a written exercise. The information sheet explained the technique of assertive requests and discussed the types of situations in which to use it. In the written exercise members are asked to write a response to situations which had come up in previous groups. Examples of these situations included the following:

1. On Saturday, you purchased a medium priced shirt/blouse at a nearby department store. On Monday, you realize that you have overspent your budget and feel that you need to return the shirt/blouse. You return to the store and say . . . .
2. You are at a committee meeting/small class and the person who is speaking is difficult to understand. You really want to understand what he or she is talking about. You ask for clarification by saying . . . .
3. You have had some new/old friends over for dinner. It's getting late and you would like to go to bed. You say . . . .

Besides a written response, members are asked to rate their discomfort in each of these situations from one (low) to ten (high). For example, as Tom is a student, he decided to use the small class alternative for situation 2 which he rated seven for discomfort. He also decided that he would rather be making his request to a male professor as he had a specific situation in mind. As homework, he wrote out a response which was: "Excuse me, Dr. Smith, but I don't understand your last point about the importance of the Jones article. Would you mind expanding this briefly?"

After the trainers explained the exercise to the members, they modeled how to role play the situations in the exercise.

Barb: (in role play) Excuse me, Sir. I purchased this blouse on Saturday and have decided that I just don't want it. I've got the sales slip here and the blouse is still in the package. I'd like to get a refund.

Rick: (as salesclerk) OK, but I'll have to get the manager, she has to approve all returns.

Barb: OK, I'll just wait right here.

Members then practiced all ten situations that were listed on the group exercise without referring to their homework. This was done in two groups of three with one trainer with each subgroup. A discussion then followed in the large group concerning the limits of this technique and other situations in which to use it.

Debi was the first to role play as agreed on in Session Two. She presented a situation that involved asking for a raise at work and seemed to find a response that she could effectively role play. Phyllis, who worked at a residential treatment center, then role played a situation in which she requested one of the clients to leave her office so that she could get some work done (the client usually dropped over to just chat). She tried two different responses before she found one that felt somewhat comfortable. She said that she felt very guilty for having to ask someone to leave because the residents (her clients) did not have many people to talk with, and chose the response that showed a lot of empathy for the client and suggested another time to get together.

After the break, the trainers reviewed the use of contingency contract to help work on specific goals. The members again had prepared for this by reading an information sheet (Hall and Rose, 1978) and by completing a brief written assignment. The information sheet explained the purpose of the contingency contract, how to incorporate the survey of reinforcers in writing a contract, the format to use when writing a contract, and five examples of contracts (from former group members). Each member had then agreed to write a first draft of a contract for Session Three and all but Ruth had done so.

The group discussed the major points of the information sheet and briefly reviewed the first draft contracts that they had written. Next, the members worked with their buddies to polish up their first draft. Examples of three acceptable contracts were the following:

1. I agree to tell my roommate this week that it really bothers me when she does not keep the bathroom clean when it is her turn to clean it. If I do this, I will buy the new Billy Joel album. To insure that I complete this assignment, I will give the money for the album to my buddy, who will either buy the album if I talk with my roommate or donate it to a charity of his choice if I don't.

2. If I speak up in class one time this week, I will then get to spend Tuesday evening with Bob without doing any homework.

3. If I talk with my husband in a nondefensive, assertive manner this week about how he makes me feel when he calls me names, then I will be able to call my friend, Betty, long-distance to talk for 30 minutes. I will not call Betty until I do speak to my husband in the above mentioned manner.

Andrea's contract read: "When I am assertive this week, I will read one of the books I have been meaning to read." The trainers had to work with her to specify the situation and a type of response, and a specific reinforcer given by the buddy.

After rewriting contracts with their buddies, each member briefly described his/her contract and they agreed to work on the contract with their buddies serving as monitors.

Next, Tom described a recent situation involving his girlfriend. She had been late in meeting him, and he said that he reacted very angrily. He practiced a more assertive way of expressing his anger over her being late and seemed to find that first trying to find out why she was late was important to include as well.

Andrea presented a situation that occurred at a bar. She and a friend had decided to get together to discuss old times when two men came over to their table and asked if they could get into the conversation. Andrea didn't want them to stay, but didn't say anything. Her friend finally demanded that they leave at once or she would call the police. Andrea wanted to find a better way of asking them to leave and received several suggestions from the others. She practiced asking them to leave in a firm, but pleasant voice and during the re-rehearsal, practiced repeating this request over and over until they left.

Susan described a situation that had just occurred. She had been at a family picnic when her father-in-law began degrading blacks for being lazy and not working. When she was asked if she agreed, Susan stated that she had become so angry that she could not talk and just walked away. She practiced saying that she didn't agree in a short, nondefensive statement.

Ruth again brought in a situation that was very complex. Although Rick had met with her before the meeting, she included more about how this related to her childhood and how deep rooted this problem was. This situation concerned another office worker whom she had "told off" in a very aggressive way. However, at the end of ten minutes, she still had not role played so that Rick asked her to role play this at the beginning of the next session.

The new assignments for Session Four were the following:

1. one successful and one problematic diary entry;
2. one buddy contact during the week;
3. read information sheet on assertive expressions;
4. work on contingency contract completion;
5. read assignment from Alberti and Emmons that related to expression of feelings and talking with close friends.

After the assignments were agreed to by the members, session evaluations were completed and the meeting ended.

Discussion of Session Three

From the evaluations, the members reported that the role playing was becoming easier and that they were able to work out more realistic responses to their problematic situations. Tom said that "It helped me to focus on my specific problem." Susan said, "I was very pleased with myself during the role play with Tom. I think the group is becoming more at ease with each other—at least I am." Ruth even stated, "Role playing becomes a little more familiar; it's good to try to empathize." Even though she had not role played a response to her own situation, she did role play the "other" person in two other behavioral rehearsals.

The mean satisfaction rating for this session was 5.17 which is up from 4.83 for Session Two. The participation percentages for Session Three are shown in Table 1-3.

TABLE 1-3 Participation Percentages for Session Three

Barb	16.1%	Leaders	53.9%
Rick	37.8	Members	46.1
Phyllis	5.7		
Andrea	4.0		100.0%
Tom	11.0	Standard Deviations	
Debi	8.4	Overall	11.19
Susan	3.3	Members	4.11
Ruth	13.7		
	100.0%	Mean Percentages	
		Overall	12.50
		Members	7.68

Although the percentages for the trainers stayed about the same from Session Two (Barb was 19 percent and Rick was 38 percent), there was still concern about the balance of the leader-leader ratio and the leaders-members ratio. The trainers had attempted through agenda planning to reduce the participation of the senior leader and the leaders overall. However, this had not occurred. So they agreed to continue assigning the longer agenda items to Barb, and Rick agreed to reduce his comments to a brief one or two sentences and to increase his latency to five seconds before initiating comments or questions.

Tom (11.0 percent), Debi (8.4 percent) and Ruth (13.7 percent) were all near the group overall mean of 12.5 percent participation (which would represent equal participation in the group). The other three members had lower participation percentages, so the trainers planned to encourage these three to talk more at Session Four. The mean percentage of member participation increased from 7.18 percent at Session Two to 7.68 percent at Session Three which was encouraging. However, the standard deviation also increased which indicated that there was a larger variance in member participation than in Session Two.

As mentioned above, Ruth again had difficulty in specification of her target situation. She was encouraged for improvement from the last session and Rick agreed to talk with her before the next session to go over her description. She was to call in during the week and, if necessary, they would meet immediately before the next session as well. Ruth and her buddy also agreed to work on selecting a situation for role playing. It should be pointed out, however, that Ruth did participate in two role plays during Session Three (Susan's and Debi's) even though she did not have time to role play her own situation.

As mentioned, the productivity percentage for Session Three was 75.0 percent, which was a drop from each of the other two sessions. The main problem with assignment completion was the diary situations, but due to the fact that members were bringing in situations anyway, the trainers did not plan to take any special action.

SESSION FOUR

Goals for Session Four were to continue practicing situations from member diaries, to practice the technique of assertive expressions (Hall and Rose, 1978) and to choose a new buddy for the last two sessions. The agenda followed the result format.

All six members were present for Session Four. Out of the seven assignments given each member, Tom wrote only one diary entry (which was an improvement for him), and he and Debi did not make their buddy contact. Thus, the productivity score was announced by Barb as 92.9 percent, up from 75.0 percent at Session Three.

The trainers inquired about the buddy contacts during the review of assignments. Ruth and Phyllis reported that their contact was very helpful as Ruth was able to work on a more specific situation. Andrea and Susan said that they found this contact very helpful and were glad that they had a chance to meet outside of the group. They met for lunch and were able to work on a problem situation that happened to Susan during the week. She and her husband lived in a house with another couple, and Susan was bothered that some of the household chores were not getting done. Although she did not role play at the buddy contact, she decided on a way of handling it and wanted to practice in the group.

The group exercise on assertive expression followed the same format as for assertive refusals and assertive requests. The leaders briefly introduced the exercise, modeled how to practice the situations and then divided the group in half. All members had read the information sheet on assertive expressions and had completed the written assignment.

In this exercise, trainers in the subgroups presented the same eleven situations that were on the written exercise and asked the members to respond. They could use a response that they had planned or they could use a new one. The other members gave feedback to the role player about the effectiveness of his/her response and what he/she could do to improve it. Examples of these situations were as follows:

1. A friend of yours is continually late in meeting you for lunch. (Assume you are annoyed with this.) You say . . . .
2. Assume that you have missed most of the assertiveness training group meetings and someone criticizes you for this. You say . . . .
3. Give a compliment to someone in the group about an article of clothing.
4. Praise someone in the group for a personal attribute (e.g., kindness, generosity, warmth, honesty, etc.).

For the situations involving the giving and receiving of criticism, one of the trainers was the "other" person in the role play and would ask one of the members to play the "client." One of these brief role plays involved Debi responding to Barb. Barb read situation 1 (above), and after a brief hesitation, Debi replied, "You know, I'm not really happy that you're late again. This is the third time in a row that I've had to wait for you." Others in the group began commenting:

Susan: I thought you really said what you were feeling, Debi. You kept good eye contact with Barb (in role of friend), and it was even stronger than most assertive things we've been doing. But I think you needed to be stronger.

Tom: I don't know. I thought you were very direct and strong, too. You really said some assertive statements. But, didn't you say that you weren't happy that you're friend was late again? Maybe you would be more assertive if you used a positive feeling like "I'm feeling angry because you're late again, Barb." Let her know that you feel that way.

Debi: Hey, that's good, that feels "right" too. That's a hard situation for me. Anyone else have any suggestions for improvement?

Phyllis: Yes, I thought your response was good, too, but it was a little negative overall, don't you think. I know this is skipping ahead, but I remember reading that sometimes it's good to let the person know that you care about them or like, for you, Debi, that you enjoy eating lunch with this person. Does that help any?

Debi: Well, that sounds good, but would I be letting my friend off the hook by saying something nice?

Phyllis: The example in the information sheet said that criticism is often easier to handle when we give some positive with it. It might be worth a try.

Debi: OK, I think I can try it in this situation.

The discussion for this situation was more lengthy than for most of the others. However, the group members gave more feedback in this exercise than in the previous "techniques" exercises. Also, Debi had recently been confronted with this situation so that it was extremely relevant for her. Debi was also encouraged by one member to try and respond more quickly, as her hesitation might give her a chance to become more anxious and not respond as assertively as if she responded right away. Debi agreed to this suggestion and re-rehearsed her response.

Debi: You know, Barb, I really like having lunch with you, but I've been sitting here for 20 minutes wasting my time. This is the third time this has happened in the last couple weeks. Is there anything wrong? Is there anything you're mad at me about? I'd really like to know.

After completing all of the practice the group then briefly discussed the appropriateness of this technique for certain kinds of situations and gave feedback about the exercise.

For the situations involving the giving and receiving of praise, Barb went around the group and asked members to take one of the praise situations and direct it to someone in the group. For instance, Barb asked Andrea to give someone a compliment about an article of clothing. She paused and then said, "Ruth, your outfit looks really nice on you. Those colors really complement each other." Ruth responded, "Why, thank you. This is one of my favorite outfits. That makes me feel good to know that someone else likes it, too." Each person practiced giving and receiving at least one compliment. Group members reported that even though this was an exercise, it really felt good to hear the praise.

Before the break, Ruth and Andrea described situations from their diaries to role play. Ruth had been working on her "office" situation from last week and gave about a two-minute description. She obviously had been working on this situation and had focused on one particular time when she was talking with the coworker that she didn't like. The leaders and members gave her a lot of praise during and after the behavioral rehearsal, which she completed easily within the 10 minute limit. Ruth was very pleased, as evidenced by the assertive way she handled this praise. She thanked each person for the compliments and then stated that she had worked hard on this and she was glad the others felt the same way.

Andrea presented a situation that involved her father and mother. They had asked her about her new roommate and she was having a difficult time coming up with a response for them. She had put them off the first time but she knew they would ask again on Sunday when she went over for dinner. One of her male friends, Dave, had moved in and, although they each had their own bedroom and were not romantically involved, Andrea felt very uneasy telling her parents about him. The group was able to help her come up with a satisfactory response and Susan asked her to tell them next week what happened.

After the break, the trainers went over the buddy system again very briefly. The members then selected their own buddies, although it was stipulated that they could not select their last buddy. Phyllis and Susan paired off as they lived near each other outside of Madison. Ruth and Debi became buddies, and Tom and Andrea agreed to be buddies. Each team set up a time and place to meet, and actually made an initial plan for this meeting. The leaders moved from team to team to help in the selection of this initial plan.

Tom, Debi, Phyllis, and Susan all presented situations during the second hour of the group. Tom had another situation concerning his roommates and the house budget. His roommates wanted to buy a lot of orange juice which Tom thought to be too expensive for his income and didn't want to buy. He was able to come up with a response that offered an alternative to his roommates so that they could have their orange juice and he wouldn't drink or help pay for it.

Debi's situation concerned her boyfriend who wanted to come up to her room after their last date. Debi had refused but didn't feel comfortable with her response. She practiced saying that she had a great time but that she needed to call it an evening as she had to be at work the next morning at 7:30. She felt that she would feel more comfortable with this situation next time.

Phyllis' situation involved two of her employees who were custodians at her agency. Bill, the older custodian, said that he saw Bob, who had been working there only a month, take some carpet shampoo home with him. Phyllis knew that if Bill said this, it was most likely true and she would have to confront Bob. Phyllis stated that she didn't know what to say in this situation and needed some suggestions. After a number of other suggestions, Ruth proposed that she call him into her office and tell Bob that she couldn't find the carpet shampoo and ask if he knew where it was.

Phyllis, though still anxious about it, decided that Ruth's suggestion would be the best alternative and role played it effectively with Tom playing her employee, Bob. They role played it three times and each time Tom responded differently (upon request of Phyllis), as she did not know how Bob would respond. Although Phyllis herself was not satisfied with her response, the feedback was positive: "Your eye contact was great!" "You responded quickly and you seemed very relaxed."

Susan presented the last situation of the evening. She was interested in transferring from her job to one in another department, but was afraid to ask her supervisor about it. Ruth suggested that she go to the personnel department and check it out first to see if it was really available. Susan liked this approach and rehearsed what she would say to the personnel director.

The new assignments to be completed for Session Five were:

1. two diary entries—one successful and one problematic;
2. one buddy contact with "new" buddy;
3. read information sheet on assertive defensive techniques and complete written exercise;
4. read Alberti and Emmons text for chapters about situations appropriate for above techniques.

These assignments were reviewed with the members and the session evaluations filled in. The meeting concluded on time.

Discussion of Session Four

The mean satisfaction score for this session was 4.17 which was a drop from 5.17 for Session Three and the lowest so far. The leaders theorized that this drop had to do with the focus on Phyllis' situation although it seemed that everyone was involved. Susan rated the session a three but did not give any comments. She had described a very uncomfortable situation, however, and did not have adequate time to re-rehearse and explore other alternatives. Andrea rated the session a two with the comment that she felt that her role plays were not useful. As her participation percentages revealed, she scarcely participated in the interaction at all. Phyllis gave the session a four and said, "the role plays get rather lengthy." The other three gave either fives or sixes, and wrote fairly positive comments.

Ruth gave the session a six and said, "Rapport increased, ease of talking increased as does interplay." She did comment that, "For me, getting to the point" was something she needed to work on. She improved this session but would continue to need help with her next situations.

The participation percentages for Session Four are shown in Table 1-4:

TABLE 1-4   Participation Percentages for Session Four

Barb	10.5%	Leaders	43.3%
Rick	32.8	Members	56.6
Phyllis	15.9		99.9%
Andrea	2.5		
Tom	9.9	Standard Deviations	
Debi	8.6	Overall	9.00
Susan	11.1	Members	4.34
Ruth	8.6		
	99.9%	Mean Percentages	
		Overall	12.49
		Members	9.43

The percentages (representing participation) for all members except Andrea were approaching the goal of 12.50 percent. For Session Five the trainers decided to incorporate Andrea more in the group exercise feedback and to include her more in the initial stages of the session to encourage her overall participation. The other members, as mentioned, made a substantial increase, which could not help explain the low satisfaction ratings.

The amount of participation estimated for Rick (32.8 percent) was still too high, although Barb decreased substantially from 16.1 percent for Session Three to 10.5 percent for this session. The trainers said that even though they had planned out a strategy to increase Barb's participation and decrease Rick's, this plan broke down. Rick seemed to have more comments during the role plays while Barb stated that her main concern was getting smoothly through the steps of behavioral rehearsal. It must be noted, however, that the trainers dropped from about 54 percent of the participation at Session Three to about 43 percent for this session. The goal had been 40 percent for the trainers so that even though the leader-leader ratio was unsatisfactory, the trend of total leader participation was in the right direction.

Correspondingly, the mean percentage for member participation increased from 7.68 percent to 9.43 percent, while the standard deviation for members stayed relatively the same (4.11 percent to 4.34 percent). The overall standard deviation decreased while indicated that there was less variation between all participation than at Session Three. Again, the goal here was to lower the standard deviation of participation percentages to less than 5 percent, which would reflect 20 percent participation per leader and 10 percent per member.

The trainers planned to have members "lead" role plays at Session Five, which would theoretically help accomplish our participation goals as well as provide members with valuable ingroup leadership (assertive group behavior) experience. The trainers did notice that members tended to ask Rick almost all of the questions concerning assertiveness and his answers represented the largest part of his participation. The trainers decided that Rick should try to incorporate members in answering these questions and answer himself only if absolutely necessary.

The trainers also noticed that the quality of member feedback to other members during role plays was improving. Although this could not be seen in the data, both trainers did notice that members were giving more spontaneous, specific, and sophisticated feedback and this represented the largest change in assertive ability in the group for this session.

They were concerned about the low satisfaction rating and would ask about member opinions at Session Five. The productivity score for this session was 93 percent, which was considered satisfactory, and attendance and promptness were perfect.

SESSION FIVE

Session Five included a change in the approach to the role play situations. Members led some of the behavioral rehearsals with coaching by one of the leaders. The goals for the session were to continue the practice of assertive responses to diary situations, to shift some leadership of role plays to members, and to practice defensive assertive techniques. The agenda followed the usual format.

Again, all six members were present and on time. Phyllis informed the group that she would have to miss the final meeting as she had to go out of town for a meeting. Barb reviewed the assignments with the group and found that the productivity score was 66.7 percent, down from 93 percent at the previous session. Although each member had agreed to write two diary situations, only Debi had done so. Phyllis, Andrea, Susan, and Tom had one and Ruth did not write any. Only Phyllis and Ruth had completed their contingency contracts and everyone had contacted their buddy. In fact, members were very enthusiastic about their contacts as they reported on them.

The members read an information sheet on defensive assertive techniques in preparation for this session and had completed a written exercise (Hall and Rose, 1978). These techniques are discussed elsewhere by Booraem and Flowers (1975). The defensive techniques included time out, broken record, negative assertion, clipping, and anger starvation. After reviewing the important points from the information sheet, the trainers modeled the practice exercise. They presented a situation which was taken from the exercise on assertive refusals. This situation involved telling a salesperson that you were not interested in buying magazine subscriptions. Instead of a basic, assertive "No," the leaders modeled the use of broken record which has the client keep repeating his/her refusal until the salesperson acknowledges it.

The trainers also demonstrated the use of time out by Rick responding to a request to join a community group by saying that he couldn't make a decision at this time but that he would get back to the requester (Barb) the next day with a decision. They then demonstrated the use of clipping. Rick played a roommate who said to another roommate, Barb, "The T.V. was left on all night!" Rick acted as though he were very angry. Barb then replied, "Yes, I noticed the T.V. was left on." Members asked questions about these techniques to clarify their use. Next the trainers divided the members into dyads and had them practice each of the defensive techniques. These situations included:

1. Your teenager is making a strong argument for extending his/her normal curfew for a special event. You're not sure about this event. Use anger starvation and assume that your teenager is very angry. *Or* you're not sure what you want to say. Use time out.

2. A salesclerk is exerting a lot of pressure to get you to buy a shirt that doesn't really fit right. Use broken record.
3. You generally make the morning coffee. On this particular morning, you didn't and your spouse/roommate says, "The coffee isn't made!" Assume he/she looks somewhat angry and use clipping or negative assertion.

Next, the trainers began the behavioral rehearsals. As members now could volunteer to lead every other role play, the trainers led a discussion about the important attributes and functions of leaders in this group. Then, Susan, Tom, and Phyllis volunteered to lead the second, fourth, and sixth role plays respectively. The trainers would lead the other role plays in order to continue the modeling of the appropriate leadership behaviors.

Ruth presented her situation first with Rick as leader. She described a recent situation involving her son. The son wanted to use the car when Ruth had other plans. Usually, she gave in right away if her son persisted, but this time she had tried to be assertive and had almost succeeded. She practiced a version of the broken record technique but included statements about what she did like about her son and offered to work out a compromise. The group gave her several good suggestions which she incorporated into her response. She felt very good about how she came across and the others gave her a lot of positive feedback.

Susan led the next role play which was presented by Andrea. Andrea described a situation when she was served a "wilted" salad at a local restaurant. She had sent it back for a new salad at the restaurant, but the "new" one turned out to be as bad as the first. However, she was too uncomfortable to send back this second one. Susan guided Andrea through the role play with minimal coaching by Rick.

> *Susan:* OK, does everyone understand the situation? (Pause; everyone nodded that they did.) And your goal, here, Andrea, is to send the second salad back and to get a good salad in return. Right?
> *Andrea:* Yeh, that sounds like it.
> *Susan:* OK, let's role play it. Let's see . . .
> *Rick:* (coaching) Why don't you ask everyone for some suggestions on how to handle this one?
> *Susan:* Oh, I forgot that part. Does anyone have a suggestion on how to handle this one? Would you like some suggestions, Andrea?
> *Andrea:* I guess so.

After a few suggestions, Andrea decided that she will basically repeat her first response by describing the unacceptable condition of her salad and that she wants a fresh salad brought to the table. She practiced this response and felt very satisfied about it. Then Susan asked the group for feedback.

Ruth:	I thought you handled it very assertively. Your voice was very firm and you didn't hesitate to call the waitress back.
Tom:	It looked like the waitress even looked a little guilty. Right Debi? (Debi had played the waitress.) Anyway, I thought you were very effective. You had really good eye contact and your use of humor was very appropriate. I hope that the waitress would take you seriously.
Susan:	Anything else?
Phyllis:	Yes, I watched your face while you were making the request and you looked a little angry and firm.

There weren't any suggestions for improvement and Andrea felt that she didn't need to role play again. At that point, Rick asked the group to give Susan feedback about her leadership.

Andrea:	I felt real good having you lead the role play. You kept it moving and I felt like I accomplished something by the end.
Tom:	Yeh, you kept asking questions in the beginning to help get us all involved in the conversation. That's important.
Debi:	You didn't need that much help from Rick, either. You kept to the steps of behavioral rehearsal without making me feel like you were. It was real smooth.
Susan:	(blushing) Gee, I didn't know I did so well . . . .
Phyllis:	I remember when you helped clarify the goals as well. I was a little confused at that point and you summarized them real well.
Ruth:	I thought you did a good job too. I don't think I could do as well.
Rick:	With all of these good comments, it looks like we may be out of a job, Barb. But I agree, you guided Andrea through the steps very smoothly and you were able to get everyone to participate. Great!

After the break, Barb led the next role play in which Phyllis described a situation that had happened at work. One of the residents began to gossip to Phyllis about another resident, and Phyllis practiced asking her not to continue in a firm tone of voice. She was satisfied with her response but was unsure if she would be able to do it next time.

Tom led the next role play with Barb coaching. Debi presented a situation in which a friend kept asking her a stream of personal questions. Debi felt extremely uncomfortable when it really happened and ended up telling more than she had wanted. She practiced saying that she was uncomfortable answering these kinds of questions and would rather talk about something else. Debi wanted to work on better eye contact and a smoother delivery of her statements.

The group felt that she definitely improved between her first and second role plays, and Debi herself stated that she felt much better about it.

Tom did not require any coaching from Barb and received a lot of positive feedback from the group. Debi said that she felt very much at ease with Tom leading. Phyllis said that she was really surprised how easily Tom went through the steps of behavioral rehearsal. Andrea mentioned that she forgot that a nontrainer was leading the role play. Tom smiled all through the praise and thanked the group for their comments.

Neither Tom or Susan wanted to present a situation, so Andrea came up with another one. Phyllis led the role play and Rick coached. She described another situation with her father in which he was asking her a lot of questions about her boyfriend. She practiced telling her father she wasn't comfortable with the questions and that she would prefer that he wouldn't ask them. Andrea stated that she had been helped a lot by Debi's role play as the suggestions fit her situation as well. By the second rehearsal, she said that at least she knew what to say even though she might be nervous if it happened again.

Phyllis needed more coaching than the others as she let the conversation wander several times. The group members got involved in how Andrea's father treated her overall and began asking her about how it had affected her as she grew up. Phyllis seemed to lose the leader role at these points and was coached by Rick to bring the group back to the specific situation. From the time she set up the role play, however, Phyllis became more directive and the role play finished within the 10-minute limit.

Although she wasn't very positive about her leadership, the others gave Phyllis good feedback. Tom commented that she was very empathetic with Andrea and with the group members as they gave their suggestions. Susan said that Phyllis had leaned forward in her chair as she led and kept good eye contact, which made her feel that Phyllis was in charge. Phyllis looked somewhat surprised at the feedback and also commented that she did better than she thought.

Susan and Tom agreed to role play first at Session Six.

The new assignments were:

1. two diary entries—one successful and one problematic;
2. one buddy contact;
3. Alberti and Emmons book—review chapters of interest;
4. buy another book on assertiveness and bring to Session Six;
5. Read and complete the review of assertive techniques information sheet and written exercises.

Buddies set times to meet and planned what they would do together. Session evaluations were filled out and the meeting ended on time.

Discussion of Session Five

The mean satisfaction ratings by the members for this session was 5.6 which was an increase from 4.2 at Session Four. Susan wrote on her evaluation that she found it very useful to be a role play leader. Debi wrote, "very good role plays . . . things were focused well." Ruth stated that "role playing is easier" and that "communication is more personal now." Phyllis liked her chance to lead a role play and Andrea wrote "really just practicing being more assertive and role playing" were good this session. Tom commented that at this session he received "more help where I needed it." The participation rates reflected this increased satisfaction.

TABLE 1-5   Participation Percentages for Session Five

Barb	13.7%	Leaders	35.6%
Rick	21.9	Members	64.4%
Phyllis	6.8		100.0%
Andrea	7.1		
Tom	10.0	Standard Deviations	
Debi	12.8	Overall	4.94
Susan	16.0	Members	3.53
Ruth	11.7		
	100.0%	Mean Percentages	
		Overall	12.50
		Members	10.73

Most noticeable was the drop in the percentage of leader participation, from about 44 percent for Session Four for both leaders to 36 percent for Session Five. Rick's participation decreased from 33 percent to 22 percent with the "new" format of having members lead role plays. Andrea and Phyllis had the lowest individual percentages but their evaluations indicated that they were very satisfied with the session. The mean percentage for members was 10.73 percent which was above the 10 percent goal that had been set. Also, the standard deviation for the entire group dropped from 9 percent at Session Four to below 5 percent for this session.

Ruth again described her situation and role played within the 10-minute limit. By this session, she had learned the skill of behavioral rehearsal and was able to present appropriate situations two weeks in a row.

Although not everyone role played, each member participated more than in earlier meetings (as the percentages indicate). The group exercise also involved everyone and included more complex situations in which the members had to respond more than once to the "antagonist."

Also impressive about this session was the ability of the members to lead role plays and to give feedback to these leaders. During each of the role plays, member suggestions indicated thinking about the appropriateness of the defensive techniques for these situations and the members were asking for more stress in the role plays. The trainers planned to have members lead role plays at Session Six as well.

As mentioned before, the productivity score for this session was 66.7 percent, which mainly reflected that diary situations were not written up. However, the trainers were impressed with the types of situations being presented so no plans were made concerning these assignments. Attendance and promptness were both perfect.

SESSION SIX

The goals for Session Six were to continue practicing an assertive response to diary situations, to practice at least five of the assertive techniques, to select three methods for continuing assertive practice after the group ended and for at least three members to lead one role play or the discussion of other agenda items. The agenda followed the same format described in Session Two.

Five of the members attended Session Six. Phyllis who made up the meeting the evening before was absent because of an out of town meeting. Barb computed the productivity score for this session at 83.3 percent, with five assignments given per member. Susan and Phyllis had not been able to have a buddy contact, Tom didn't write either diary situation, Debi didn't write up a problematic diary situation.

Next Debi reviewed the assignments with Barb coaching. She asked members to describe their successful (assertive) experiences. Susan mentioned that she had finally gone to the personnel director to inquire about a new job and had already been interviewed this week. She was very satisfied with how she responded both with the personnel director and with the job interviewer. Andrea said that she had talked with her father about her male roommate and that the conversation went smoothly. There were some uncomfortable moments, but neither one got very upset, and they even went out for a beer later. Members and leaders applauded and cheered as each member presented these successful situations.

After the assignments had been reviewed, the group gave Debi feedback on her leadership. Tom thought that the agenda item was a tough one to lead, but that Debi had maintained good eye contact with everyone and that helped keep people interested. Ruth liked how Debi asked the members for comments if the group became too quiet.

At this point, Barb introduced the group exercise that reviewed all of the assertive techniques (Hall and Rose, 1978). All of the members had read the information sheet describing the exercise and had completed the written exercise before the meeting. For the written exercise, they had to write responses to

35 situations using specified assertive techniques. After Barb had explained the exercise to the total group, she divided them up into dyads and assigned them two or three techniques. The dyad then summarized the significance of this technique to the rest of the group and demonstrated a nonassertive and an assertive application to one situation. These situations were very similar to those used in the previous sessions.

> *Susan:* You can use the broken record technique when you have to be persistent with someone like a salesperson or some other person with whom you do not wish to enter into a relationship. The book recommended that you use it with nonfriends ordinarily, although there are situations in which it might be used with a friend where he or she is trying to manipulate you. We have a role play to demonstrate what we mean.
>
> *Andrea:* Excuse me, ma'am, but I'm selling Globe Encyclopedias and I notice your children are about ready to need a set of these. What grade are they in?
>
> *Susan:* I don't think that's important. Although I'm sure you have a fine offer, I'm not interested.
>
> *Andrea:* Most of the concerned parents in your neighborhood have ordered a set. I'm sure you wouldn't want your children to get behind in school would you?
>
> *Susan:* I am very concerned about my children, but I just am not interested.

Andrea and Susan continued their role play in order to demonstrate the persistence of the broken record technique. Upon conclusion of the role play, other members gave feedback from the criteria of assertiveness and from the information sheet that included broken record.

Next, Barb went around the group, and asked members at random to respond with a specific technique to one of the situations from the group exercise sheet. Brief discussions followed each response concerning appropriateness and relevance to other situations. The trainers continually emphasized the sequence in deciding to use defensive techniques. Rick mentioned that it was important to reserve these techniques to situations in which the basic techniques had failed. And then only if the member felt pressured and if the relationship could handle it. Although the leaders had planned to take only 20 minutes for this exercise, it continued for the entire first half of the meeting. However, members did agree to continue it as they felt that they were able to "pull things together" by using this exercise. Several questions and comments concerned the ethics of using the techniques in certain situations. The leaders purposely stayed out of the conversation as much as possible and tried only to comment when there was a question on definition.

After the break, the members were asked to re-order the remaining agenda items. They decided to role play until 8:45 at which time they would have the other group exercise. They also agreed that they didn't need one of the trainers to model leading the first role play so Ruth and Debi volunteered to lead. Andrea didn't want to lead and, although she was strongly encouraged by everyone, she stuck to it and assertively refused.

Ruth led the first role play and Tom presented. He had another situation with his girlfriend. This time, she wanted him to park in a no parking zone while they ate at a restaurant and he didn't want to. An argument ensued and Tom wanted to find a better way of handling it.

Andrea suggested that he firmly say that he wouldn't feel comfortable parking there and he would continue looking for a space. He thought he would try that and, after practicing, he felt as though he could handle it next time.

Susan presented the second situation while Debi led. Susan described a situation from last week when her husband made a rude remark about her cooking. She got very angry and yelled back at him. Tom suggested that she use a form of clipping in that she reflect her husband's remark and then taste the spaghetti herself. Then she could make a decision whether he was right or not. However, in either case, she had to then continue to respond to his rude remarks. She practiced expressing her feelings about his remarks and how she didn't (or did) agree with him. Ruth felt that Susan used a very firm and calm voice throughout the role play which surprised Susan. The other members agreed to the comment, and also mentioned that her response latency was brief and that she didn't get defensive during the role play. Susan was pleased with her response and promised to let us know if this situation happened again.

Because of the length of the exercise and due to the number of comments with each of these two role plays, there were only two situations presented. Next, Tom led the group exercise concerning what to do after the group had ended (Hall and Rose, 1978). The members read a brief information sheet which explained the purpose of the exercise. After questioning the leaders about the exercise, Tom divided the group into dyads and asked each pair to come up with at least four ways of continuing to practice assertiveness after the group had ended. Later in the discussion, Ruth suggested that they could read books about assertiveness and even take an advanced course. Susan thought that she might try role playing with her husband when a difficult situation occurred. Andrea mentioned that the group could get together later to see how each other is doing. She also suggested that they could continue the buddy system with each other. The members liked this idea and exchanged phone numbers. Debi mentioned using diary entries to help focus situations and contingency contracts if they were helpful.

After this group discussion had been completed, the group gave Tom feedback about his leadership. Debi liked how easily Tom got each person to participate and how smoothly he directed them to go from dyads to the large group.

Ruth thought that he praised what everyone said during the exercise just like the real leaders. Tom again was very pleased with this feedback and stated that he really enjoyed leading the group.

Finally, the trainers arranged times in one week to interview each member individually and asked if the members would be interested to get together for a follow-up session in three to six months. Everyone agreed and even arranged to get together in one month at a local pub. Session evaluations were then filled out and the meeting ended on time.

Discussion of Session Six

The mean satisfaction rating for this meeting was 5.8, the highest of all sessions. The members commented mainly about the positive aspects of the session, although two members did say they didn't feel totally comfortable with some of the assertive techniques and wanted more practice. Susan said that she was "not as nervous during role plays." Debi said that she found the role playing useful and leadership of role plays very helpful. Ruth, Tom, and Andrea all commented that they thought the review of assertive techniques exercise was very useful. Although only two members were able to present situations for role plays, everyone had a chance to participate.

TABLE 1-6   Participation Percentages for Session Six

Barb	13.3%	Leaders	36.8%
Rick	23.5	Members	63.0
Phyllis (absent)			
Andrea	8.7		99.8%
Tom	11.9	Standard Deviations	
Debi	8.7	Overall	5.3
Susan	15.7	Members	4.17
Ruth	18.0		
	99.8%	Mean Percentages	
		Overall	14.3
		Members	12.60

All member percentages were increased from Session Five but there was one less member present. However, the standard deviation remained around 5 percent which was the goal. The leader percentages stayed relatively the same as Session Five. Together, the trainers participated about 37 percent of the time during the session compared to about 63 percent for the members. This percentage for leaders (37 percent) was below the goal of 40 percent, as it also had been for Session Five.

The group members had been able to take over much of the leadership skills in the group by this session. Debi had reviewed the assignments, Tom had led a group exercise, and Ruth and Debi led role plays. Although the productivity score was only 83 percent, the trainers felt that the members were very prepared for this session as evidenced by their participation in the exercise on assertive techniques. The postgroup interviews were planned for one week from the last meeting and followed the same format as the pregroup interviews.

POSTGROUP INTERVIEW

The purpose of the postgroup interview was two-fold. First, a reassessment took place using the measures used at the pregroup interview: the Gambrill-Richey Assertion Inventory and the role play test. Second, members were asked to evaluate the program, both in writing and verbally. All of the interviews took place one week following the sixth session on the same evening that the group had been meeting (Thursday). Each leader interviewed the same three persons that he/she had interviewed at the pregroup meeting. These interviews lasted about 45 minutes each.

When a member arrived, he/she was asked to first complete the Assertion Inventory and the Postgroup Information Sheet. The information sheet was similar to the one used at the pregroup interview, but included questions concerning program evaluation and self-assessment of procedures and activities in the group. This list included role plays (led by leaders or led by members), diaries, the buddy system, the text (Alberti and Emmons), the criteria of assertiveness, the assertive techniques exercises, and the leaders themselves. The information sheet also asked each member to list three situations in which he or she felt more assertive and three situations in which he or she needed more practice. Each member then rated his/her overall assertiveness as a person and could write in additional comments and suggestions.

The role play test was conducted in the same fashion as at the pregroup interview. When a member completed the written work, one of the leaders reviewed the basic steps in the role play test and then administered the test.

Results

The results of this study have been assessed primarily on the basis of the pre- and posttesting with the two tests. The first (Assertion Inventory) provided both a response probability score and an anxiety or level of disturbance score. (In both cases, the lower the score, the better.) Table 1-7 shows the results of the Assertion Inventory for response probability and for level of disturbance.

TABLE 1-7 Assertion Inventory Scores

	DEGREE OF DISCOMFORT		
Member	Pretest	Posttest	Change
Ruth	74	47	− 27
Susan	95	101	+ 6
Debi	159	161	+ 2
Tom	128	55	− 73
Andrea	107	77	− 30
Phyllis	133	125	− 8
Lana	76	Dropped out	
Sara	116	Dropped out	
Average[1]	116.00	94.33	− 21.67
Standard Deviation	30.23	43.63	29.14

	RESPONSE PROBABILITY		
Member	Pretest	Posttest	Change
Ruth	115	107	− 8
Susan	101	103	+ 2
Debi	132	103	− 29
Tom	123	117	− 6
Andrea	115	106	− 9
Phyllis	123	121	− 2
Lana	77	Dropped out	
Sara	126	Dropped out	
Average[1]	118.17	109.50	− 8.67
Standard Deviation	10.52	7.64	10.76

[1] Data for "dropouts" *not* included in any summary statistics.

The role play test provides three sets of data. Two are self assessment measures by the client while the third is a more objective score by trained raters. For each role played situation in the test, the client rated how uncomfortable he/she felt (subjective units of discomfort = SUDS) and how satisfied he/she felt with his/ her response (see Table 1-8). The third score was obtained by "blind" observers rating the audio-taped responses (see Table 1-9).

As we review the data we have evidence that all of the members showed changes on almost all of the measures in the desired direction. On the one objective measure, assessment by the rater of the role play test, both Ruth and Phyllis showed slight shifts in the undesirable direction while all others showed moderate to large shifts in the desired direction. Only Ruth showed a decrease in her satisfaction level with her responses and no change at all on her SUDS or anxiety level on the role play test (see Schinke and Rose (1976) for a detailed description of this instrument). On the Assertion Inventory (see Gambrill and

TABLE 1-8 Role Play Test Scores: Self-Assessment by Members

	SUDS (SUBJECTIVE UNITS OF DISCOMFORT)		
Member	Pretest	Posttest	Change
Ruth	2.72	2.72	.0
Susan	2.27	1.82	− .45
Debi	3.64	3.45	− .19
Tom	2.64	1.36	− 1.28
Andrea	1.82	1.55	− .27
Phyllis	3.18	2.82	− .36
Lana	2.09	Dropped out	
Sara	2.00	Dropped out	
Average	2.71	2.29	− .42
Standard Deviation	.64	.83	.45

	SATISFACTION		
Member	Pretest	Posttest	Change
Ruth	3.82	3.45	− .37
Susan	3.45	3.73	+ .28
Debi	2.82	3.64	+ .82
Tom	4.09	4.55	+ .46
Andrea	4.27	4.64	+ .37
Phyllis	2.55	3.18	+ .63
Lana	4.55	Dropped out	
Sara	3.73	Dropped out	
Average	3.50	3.86	+ .36
Standard Deviation	.69	.60	.41

TABLE 1-9 Role Play Test Scores of Assertiveness: Assessment by Rater

Member	Pretest	Posttest	Change
Ruth	3.55	3.36	− .19
Susan	2.45	2.55	+ .10
Debi	2.18	3.27	+ 1.09
Tom	2.00	3.45	+ 1.45
Andrea	2.55	2.82	+ .28
Phyllis	3.00	2.91	− .09
Average	2.62	3.06	+ .44
Standard Deviation	.57	.35	.67
Overall Reliability = 82%			

Richey, 1975, for a detailed description of this instrument), Susan and Debi showed no decrement in anxiety while the others showed small to large decrements. Susan also showed no decrement in her response probability while all the others showed a small decrement and Debi showed a large one.

In summary it appears that Ruth showed shifts in the desired direction on only two of the five measures. Debi showed shifts in the desired direction on three of the measures, Phyllis and Susan on four, and Andrea and Tom on all of the measures.

Although these results are not unequivocal, they suggest at least a moderate success rate in the group. If we compare these shifts to other groups in which a similar approach has been used and similar measures applied, these mixed results are not unusual.

Discussion

The group presented in this paper was typical of most of the assertive training groups run under the auspices of Interpersonal Skill Training and Research Project in terms of process and outcome.

The leaders have shared their planning and their leadership activities, their mistakes and their successes with the reader. They have tried to show how they dealt with the myriad of problems that arose in this typical group.

They successfully dealt with their own tendency to dominate the interaction. They dealt less successfully with the discrepancy between the two leaders in providing leadership. They dealt effectively with an effusive but off task member for whom the structure of the group was initially something to avoid.

Whether or not the members changed dramatically as evidenced on the self-report and objective measures, they all valued the group highly and felt it was an important and useful experience.

REFERENCES

Alberti, R. E. and Emmons, M. L. *Stand Up, Speak Out, Talk Back!* New York: Pocket Books, 1975.

Booraem, C. D. and J. V. Flowers. A procedural model for the training of assertive behavior. University of California-Irvine, unpublished manuscript, 1975.

Eisler, R. M., M. Hersen, and P. M. Miller. Effects of modeling as components of assertive behavior. *Journal of Behavior Therapy and Experimental Psychiatry*, 1973, *4*, 1-6.

Galassi, J. P., M. D. Galassi, and C. M. Litz. Assertive training in groups using video feedback. *Journal of Counseling Psychology*, 1974, *21*, 390-94.

Galassi, J. P., M. P. Kostka, and M. D. Galassi. Assertive training: a one year follow-up. *Journal of Counseling Psychology*, 1975, *22*, 451-52.

Gambrill, E. D. and C. A. Richey. An assertion inventory for use in assessment and research. *Behavior Therapy*, 1975, *6*, 550-61.

Goldfried, M. R. and T. J. D'Zurilla. A behavioral-analytic model for assessing competence. In C. D. Spielberger (ed.), *Current topics in clinical and community psychology*, vol. 1. New York: Academic Press, 1969, pp. 151-96.

Hall, J. A. and S. D. Rose. *Assertive problem solving in groups: training manual.* University of Wisconsin-Madison, unpublished manuscript, 1978.

Hall, J. A., D. Lodish-Hall, and S. D. Rose. The Relationship of participation to outcome in assertiveness training groups. University of Wisconsin-Madison, unpublished manuscript, 1978.

Hedquist, F. J. and B. K. Weinhold. Behavioral group counseling with socially anxious and unassertive college students. *Journal of Counseling Psychology*, 1970, *17*, 237-42.

Hersen, M., R. M. Eisler, and P. M. Miller. An experimental analysis of generalization in assertiveness training. *Behavior Research and Therapy*, 1974, *12*, 295-310.

————, M. B. Johnson and S. G. Pinkston. Effects of practice, instructions, and modeling on components of assertive behavior. *Behavior Research and Therapy*, 1973, *11*, 443-51.

Lomont, J. F., F. H. Gilner, N. J. Spector and K. K. Skinner. Group assertion training and group insight therapies. *Psychological Reports*, 1969, *25*, 463-70.

MacDonald, M. L., C. U. Lindquist, J. A. Kramer, R. A. McGrath and L. L. Rhyne. Social skills training: The effects of behavior rehearsal in groups on dating skills. *Journal of Counseling Psychology*, 1975, *22*, 224-30.

McFall, R. M. and D. B. Lillesand. Behavior rehearsal with modeling and coaching in assertive training. *Journal of Abnormal Psychology*, 1971, *77*(3), 313-23.

McFall, R. M. and A. R. Marston. An experimental investigation of behavior rehearsal in assertiveness training. *Journal of Abnormal Psychology*, 1970, *76*, 295-303.

McFall, R. M. and C. T. Twentyman. Four experiments on the relative contributions of rehearsal, modeling, and coaching to assertion training. *Journal of Abnormal Psychology*, 1973, *81*, 199-218.

Percell, L. P. Assertive behavior and the enhancement of self-esteem. In R. E. Alberti (ed.), *Assertiveness.* San Luis Obispo, Calif.: Impact Publishers, 1977.

————, P. T. Berwick and A. Beigel. The effects of assertive training on self-concept and anxiety. *Archives of General Psychiatry*, 1974, pp. 502-4.

Rathus, S. A. An experimental investigation of assertive training in a group setting. *Journal of Behavior Therapy and Experimental Psychiatry*, 1972, *3*, 81-86.

Rimm, D. C., G. A. Hill, N. N. Brown and J. E. Stuart. Group assertive training in the treatment of inappropriate anger expression. *Psychological Reports*, 1974, *34*, 791-98.

Rimm, D. C., M. Keyson and J. Hunziker. Group assertive training in the treatment of antisocial aggression. Unpublished manuscript, Arizona State University, 1971.

Rose, S. D. *Group therapy: A behavioral approach.* Englewood Cliffs, N.J.: Prentice-Hall, 1977.

———— and S. Schinke. Assertive training. In H. H. Grayson and C. Loew (eds.), *Changing approaches to the psychotherapies.* New York: Spectrum Publications, 1978.

Schinke, S. P. and S. D. Rose. Interpersonal skill training in groups. *Journal of Counseling Psychology*, 1976, *23*, 442-48.

Serber, M. Teaching the non-verbal components of assertive training. In R. E. Alberti (ed.), *Assertiveness: Innovations, applications, issues.* San Luis Obispo, Calif.: Impact Publishers, 1977.

Shoemaker, M. E. and T. L. Paulson. Group assertive training for mothers: A family intervention strategy. In E. J. Mash (ed.), *Parenting: The change, maintenance, and direction of healthy family behaviors.* New York: Brunner/Mazel, 1976.

Thorpe, G. L. Desensitization, behavior rehearsal, self-instructional training and placebo effects on assertive-refusal behavior. *European Journal of Behavioural Analysis and Modification*, 1975, *1*(1), 30-44.

Wolpe, J. *The practice of behavior therapy.* New York: Pergamon Press, 1973.

2

group problem solving
with the elderly

INTRODUCTION

The term problem-solving has been used by helping professionals to explain a particular process between client and worker which leads to the resolution of problematic situations experienced by the client. William James (1890) was one of the earliest proponents of the benefits of using systematic problem-solving processes for learning. Since then, aspects of problem-solving have been incorporated into many different theories of learning (see for example, Mowrer, 1947; Hilgard, 1956). Many recent theorists have recommended the use of problem-solving methods for the treatment of diverse problematic situations (see for example, Perlman, 1957; Hallowitz, 1974; Mahoney, 1974).

Problem-solving intervention methods have the potential for wide application in helping clients to resolve problematic situations. Components of problem solving have been used extensively by psychiatrists, psychologists, and social workers as a part of their clinical practice. For example, the discussion of response alternatives and consequences is a long-standing practice of directive therapy approaches (Rotter, 1954; Kelly, 1955). Despite the use of problem-solving procedures in clinical practice, problem-solving procedures have not been clearly specified. Little research has been undertaken to verify the effectiveness of the components of the problem-solving process or to evaluate the effectiveness of a problem-solving approach to group treatment.

EVALUATIONS OF GROUP PROBLEM SOLVING

In evaluating group problem-solving procedures with adults, Coche and Flick (1975) found problem-solving training groups significantly improved hospitalized psychiatric patients' abilities to solve interpersonal problems. Toseland (1977), in an uncontrolled group study, found problem solving to be effective in increasing social skills of older adults. Other than these studies the only tests of the direct application of problem-solving training to behavioral difficulties has been a handful of studies employing "thinking skills" as part of therapeutic procedures (see, for example, Giebink, Stover, and Fahl, 1968; Mahoney, 1974; McGuire and Sifneos, 1970). By far, most of the evaluation of problem solving has been done by child psychologists interested in training young children to learn how to problem solve and teaching parents how to help their children problem solve (see, for example, Shure and Spivack, 1975a; Shure, Newman, and Silver, 1973; Shure and Spivack, 1972; Shure and Spivack, 1957b).

PROBLEM SOLVING
AND COGNITIVE BEHAVIOR THERAPY

Mahoney (1974) suggests that the lack of specificity in regard to problem-solving components and the lack of research on the effectiveness of problem solving is due to a failure to define and measure problem-solving ability adequately. The failure can, in part, be attributed to the fact that problem solving is a cognitive process which results in behavioral outcomes. The cognitive processes which occur in problem solving mediate between a particular stimulus such as a problematic event and a particular response to the problematic event. Early in the history of operant behavior therapy, the focus of theory and practice was on the overt response consequences and resulting behavior patterns. Problem-solving processes are largely covert cognitive operations. Thus, despite the widespread use of problem-solving procedures by clinicians, applied behavior therapists have been reluctant, until recently, to specify and measure the covert cognitive process of problem solving.

Applied behavior therapists have now begun to show an increasing interest in covert cognitive behavior (see, for example, D'Zurilla and Goldfried, 1971; Mahoney, 1974). Operant behavior theorists have also become increasingly interested in covert cognitive events which occur between response consequences and the performance of a behavior. Both behavior theorists and applied behavior therapists have become increasingly aware of the function of covert problem solving in response performance.

GENERAL PROBLEM-SOLVING SKILLS

Despite the lack of evidence for the effectiveness of problem solving in group treatment, the importance of the problem-solving process should not be underestimated. Unlike the emphasis on discrete response training in some behavioral group methods, problem solving is focused on a set of general skills which are helpful in handling diverse problematic situations. Studies have shown that emtionally distressed individuals are poor problem solvers (see, for example, Spivack and Levine, 1963; Platt and Spivack, 1972a and b; and Platt, Scura, and Hannon, 1973). They tend to use more impulsive and aggressive solutions to problematic situations and are less capable of means-ends thinking than their "normal" peers (Shure and Spivack, 1972).

PROBLEM SOLVING DEFINED

There is no single universally accepted definition of problem solving. One of the most widely used definitions is provided by D'Zurilla and Goldfried (1971). According to them problem solving is:

> a behavioral process, overt or cognitive in nature, which makes available a variety of potentially effective response alternatives for dealing with the problematic situation and increases the probability of selecting the most effective response from among these various alternatives (p. 108).

The problem-solving process can be divided into a series of six interrelated component steps: general orientation, defining the situation, problem-solving orientation, generation of alternatives, decision making, the evaluation and implementation of the problem solution. Although there is a lack of empirical evidence for the effectiveness of the overall problem-solving process, there is a considerable amount of evidence for the effectiveness of each of the above components. This evidence will be presented in conjunction with the detailed explanation of each of the problem-solving steps as they were applied in one particular project and in one particular group for the elderly.

FORMING THE GROUP

In this project group participants were recruited by newsletter, posters, and personal contact with the staff of three community agencies for older adults in Dane County, Wisconsin, as part of the research program of the Interpersonal Skills Training and Research Project of the School of Social Work, of the University of Wisconsin (Madison). Two of the agencies were coalitions of small religious, private, and public groups of older persons in Madison. One agency was a senior citizen center in Sun Prairie, Wisconsin.

Twenty-four persons participated in the problem-solving workshops. Five groups were formed ranging in size from three to six participants. All volunteers were sent a letter explaining the purpose of the group workshop, as well as the time and place of the first group meeting.

Leaders for the groups were made up of the four staff members of the participating agencies and two social work graduate students. All leaders received 16 hours of training in the problem-solving method. A detailed manual of the problem solving process described below was also provided for each group leader. (This manual is available on request from the author).

A PROBLEM-SOLVING GROUP FORMAT

As a response to posters and contact with a social worker from a nearby senior center, eight persons from a housing project for senior citizens volunteered to participate in a problem-solving group. The participants met in the community room in the housing project for six weekly 90-minute meetings. Bill and Charlie, the two male members of the group, were both retired businessmen. They stated that they wanted to participate because they wanted to learn more about how to get along with their friends. Bill, age 68, pointed out that since he had retired, he had had a lot of time on his hands which he wanted to use by getting more involved in social activities. Charlie, who retired nine years ago, was interested in the skills he could learn to confront people who were annoying him and to reduce social contacts with people whom he "didn't care to to associate with."

Six women, all homemakers, also were interested in the group workshop. Sarah wanted to participate because she was very passive. She wanted to be able to tell people about things which annoyed her. Anne and Betty stated that they needed to improve their skills in handling difficult interpersonal situations tactfully. The other three women—Hyde, Pauline, and Jan—were interested in learning more about interpersonal skills in general. In discussing why the group members wanted to participate, it became clear that the members were reluctant to discuss any interpersonal difficulties they might be having with friends or family. Since it was important for all members to share their experiences in interpersonal encounters, a group problem confronting the leader of the workshop was to increase the frequency of members discussions of difficult interpersonal situations. This was accomplished by praising all attempts by group members to explain difficult interpersonal encounters. In addition, the leader cautioned group members about being judgmental or critical concerning the way a group member handled a particular encounter. Once a group member had fully explained a situation, the other group members were encouraged to point out what was done effectively in the way the situation was handled. Once this feedback was given, the group members could suggest additional ways to handle the interpersonal encounter effectively.

A problem-solving process was used to help group members develop the social skills necessary for dealing effectively with interpersonal problems. Each session focused on particular topic areas related to developing social skills in difficult interpersonal situations. The topics for each session were: (1) initiating interactions and conversations; (2) confronting others and giving negative feedback; (3) handling service situations; (4) making requests; (5) turning down requests; and (6) responding to criticism. In the group session, all group members had an equal opportunity to practice the problem-solving method on the problematic situation of their choice. This was accomplished by asking for volunteers and then allowing persons who did not get a chance to present a situation in a given session to present their situation in the succeeding session. In this manner the problem-solving process was carried out for each situation brought to the group by each group member.

At the end of each group session, the topic for the following week's session was stated and examples of situations in the topic area were given. For example, under the topic "handling service situations," the group leader gave examples such as: "Have you ever been given a rare steak when you asked for a well done one at a restaurant?" The participants were requested to think of a problematic situation in the topic area for the next group meeting. With the help of the leader and the group members, the problem-solving method was used to find a more adequate solution to these situations.

The problem-solving method was explained and demonstrated to the group members in the first session and thereafter reviewed in each of the succeeding sessions (see the explanation of the problem-solving process below). As the group members became familiar with the problem-solving steps in each succeeding session, the group leader placed an increasing emphasis on the group members' participation and responsibility for carrying out the steps of the problem-solving process. Thus, the group leader gradually became a facilitator of the group solving process rather than a leader of the process. This transition was intended to increase the group members' ability to solve problems by themselves. In order to accomplish this, each member was given responsibility for leading a segment of the group session. In the fourth session, for example, Anne brought to the group a situation which concerned her relationship with her adult daughter. The daughter was very protective of Anne, suggesting that Anne refrain from doing things because of her age. Anne was angry because she felt that she was losing her independence. In this situation, Charlie had the responsibility of leading the group discussion using the problem-solving process. When Charlie forgot to include part of the problem-solving process, Bill reminded him of the steps in the process which he neglected to utilize. In this way, the group members helped one another, and, in the process, increased group cohesion.

THE PROBLEM-SOLVING PROCESS

The problem-solving process consists of a general orientation, defining the situation, problem-solving orientation, generating alternatives, decision making, and implementation. These six steps are not separate entities. In actual group meetings the steps merge and overlap. Before we present a case example, it is essential to explicate the unique aspects of each step in the problem-solving process.

General Orientation

The general orientation provided members of the group with an initial set of expectations. The group leader focused on providing a belief that change was possible with the involvement of the group members' own efforts. In this step, definitions of assertiveness as a social skill (as compared to aggressiveness and passivity) were given. Assertive behavior was defined as interpersonal behavior in which a person stands up for legitimate rights without violating the rights of others. Nonassertive behavior is interpersonal behavior which allows for the violation of a person's rights by others. Aggressive behavior is interpersonal behavior that violates the rights of others (Jakubowski-Spector, 1973).

The group leader asked the group members about their reasons for attending the group and explained to the members how appropriate use of social skills could help them handle difficult interpersonal situations. Several of the group members reacted with skepticism to this. For example, Jan stated that when she is passive and "doesn't get into a fight" with a neighbor who annoys her by leaving her wash in the community washing machine, she avoids trouble. The group leader pointed out that this passive behavior does not help her deal with the problem. She remains annoyed at her neighbor and has to put up with inconvenience and anger each time the problem occurs. The group leader and other group members suggested that Jan change her initial orientation to the problem and try the problem-solving process in order to use a different approach to overcoming expectations of failure and uncertainty about the value of being assertive as compared to previous passive or aggressive behavior patterns. This included emphasizing that difficult interpersonal situations arise as a normal part of life and that these problems can be solved if they are recognized and if appropriate problem-solving steps are taken.

Defining the Situation

In order to use the problem-solving process effectively, it is essential to define the problem. Without a clear definition of the problem, the solution to the problem can never be clear or specific. A clear definition of the problem includes defining all aspects of the situation in operational terms and formulating or classifying elements of the situation appropriately in order to separate relevant from irrelevant information and to identify subproblems and issues related to the problem (D'Zurilla and Goldfried, 1971).

A clear definition includes considering all the available facts and information and seeking additional information where gaps in knowledge exist (Crutchfield, 1969; Osborn, 1963). Crutchfield (1969) suggests using a five-step process: (1) identify the boundary condition of the problem situation, (2) order the facts, (3) discriminate the relevant from the irrelevant facts, (4) find gaps in existing information, and (5) specify the facts needed to have complete information about the situation.

Group members attempting to find solutions to problematic interpersonal situations must avoid the use of ambiguous or vague terms. Clarity helps others in the group participate in the problem-solving process and allows for specific solution generation. Bloom and Broder (1950) found that successful problem solvers tended to translate difficult and unfamiliar problem aspects and concepts into simpler, more concrete, and more familiar terms. Unsuccessful problem solvers tended to accept vague or unfamiliar concepts and appeared to be unable to do anything further with them.

In the first and second sessions of the group workshops, members often used vague or ambiguous terms to describe their social interactions. Sarah, for example, stated that something she wanted to work on was her relationship with her neighbor. When asked to define what specific things about the relationship she wanted to work on, Sarah said that she wanted to work on getting her neighbor to "talk better." After some discussion, clarification, and specification by the leader and the group members, "talk better" was defined as getting her neighbor to decrease her frequent references to her poor health, worries about going to the doctor, and similar unpleasant health-related comments. As the group progressed, members practiced specifying, objectifying, and quantifying their statements so that everyone in the group was able to understand exactly what were the specific problematic interpersonal interactions.

Problem-Solving Orientation

The next step in the problem-solving process used in the group workshop was the orientation to the problem and the specification of the preferred solution. In this step it was important for the group members to reduce the tendency to make an immediate and automatic response to a situation. This inhibitory set is crucial for effective problem solving. Less effective problem solvers are impulsive, impatient, and quick to give up (Bloom and Broder, 1950). The group member must learn to stop and think of the most effective response and to use the most appropriate course of action.

The orientation to problem solving also included an analysis of the group members' covert thoughts and feelings about the event. In order to inhibit impulse-ridden aggressive or passive responses, the group member must be able to identify thoughts and feelings about the event. Failure to problem solve effectively is often caused by distracting, irrelevant self-statements or self-statements and emotions that are counterproductive to problem-solving efforts. Group members' self-statements included such comments as "I can't do it," "It's no use," "I'll kill him," etc. Ellis (1962) points out that many people maintain irrational expectations and expectations which lead to frustration, disappointment, and emotional upset. Meichenbaum and Cameron (1973) and Lazarus (1966) have found that teaching cognitive restructuring in the form of positive self-statements and task-focused problem-solving statements helps with the effective solution of a problem.

An example of cognitive restructuring used in the second group meeting may help to clarify the procedure. Jan, who for years had wanted to tell cigarette smokers to stop smoking near her in crowded public places, stated thoughts such as "What a lot of nerve she's got for smoking here," "Isn't that terrible," and "I can't do anything about it." After expressing these thoughts, Jan evaluated each one according to three of Maultsby's criteria for examining the rationality of a tought. These include: is the thought (1) based on objective reality, (2) goal producing, (3) able to reduce internal conflict experienced by the person confronted with the situation (Goodman and Maultsby, 1974). Jan's thoughts led to feelings of anger ("Isn't that terrible") and fear of doing anything to change the situation ("I can't do anything about it"). Along with the leader and other group participants, Jan identified thoughts and self-statements that helped rather than hindered making a response. Each suggested self-statement is examined by asking the group members if it meets Maultsby's criteria for examining the rationality of a thought. Self-statements, such as "I can tell this person to stop smoking . . ." and "I will say . . ." are examples of the thoughts suggested by group members to replace the maladaptive thoughts expressed by Jan.

The problem-solving orientation also includes specifying the preferred emotion, behavior, and consequences that the person presenting the problematic situation would most like to see occur in the situation instead of using irrational, spontaneous responses made out of habit. The leader asked each group member who presented an interpersonal situation to specify what he/she would prefer to do in the situation and what he/she would expect to be the consequences of this action. Early goal formulation is important in problem solving. Jerome (1962) suggests that problem-solving deficits are caused by inadequate or delayed goal formulation. In the group workshop, Hyde discussed her goal of getting less angry at a garden club member who often took her gardening tools. In an encounter with this person, Hyde said that she felt like "telling her off." When she remembered her goal of getting less angry and trying to solve the situation without anger, Hyde changed her self-statement to "What can I do to let her know that when she takes my tools it makes me feel angry?" By remembering her goal and by changing her self-statement, Hyde was able to control her anger and begin to think about an effective assertive response that would lead to a resolution of the problem.

Generating Alternatives

The next step in the problem-solving process is to identify alternative solutions to the problematic situation. The procedure used to generate solutions is Osborn's (1963) method of brainstorming. Effective brainstorming consists of eliciting all possible alternatives by (1) outlawing criticism, (2) welcoming unique ideas, (3) encouraging a diversity of possible solutions, and (4) eliciting combinations and improvements of existing solutions.

The main innovation of brainstorming is in giving all group members a chance to present all their suggestions for possible solutions without criticizing the solutions while they are being given. Support for the effectiveness of brainstorming procedures (Osborn, 1963; Clark, 1955; and Maltzman, 1960) is suggestive, since controlled studies are lacking. Elements of the brainstorming process, such as ruling out criticism, have proven effective in increasing the quality and quantity of solutions in research studies (see, for example, Bayless, 1967; Davis and Manske, 1966).

In the situation mentioned earlier concerning Anne and her daughter, the leader asked the group members for ways in which Anne could get her daughter to reduce the number of times she told Anne what she could not do because of her age. A number of alternatives was generated. Jan, for example, suggested that Anne tell her daughter "that although she knew that she (daughter) was concerned about her mother, she (Anne) was able to decide for herself what she was able to do." Bill said that this kind of response would offend Anne's daughter. At this point the leader interrupted Bill and told him to hold all of his judgments about the effectiveness of the suggestions until all the possible alternatives were exhausted. The leader then encouraged more suggestions and combinations of alternative suggestions. Only after everyone responded with all the alternatives they could think of, were Bill and the other group members allowed to critique each alternative.

Decision Making

Once all the alternative solutions to the problematic situation have been exhausted, decision making is used to determine which is the best alternative. There is no single criterion for choosing between alternatives. Several different criteria act as guides in helping the group members determine what constitutes the best alternative to a problematic interpersonal situation. One criterion is to look at the utility of each of the proposed solutions in terms of the preferred emotions, behavior, and consequences specified earlier by the group member. For Hyde, remaining calm and responding assertively without anger to her fellow garden club member was the preferred emotion and behavior. The preferred consequences were that instead of arguing with the other person, Hyde would be able to solve the problem and remain friends. In examining alternatives generated by the group members, some alternatives, such as taking one of the woman's tools, would clearly provoke hostility and prevent the preferred behavior and consequences from taking place. Another suggested alternative was to explain why the woman's behavior was hindering Hyde in her own gardening work and what tools could be borrowed at specific times when Hyde was not using them. This alternative was examined by the group members and decided on as being the response that would be most likely to help Hyde reach her preferred emotions, behavior, and consequences in the situation.

Another criterion for choosing between alternatives is to evaulate them in terms of their ease of implementation and the client's ability to implement the solutions proposed. Extremely difficult solutions, although effective, may be poor choices because the group member is not likely to be able to acquire the skill or expend the energy necessary for solution implementation. For example, having Jan change her seat in a movie theater or public place when a cigarette smoker sat next to her, might be effective in helping her reduce her allergy to smoking, but would cause Jan a great deal of inconvenience, particularly in crowded places where seats near nonsmokers might be difficult to find.

The third and often the most helpful criterion for decision making is to have some empirical data concerning what constitutes an effective response. For decision making with problems caused by difficult interpersonal situations, criteria for effective use of social skills have been presented by Alberti and Emmons (1974) and by Eisler, Miller, and Hersen (1973). These criteria include: Does the solution alternative (1) explain the problematic situation to all actors in the problem as clearly and concisely as possible, (2) make a clear, concise, and direct request and/or ask for a change in the problematic situation, and (3) use a calm affect and firm but not angry tone of voice while making the request or asking for a change in the situation? These rules are based on social skills criteria for an effective response as defined by Eisler, Miller, and Hersen (1973). Thus, an effective response for Jan should include (1) telling the person who is smoking that she has an allergy and the smoke really bothers her, (2) asking the person if he/she would be kind enough to stop smoking or smoke in the hallway, and (3) making the request firmly but not with anger or a pleading tone of voice.

Once a decision is made and the solution decided upon by the consensus of the group members is identified, the participant who first brought up the situation is asked how comfortable he/she feels about implementing the solution. For example, Jan was asked if she felt comfortable about confronting a smoker in a public place. If the group member is uncomfortable with the solution, the leader goes back over step three, the problem-solving orientation and cognitive restructuring, so that the participant will focus on solution-oriented thoughts and feelings. In Jan's situation, it was also helpful to have her practice role-playing what she would say to a smoker in a public place using one of the group members who smoked cigarettes as the person with whom she practiced the response.

Implementation

The final step in problem solving is to implement the decision. Implementation of a decision can be aided by role-playing each step necessary to carry out the chosen alternative. Sometimes it is necessary for the leader to model or demonstrate a particular step or several steps in the solution. If the response is difficult for the group member to learn, several practices are necessary so that the group member learns the response well before carrying out the solution in the real world. It took Jan several practices before she felt comfortable making her response. In the initial practice, Jan made several mistakes, such as not explaining why she was asking the smoker to refrain from smoking. The leader, acting as a model, demonstrated the response (decided on previously) with another group member. In a second practice, Jan followed the changes made by the leader but was very hesitant in her responses. It was not until the third role play practice that Jan was able to make an appropriate response in a fluid, firm manner.

Even when responses are rehearsed in the group meetings, group members may have difficulty applying the practiced response in the actual situation. Assignments for group members to complete between group sessions can help an anxious member apply responses practiced in the group meeting. An initial assignment was for each group member to keep a diary of situations that they handled effectively. On the opposite page from the actual situation, the group members wrote down both cognitive and behavioral aspects of the situation that needed to be changed in order to handle the situation effectively. Logs were discussed in the group meetings. In addition, when a particularly difficult situation confronted a group member, after the response was rehearsed in the group, the member was given an assignment to try the response out with someone who made the group member feel comfortable. Jan, for example, had a friend who was a cigarette smoker. Although this friend did not smoke cigarettes near Jan, Jan asked the friend to smoke a cigarette near her so that she could practice her response. In this way Jan had a chance to practice her response outside of the group meeting before she tried the response with a stranger.

CASE EXAMPLE

Although the steps in the problem-solving process were presented separately above, they tend to merge in an actual group meeting. The whole problem-solving process can take as little as 15 minutes, once the group members understand it. In order to demonstrate how the whole problem-solving process is utilized in a group meeting, the following portion is presented. It occurs early in the second group meeting after a brief review of the first one and a review of the problem-solving process.

Group leader (Anne):	Today we will focus on difficult interpersonal situations where you want to confront a person or give negative feedback to someone regarding an action or an event which you consider to be a violation of your rights. For example, you are on a bus and someone sitting next to you is playing a radio which is annoying you. This kind of situation calls for you to confront the person with the fact that the radio is annoying to you. Does everyone understand what I mean by situations in which you want to confront a person or give negative feedback? (Looking around the group.) Good. Who has a situation in this area that they would like to discuss?
Group member (Bill):	Well—I'm not sure if this is one but—we have a rule here (a private housing project) that each tenant has one place to park their own car. The spots are numbered. The daughter of a woman who lives in my building unit visits her mother almost every day. When her mother's car is parked in their parking place, she puts her car in my spot—like when I'm out shopping. I didn't say anything the first few times—but it annoyed the hell out of me! Last Saturday, it happened again and as I pulled up, this woman comes out of the building from her mother's house—I really gave it to her. Afterwards I felt like I shouldn't have—you know what I mean.
Anne:	Is the situation clear to everyone?
Group member (Betty):	Good for you, Bill, these people should know better.
Anne:	Is the situation clear to you Sarah?
Group member (Sarah):	Well—I'd like to know what you said to her Bill?
Bill:	I told her she had some nerve parking in my spot and if she did it again I'd have her car

	towed away—I said it in more "descriptive" terms though. (Laughter from the group members)
Anne:	I'd like to know if there is a place for the woman to park.
Bill:	Yeah, in the visitors' parking lot.
Anne:	I see. So the fact is this woman parked in your spot, you let it go a few times, and then you got angry.
Bill:	Yeah—now I avoid Mrs. K.—the woman's mother—I feel kind of funny.
Anne:	Is everyone clear about the situation? Good. Who remembers the next thing we do when trying to find a better method of handling a situation?
Group member (Charlie):	We all say how else it could be handled.
Anne:	Well that's an important step Charlie—but first there is another step. Does anyone recall—what about how Bill's thoughts affected his actions.
Bill:	Oh yeah—I remember—first, I'm supposed to tell you what I was saying to myself and find something better to say. I was really angry. When I saw that car there, I said to myself, "She's got some nerve," "She has no respect." I was sitting in my car for a while getting more and more angry—when she came out, I was steaming!
Anne:	You got pretty worked up!
Bill:	Yeah—I suppose that's why I let her have it.
Anne:	What would you have preferred to do Bill?
Bill:	I would have liked to be less angry and given her some kind of warning; after all, it was the first time I spoke to her.
Anne:	(to the other group members) What could Bill have said to himself?
Sarah:	He could have said, "No sense getting all upset—I'll have to speak to her about the visitors parking."
Charlie:	He could have said, "I'm not gonna let this get me angry, but I'd better tell her that she's not supposed to park in my spot."
Anne:	How does that sound Bill?
Bill:	That would help me to remain calm. I took it personally. I could have said, "Maybe she doesn't realize how inconvenient it is for me," and what Charlie said about not letting it get me angry.

Anne:	Good. You can practice that later once we figure out a solution. Charlie, now for the next step—do you remember you said it before.
Charlie:	We all think of ways to handle Bill's situation.
Anne:	Exactly. Does anyone have any suggestions? Remember everyone's suggestion is welcome—we won't figure out which one is best until we have all possibilities. I'll write all the possible solutions down so we can refer back to them later.
Sarah:	Bill, maybe she didn't know about the visitors' parking. You could have told her about it and told her about how the parking spot she is in is reserved for you.
Charlie:	You could tell her mother to tell her not to park in your spot.
Sarah:	You could have told the building manager to tell her.
Anne:	You have any ideas Betty?
Betty:	I'm not one to speak up but maybe you could tell her about the visitors' parking and ask her not to park in your spot again.
Anne:	Anyone have any other solutions?
Bill:	What if she knows about the visitors' parking and is parking in my spot anyway?
Anne:	For now, let's assume she doesn't know—but that's a good point Bill. After we decide on a solution we will make a point of going over the situation in which you have acted in an appropriate manner—not angry or passive—and you still don't solve the problem. Okay?
Bill:	Yeah—first I want to learn how to remain calm in the first round. (Laughter from the group.)
Anne:	Okay then, we are ready to decide on one of the alternatives. Do you remember the three criteria for an effective response?
Bill:	First, you explain the situation, then you ask for a change, and you remain calm but firm.
Anne:	That's right Bill—I'll read the alternatives again (reads the alternatives). Which one fits the criteria best? (Here the group members discuss each alternative.)
Anne:	Well, it seems that the consensus of the group is that it would be best to explain to the woman about the visitors' parking and about

	the fact that this is your spot. Then you could ask the woman not to park in your place from now on. This solution is a combination of a couple of alternatives. What do you think about the solution Bill?
Bill:	It sounds good—but I'm not sure I'd be able to say it without getting angry or using the wrong words.
Anne:	Bill why don't you and someone practice the solution. Practice what to say. Also Bill remember to practice saying things to yourself that will help you remain calm. Is there someone who will volunteer to play the lady? (No response.)
Anne:	Okay, I know this role playing is new for all of you. I'll play the woman this time. Bill, you direct me—how should I act?

Bill goes on to direct Anne and they play out the situation. After the practice, group members give Bill some feedback on his performance and the practice is done a second time. After the second practice, Bill feels confident of his ability to handle the situation should it come up again and the group moves to a new problem concerning noisy neighbors that Sarah brings to the group.

Evaluation Problem-Solving
Group Effectiveness

The group members reported a high degree of satisfaction with their participation in the problem-solving group. They reported learning to use the problem-solving method and applying the social skills training in a variety of situations. Bill reported using the social skills he learned to increase his participation in social activities by asking to join several recreational groups at the senior center. By the end of the group meeting he was involved in the men's pool tournament and had joined a group from the senior center which swam at the YMCA in a nearby town. Charlie reported that he was able to speak up in a large meeting, and request that a neighbor curb her dog. Before the group meetings, Charlie had wanted to do something about these situations. During the group, he learned how to respond effectively.

The six women who participated in the workshop also reported using social skills in a variety of situations. Anne reported being able to decrease her daughter's comments about not participating in activities in which Anne wanted to participate. After several weeks of practice, Jan reported asking a cigarette smoker to refrain from smoking in her home. Jan also reported asking a person in a movie theater to stop smoking. Sarah and Hyde both reported being able to make requests for information and help. Sarah, for example, was able to ask her family doctor some questions about back pains for which the doctor had been treating her for two years. Hyde was able to ask a neighbor for a ride to town when the neighbor was going shopping. Hyde had been reluctant to impose on this neighbor, although it was difficult to go shopping in town. When she did ask the neighbor, she found they enjoyed riding into town together. Pauline also reported a number of changes. She was able to ask for the return of an item which had been borrowed over three months ago and she refused to allow a salesman into her apartment, thereby avoiding spending a long time trying to convince the salesman that she didn't really need the item he was selling.

In addition to the results reported by the individual members of the group described above, a behavioral role play test was used to evaluate the effectiveness of all five group workshops which were sponsored by the Interpersonal Skill Training Project of the University of Wisconsin. Five discussion groups acted as control groups. These groups were compared to the problem-solving groups on the change evidenced in the behavioral role play test.

The behavioral role play test consisted of eight audiotaped situations. The situations were obtained through interviews with 50 persons aged 55 and above. These older persons were asked to state a number of interpersonal situations which they found difficult to handle and relevant to their everyday life in any of the six areas to be covered in the group sessions. Eight of the most relevant situations were placed on a cassette tape. Four of the situations were used as examples by the group leaders in training group members to use the problem solving approach. Four situations were not used in the group meeting and constitute a measure of the effectiveness of the problem-solving approach for untrained situations.

Each group participant was asked to give a response to each situation as if the situation were actually occurring. Responses to the situations were taped and rated by two trained coders. Ratings of the situation on a five-point score were made based on a codebook for the most appropriate to the least appropriate response. The codebook was developed by asking eight experts in the field of gerontology what constituted a response at each score level.

The results indicate that the problem-solving groups were significantly more effective than discussion groups in increasing group members' skills in interpersonal interactions. As compared to the discussion groups, on both the trained role play test situations ($t = 2.78$, $p < .01$) and the untrained situation ($t = 3.55$, $p < .01$), the problem-solving group members significantly increased their social skills. The problem-solving groups were effective in helping the members solve interpersonal problems brought to the group meeting and were also effective in increasing members' social skills in new untrained situations. In a three month follow-up the group members maintained the social skills which they learned in the problem-solving groups.

Overall, the findings suggest that problem-solving training is an effective method of increasing the problem-solving and social-skills abilities of older adults. An important unanswered question is the effectiveness of problem-solving processes with problematic situations of varying complexity. Perhaps problem solving is most effective for relatively complex problematic situations, whereas other treatment approaches, such as social skills role playing groups, may be more effective for less complex problematic situations where a response can be easily modeled and practiced. Future research should address itself to this question as well as to the effectiveness of problem solving with a wide range of problematic situations.

REFERENCES

Alberti, R. and M. Emmons. *Your perfect right: A guide to assertive behavior.* San Luis Obispo, Calif.: Impact Publications, 1974.

Bayless, O. L. An alternative pattern for problem solving discussion. *Journal of Communication*, 1967, *17*, 188-97.

Bloom, B. S. and L. J. Broder. *Problem solving processes of college students.* Chicago: University of Chicago Press, 1950.

Clark, C. H. *Brainstorming.* Garden City, N.Y.: Doubleday, 1955.

Coche, E., and A. Flick, Problem solving training groups for hospitalized psychiatric patients, *Journal of Psychology*, 1975, *91*, 19-29.

Crutchfield, R. S. Nurturing the cognitive skills of productive thinking. In *Life skills in school and society.* Washington, D.C.: Association for Supervision and Curriculum Development, 1969.

Davis, G. A. and M. E. Manske. An instructional method of increasing originality.. *Psychonomic Science*, 1966, *6*, 73-74.

D'Zurilla, T. and M. Goldfried. Problem solving and behavior modification. *Journal of Abnormal Psychology*, 1971, *78*, 107-26.

Eisler, R. M., B. M. Miller, and M. Herson. Components of assertive behavior. *Journal of Clinical Psychology*, 1973, *29*, 295-99.

Ellis, A. *Reason and emotion in psychotherapy.* Secaucus, N.J.: Lyle Stuart, 1962.

Giebink, J. W., D. S. Stover, and M. A. Fahl. Teaching adaptive responses to frustration to emotionally disturbed boys. *Journal of Consulting and Clinical Psychology, 32*, 366-68, 1968.

Goodman, D. and M. Maultsby. *Emotional well-being.* New York: C. Thomas Company, 1974.

Hallowitz, D., Problem-Solving Through Social Work Treatment in Francis J. Turner (ed.), *Social work treatment: interlocking theoretical approaches,* N.Y.: Free Press, 1974, p. 112.

Hilgard, E. *Theories of learning*, 2nd ed. New York: Appleton-Century-Crofts, 1956.

Jakubowski-Spector, P. Facilitating the growth of women through assertive training. *The Counseling Psychologist*, 1973, *4*, 75-86.

James, W. *The principles of psychology*. New York: Holt, Rinehart and Winston, 1890.

Jerome, E. A. Decay of heuristic processes in the aged. In C. Tibbitts and W. Donahue (eds.), *Social and psychological aspects of aging*. New York: Columbia University Press, 1962.

Kelly, G. A. *The psychology of personal constructs II: Clinical diagnosis and psychotherapy*. New York: Norton, 1955.

Lazarus, R. S. *Psychological stress and the coping process*. New York: McGraw-Hill, 1966.

Mahoney, M. J. *Cognition and behavior modification*. Cambridge, Mass.: Ballinger, 1974.

——. Clinical issues in self-control training. Paper presented to the American Psychological Association, 1974.

Maltzman, I. On the training of originality. *Psychological Review*, 1960, *67*, 229-42.

McGuire, M. T. and P. E. Sifneos. Problem solving in psychotherapy. *Psychiatric Quarterly*, 1970, *44*, 667-73.

Meichenbaum, D. and R. Cameron. Training schizophrenics to talk to themselves. *Behavior Therapy*, 1973, *4*, 515-34.

Mowrer, O. H. On the dual nature of learning: A reinterpretation of "conditioning" and "problem solving." *Harvard Review*, 1947, *17*, 102-48.

Osborn, A. F. *Applied imagination: principles and procedures of creative problem solving*, 3rd ed.. New York: Scribner's, 1963.

Perlman, H. A. *Social casework: A problem solving process*. Chicago: University of Chicago Press, 1957.

Platt, J., W. C. Scura, and J. R. Hannon. Problem solving thinking of youthful incarcerated heroin addicts. *Journal of Community Psychology*, 1973, *1*, 278-81.

Platt, J. and G. Spivack. Problem solving thinking of psychiatric patients. *Journal of Consulting and Clinical Psychology*, 1972, *39*, 148-51. (a)

——. Social competence and effective problem solving thinking in psychiatric patients. *Journal of Clinical Psychology*, 1972, *28*, 3-5. (b)

Rotter, J. B. *Social learning and clinical psychology*. Englewood Cliffs, N.J.: Prentice-Hall, 1954.

Shure, M., S. Newman, S. Silver. Problem solving thinking among adjusted, impulsive, and inhibited head start children. Paper presented at the meetings of the Eastern Psychological Association, Washington, D.C., 1973.

—— and G. Spivack. A problem solving intervention program for disadvantaged preschool children. Paper presented at Eastern Psychological Association, 1972.

——. A preventive mental health program for young inner city children. Paper presented at the American Psychological Association, 1975. (a)

————. Training mothers to help their children solve real life problems. Paper presented at the Society for Research in Child Development, 1975. (b)

Spivack, G. and M. Levine. Self-regulation in acting-out and normal adolescents. Report M-4351. Washington, D.C.: National Institute of Health, 1963.

Toseland, R. A problem solving workshop for older adults. *Social Work*, 1977, *22*(4), 325-27.

———— and S. D. Rose. A social skills training program for older adults: Evaluation of three group approaches. *Social Work Research and Abstracts*, March, 1977, vol. 1.

TONI A. ZANDER and PHILLIPS KINDY, JR.

3

behavioral group training
for welfare parents

In the past decade an increasing number of behavioral parent training studies have emerged, presenting a variety of training approaches. Parents have been trained to systematically apply learning theory principles to a wide range of child problem behaviors, from simple conduct problems to complex behavioral chains traditionally labeled psychotic (Berkowitz and Graziano, 1972; Brown, 1972; Cone and Sloop, 1974; Shack and Barnett, 1973). The rapid development of studies in parent training is, in part, a response to the failure of traditional psychodynamic modes of child therapy to demonstrate their effectiveness. Cone and Sloop (1974) found that "little evidence exists to support the belief that 'traditional' child-psychotherapy techniques are more successful than no formal treatment in ameliorating childhood behavioral disturbances" (p. 286). Furthermore, as Berkowitz and Graziano (1972) point out:

> some parents, overwhelmed and unable to cope with the demands of a disturbing child, receive little practical guidance from the therapist, and find no ebbing of their feelings of helplessness, rage, and literal hate. . . . Such intense parental feelings may occasion significant further disorganization in the family's life. Thus, the direct and practical coping with the everyday realities of the disorganized family situation may be an important therapeutic need currently unmet by psychodynamic therapists who deal with inferences and not behavior (p. 298).

The parent-training approach to child therapy is an extension of the learning theory principles upon which behavior modification procedures are based. As Cone and Sloop (1974) state, the most important rationale for training parents in behavioral techniques is that

> logically consistent adherence to experimental analysis principles requires it. Parents and other caretaking agents invariably have control over environmental stimuli which powerfully influence their child's behavior. Moreover, control of these stimuli is vested in the parents significantly more often than 50 minutes a week. Even if professional therapists were to gain effective control over certain behavior during the usual 50-minute session, there is little reason to suppose this would generalize to the non-therapy environment. On the contrary, the deviant behavior was probably shaped and maintained by the social environment of the child in the first place. Returning him to an unchanged set of reinforcement contingencies is simply to invite retention of the problem (p. 291).

Thus, training parents to change their interaction patterns with their children may be the only way to assure that therapeutic changes in child behavior are generalized to and maintained in the 24-hour-a-day living environment.

Studies employing behavioral group methods have reported positive outcomes in the training of parents as change agents (Howard, 1970; Lindsley, 1966; Rose, 1969, 1974; Tams and Eyberg, 1976). Although additional research is needed to examine the relative efficacy of group and individual methods for training parents in child management techniques (Kovitz, 1976), the group approach has several advantages to recommend it. Group training reduces the cost to the individual parent and allows greater utilization of professional time. The group approach contributes to parent effectiveness and the maintenance of behavioral skills by exposing members to a variety of positive and negative models of parenting techniques. The leader can then use these models to demonstrate verbal and behavioral skills.

In group training, parents are exposed to the assessment and treatment of a greater variety of problematic child behaviors than they would be in individual treatment. The exposure to "change plans" for a variety of behavior problems gives the individual parent models for the treatment of future difficulties, thus decreasing parents' need for future professional involvement. A group situation provides opportunities for shared problem solving as parents help other parents develop and evaluate change plans for problematic child behaviors. Furthermore, parents often develop friendships and maintain contact with each other after the group terminates. These ongoing contacts with peers trained in the same parenting procedures provide a supportive environment for the continued use of the procedures learned in the group.

In training parents from families who are in part supported by Aid to Families with Dependent Children (AFDC), special considerations must be taken because of the particular circumstances in which the majority of AFDC parents find themselves. Most AFDC parents are single women in a fatherless family with multiple environmental problems including financial difficulties, lack of a high school education, and inadequate child management skills (Kadushin, 1974, pp. 168-77). Most AFDC mothers have a primary support group of other AFDC women which provides mutual child care aid. Because of these characteristics, it is important in training AFDC parents to provide motivation for attendance and participation in the training, repeated practice in child management skills, and assurance of the maintenance of these skills (Rose, 1972).

This paper describes an eight-session group parent training program and the application to AFDC parents. The training model outlined is a skill-oriented model which was designed to include parents of both problem and nonproblem children between the ages of 2 and 12 years. The primary goals were to provide parents with a learning theory framework and to teach parents the verbal and behavioral skills to manage their children's behaviors effectively.

GROUP COMPOSITION AND ORGANIZATION

Of the 15 AFDC parents originally referred to the parent training group, 5 women ranging in age from 22 to 47 participated. Members were recruited through a county social service agency. One member's attendance in the training program was court ordered. All members received at least partial AFDC assistance. Four members were divorced, one was married. All members lived in the same geographical area. The two leaders, one male and one female, were advanced graduate students in the Interpersonal Skill Training and Research Project of the school of social work. They were experienced in behavioral parent training in a group setting.

The sponsoring social service agency provided all group materials, funds for member transportation and babysitting costs, and monetary rewards for member attendance (25 cents per session), promptness (25 cents per session), and assignment completion (50 cents per session). In order to enhance member attendance, the agency arranged for a central accessible meeting place, a comfortable room in a neighborhood church. Leaders' fees were paid through a purchase-of-service contract with the area's technical school.

After receiving the referrals from the agency, the leaders telephoned each member, explained the purpose and method of the group, and arranged for the pregroup assessment procedure. A two-hour home observation of the parent-child interactions of each group member's family was taken by one leader and a trained agency social worker using the Interactional Analysis system developed by the Home and Community Treatment Project, Wisconsin Childrens' Treatment Center, Madison, Wisconsin. Categorizing parent and child behaviors as appropriate, inappropriate, and appropriate absent, the observations gave the leaders detailed information concerning each family member's behavioral strengths and deficits. The observation also enabled the leaders to help the parent pinpoint problematic child behaviors and identify change plans that are likely to succeed, enabling members to realize early successes in using behavioral child management techniques.   `

After the home observation, the members completed two written instruments: a 10-item Knowledge Questionnaire (Brockway, 1974) which measures the parent's knowledge of learning theory principles, and the 50-item Walker Problem Identification Checklist (Walker, 1970) which codifies the parent's verbal reports of their children's behavior.

Several members reported problems completing the written instruments: They did not understand some of the vocabulary, the behavior rating system was not clear, some of the behavioral categories were too broad. In two of the home observations, some family members were not at home, despite prior arrangements, so data could not be collected on the interactions of all family members.

Prior to the first group meeting, two social work students were trained as observers to collect data on various leader and member behaviors, including direction of interaction, frequency of participation, and frequency of reinforcement. The observers also monitored attendance, promptness, assignment completion, and member responses to the weekly evaluations.

PROGRAM FORMAT

Parents attended eight weekly two-hour sessions. In order to achieve individual and group goals in a time-limited training program, leaders provided members with a highly structured written agenda at each session. The first part of each agenda concerned teaching new behavioral principles while the second part focused on skill training.

The sequence of each session followed this general format:

1. Brief review of previous session and assigned reading from *Parents Are Teachers* (Becker, 1971).
2. Short content-oriented quiz on assigned readings, reviewed immediately in group.
3. Brief presentation and discussion of new concepts, providing a cognitive/instructional set for the specific technique to be learned during the session (Goldstein, Heller, and Sechrest, 1966, pp. 240-50).
4. Leader-led role plays, modeling new behavioral skills and illustrating behavioral principles. Written vignettes were also used to emphasize key concepts.
5. Behavioral rehearsal by members to practice new behavioral skills and to assess problematic child behaviors.
6. Home management programming. Training in treatment planning skills (e.g., assessment, monitoring, treatment, graphing, and transfer of change plans).

7. Brief review of behavioral assignments for the following week.
8. Completion of a weekly group evaluation form.

Suggestions and alternative procedures developed in subsequent groups have, at times, been included to point out alternative ways of handling various didactic and small group problems.

Session One

In session one, the primary concepts introduced were behavioral specificity and the environmental context of discrete behavior. The primary skill taught was describing a behavior in observable and measurable terms.

As the members arrived for the first session, the leaders immediately gave them 25 cents for attendance and 25 cents for promptness accompanied by such social amenities as, "I'm glad to see you here so early." Members were also reimbursed for transportation costs. These procedures were repeated at the beginning of each session in order to reinforce the desired attendance and promptness. In addition a babysitter was available at the meeting place to care for the members' children during the sessions.

At the beginning of the session, the leaders explained that they would like the group to get to know each other by breaking into dyads, introducing themselves to their "partner," and then introducing their "partner" to the group. The leaders modeled this process by introducing each other.

After the introductions, the group leaders presented an overview of the group and outlined leader, parent, and agency responsibilities. During this 10-minute presentation, the leaders observed some members looking around the room and stretching which suggested they were not attending throughout this and other "lecture" portions of the session. In order to involve members in the meeting and reduce the amount of leader participation, the trainers completed this section of the agenda by asking the members to read consecutive items on the group contract (see Rose, 1977, pp. 22-25). Leaders encouraged discussion and questions pertaining to the contract items by responding to member comments and praising their participation. After reviewing the contract, the leaders and members countersigned two copies of the contract, each retaining one copy.

At this point, a parent who had been a member of a previous AFDC parent training group briefly described her change plan for increasing compliance in her five-year-old daughter and her experience in using behavioral methods during and following the group. (The leaders had reviewed this presentation with this parent before the group session to assure she would provide useful information and serve as a positive model.) Members of the group showed interest in this parent's experience by asking several questions. The previous group member responded to these questions with appropriate terminology, operational definitions of behavioral problems, and generally positive statements (e.g., "Once you try it, it works!").

Leaders began formal training by introducing definitions of such general learning theory principles as "behavior" and "specificity." Parents were told that focusing on discrete behavior allows them to evaluate changes and makes the problem manageable. Leaders presented the criteria for behavioral specificity (i.e., that the description be observable and measurable) and introduced a specificity exercise. After reviewing the first example in this exercise, parents were asked to indicate which description of a child behavior problem was the most specific. One of the specificity examples (see Kindy, 1978, for complete list) utilized was:

> Peter, 10, has just moved into a new neighborhood. In his old neighborhood he had many friends and played outdoors with them much of the day. Dad had noticed that Peter now goes out very little and has not made any new friends in the new neighborhood. Dad asked Peter if he had made any friends but Peter said that he hadn't because the kids in this neighborhood are "too rough." When Dad asked Peter what he meant by "too rough" he said, "Oh, I don't know." Dad has decided to play more with Peter until he makes some new friends.

During the first vignettes, the leaders had to prompt members to generate discussion by asking them to explain their responses in terms of the observable/measurable criteria. By the third vignette, members began to spontaneously critique and improve upon each other's behavioral definitions.

The leaders next described the environmental context of behavior in terms of the "A-B-Cs" of behavior (antecedent-behavior-consequence). The group leaders explained that the A-B-Cs allow parents to make future predictions about the behavior and to plan an intervention strategy. Using a series of prepared scenarios, the leaders identified the A-B-C sequences in the first scenario and then asked the group members to specify in writing the antecedents and consequences in several other situations. Sample scenarios included:

> Stacy, 4, is a very active child. She frequently runs instead of walking in a normal gait. This behavior is okay out-of-doors but indoors Mom says it's "really nerve-racking." When Mom observes Stacy running, she yells at her to stop. Stacy usually stops after the third yell, when Mom says she'll spank her if she does it once more. Stacy seems to do more running when Mom is busy, for example, diapering the baby, or making dinner.

> Wilma has just moved to a large city school from a small country school. She brings home a slip of paper from her fourth grade teacher that says, "Wilma is not working up to capacity. Her spelling papers are messy and often incomplete. This is unusual for Wilma whom we know can do the work. If there are home problems and I can be of assistance, please feel free to contact me. Sincerely, Mr. Jones." Wilma's parents are angry and

embarrassed by this. They tell Wilma that her teacher is a no-good busy-body and that she cannot ride her bike until her grades improve.

At this point in the meeting, each parent was asked to select two behaviors of their children that they would like to change, using the Walker Problem Behavior Identification Checklist (Walker, 1970) and data gathered in the pregroup home observations. With the help of the leaders the group members targeted the following behaviors: making beds in the morning and completing household chores (Shirley); climbing in window and appropriate play (Rosemary); enuresis (Sally); compliance to commands, bed-time crying, and sitting down when told "no" (Chris). Parent trainers asked parents to check each other's descriptions for behavioral specificity.

One member, Mary, stated that she was unable to identify any child behavior problems. She said she had planned on working on a behavior of a child for whom she babysat but the child had recently moved. Several members suggested possible problem behaviors, none of which Mary considered problematic. Since there was only one child present during the home observation, the leaders were unable to offer additional suggestions. In order to keep Mary in the group and maintain group cohesiveness (Mary knew several other members), the leaders asked Mary to observe her children's behavior over the next few days to try to pinpoint a problem behavior she may have overlooked. The leaders arranged to telephone Mary in three days to provide assistance, if needed, in describing the selected behavior in specific terms.

Near the conclusion of the meeting, the leaders presented the rationale for using a buddy system and assigned buddies according to parenting skills, with a more skilled parent assigned to a less skilled parent. The leaders explained that members were expected to contact their "buddy" at least once during each week of training to provide encouragement to each other on their home management programs and to provide mutual assistance on reading materials, assignments, and child management difficulties. The leaders then role played a buddy phone contact to demonstrate how these contacts should be both encouraging and supportive and task-oriented. Members exchanged phone numbers and arranged a time to call each other before the next meeting.

Finally, members completed an evaluation of the session which asked the following questions: (1) "What did you like most about this session?" (2) "What did you like least about this session?" (3) "What did we talk about that you did not understand and would like to talk about more?" (4) "What suggestions do you have concerning the group, the leaders' behavior, what we did today, or what you'd like to do at future meetings?" (5) "Rate how useful this session was in helping you manage your child" (1 to 10 scale, 10 being high). (6) "Rate your desire to return to this group next week" (1 to 10 scale, 10 being high). This self-report evaluation form given at the end of each session provided leaders with a measure of group attraction and cohesion. The evaluation aided in the planning of future sessions by incorporating member suggestions and reviewing content areas that participants indicated they did not understand.

Intersession assignments were to: (1) complete the behavior-in-a-situation form for the two problem behaviors identified in session one; (2) read Unit One in *Parents Are Teachers*; (3) call buddy.

Session Two

In session two, the primary concepts introduced were operant control of behavior through contingency management and principles of reinforcement. The principal skills taught were reinforcement of appropriate behavior and monitoring procedures.

Beginning with the second session, members received 50 cents for assignment completion, which was delivered in the same manner and at the same time as the reinforcement for attendance and promptness. In session two, Shirley said that she had completed the behavior-in-a-situation form but had not had the time to read the book because she had to take her children to the doctor during the week. Throughout the group, leaders ignored excuses for noncompletion of assignments but verbally reinforced the member for the assignments she did complete. In this case the leader said to Shirley, "Well, I'm glad you were able to complete the forms. They will help you when it comes to counting these behaviors and making a plan to change them. Did you find your buddy contact helpful?" Shirley, of course, did not receive the 50 cents. In cases where members were not able to complete the assignments because of lack of understanding or other skill deficits, the leaders would answer the member's questions about the material and demonstrate how to complete the assignment and allow the member to earn the 50 cents for assignment completion if she did the assignment by the next week.

During the session members were taught the three categories of consequences: reinforcement, punishment, and extinction. After defining each of the categories, the leaders gave examples of the different consequences from prepared sample scenarios, identifying the ways in which the behaviors were reinforced. Parents reviewed the other examples, identifying the consequences and discussing the way in which the consequences were likely to influence the behavior in the future. (In other groups, the film "Who Did What To Whom" [Mager, 1972] has been used to teach control of behavior through manipulation of consequences). Throughout the discussion, the leaders referred back to the basic learning theory principles (e.g., "Yes, as I mentioned before the behavior we are concerned with is controlled by what happens after it, just as in this example." "That's a good point. You are more likely to increase or decrease a behavior in the future if you use the consequence right after the behavior occurs.") and prompted members to relate their comments about the scenarios to the principles being taught.

Parents were given a checklist outlining the criteria for the effective use of behavioral praise or positive reinforcement (see Kindy, 1978). The leaders gave the theoretical rationale for each item on the checklist and demonstrated the ways in which the example met the criteria for reinforcement. Members were divided into two subgroups. Each subgroup determined how well one of the examples of reinforcement in the exercise met the criteria on the behavioral praise checklist and then discussed their evaluation with the other subgroup. An example of one of the items in the reinforcement exercise 1 (see Kindy, 1978) is the following.

> Johnny (4) is a very shy boy. In school he usually plays by himself and only occasionally approaches and talks with other children. His teachers are worried that he will not learn how to make friends or play with other children. The teachers decide that they will each take turns watching Johnny for the four hours he is at school. Each time that Johnny starts talking with another child the teacher will drop a small piece of candy into a paper cup so that he can hear it. Johnny has been told that at the end of each hour he can have all of the candy in the cup.

Several issues related to reinforcement were raised by group members. Members stated they felt uncomfortable with the idea of using token rewards because it seemed "like bribery" to them. Parents also expressed concern about rewarding children for day-to-day behaviors (e.g., picking up toys, brushing teeth) because these behaviors were "for their (the children's) own good and they should just be expected to do them."

In response to the bribery issue, the leaders explained that bribery refers to a situation where someone is paid to do something illegal or a situation where someone is rewarded for not doing something they were supposed to do. The use of reinforcement, on the other hand, involves setting up the terms of the reward beforehand; the receipt of the reward depends upon the performance of "appropriate" behavior.

The leaders continued by outlining three different types of reinforcement: token reinforcement, activity reinforcement, and social reinforcement. After giving examples of each type of reinforcement, leaders again asked members to form subgroups and instructed them to develop a role play situation demonstrating the appropriate use of behavioral praise. Each subgroup then presented its role play to the larger group for feedback on how well it met the criteria. Using the group feedback, role plays were rehearsed to success. Although some of the members initially expressed reluctance to participate in a role play ("I'm not a good actor;" "I don't know if I can do it"), with encouragement and prompting from the leaders ("No one here is a great actor;" "Make a game out of it;" "Practicing it will help you understand how to use reinforcement") all members took part in the role plays. The laughter and praise statements during the role plays indicated all members were enjoying themselves and were reinforced for their participation. (In other groups leaders have had to shape role playing in reluctant members by having them read out prepared lines from the scenarios, act as the "director" of the subgroup role play, etc.)

During the home management part of the session, the behavior-in-a-situation exercise was reviewed and the problems encountered in completing the form were discussed. Leaders explained baseline monitoring procedures and modeled a variety of ways to count behavior when observed at home (e.g., frequency, interval, time sampling). Members paired off with their buddy to select an appropriate and convenient monitoring plan for the one child behavior they wished to work on first. Parents then presented their counting system to the larger group for additional feedback.

Mary still had not identified a behavior (which she regarded as problematic) in one of her children. When the leaders contacted her between the first and second sessions they suggested that she use the behavior-in-a-situation form to specify any behavior of her children, positive or negative. After the group, the leaders reviewed these forms in detail with Mary and suggested a number of potential problem behaviors she may wish to change. Mary said that she did not regard any of these behaviors as problems. The leaders had noted that she gave commands to the one child that was home in a loud voice and suggested that she might want to work on getting compliance by using a normal tone of voice. Mary, however, defined the loud voice as her problem, having nothing to do with the behavior of her children. The leaders said that she would get much more out of the group if she worked on a behavior and suggested that she identify a positive behavior that she would like to teach her children to do more often, but she "could think of nothing." The leaders said that she could stay with the group and listen, which she agreed to do. The leaders were concerned that their attention to "not-finding-a-problem" behavior might be reinforcing that behavior and agreed between themselves to ignore all "having no problems" talk in the future.

Intersession assignments were to: (1) monitor the selected child behavior; (2) list praise words and phrases used in their family during the week; (3) read Unit Two in *Parents Are Teachers*; and (4) call buddy. Leaders contacted each member at midweek to monitor her progress on the initial child behavior monitoring assignment and to offer any help the member might need in implementing the monitoring. Sally and Rosemary had "forgotten" to begin monitoring and assured the leader that they would begin that day. Chris had found that monitoring compliance to commands for the entire day took too much time. The leader helped her devise a time-sampling monitoring procedure which would limit the record keeping.

In session three, the primary concepts introduced were principles of extinction and punishment. The primary skills taught were ignoring and time-out.

On the evaluations for the second session, two members indicated that they would like the leaders to finish the group on time rather than running 10 to 15 minutes overtime as in the first two meetings. One member pointed out that she had to get out on time to catch the bus home. To alleviate a potential problem of reducing the attractiveness of the group for some members, and to model contracting and programming and the use of contingencies, the leaders began this session by suggesting that the group help them develop a plan to increase "finishing on time" behavior. Chris jokingly suggested that the leaders should be fined for running the group overtime and the group laughed at the idea. The leaders said that they would agree to negotiate a fine but would also like to be rewarded for finishing on time (modeling the use of reinforcement for an incompatible behavior along with a response cost system). The group developed the following contract with the leaders: Each member will receive one quarter at the beginning of each session from each leader. If the leaders finish the session on time according to the wall clock in the hall, each member will return the quarter to the leaders along with social praise for completing the session on time. If the leaders do not finish the session on time, the members can keep the quarters. This contract was carried out for the remainder of the sessions in order to model consistency in programming, appropriate use of contingencies, and fading and maintenance of change procedures. In session four, the leaders inadvertantly ran the session overtime. The members wanted to return the contingency money, saying "you only went five minutes overtime" but the leaders insisted that they follow through with the response cost program. In the sixth session, the leaders and members renegotiated the contract and replaced the money contingencies with paper tokens created by one member for "good job" and "bad job." In the eighth session, the tokens were dropped and the "finishing on time" behavior was maintained by social reinforcement alone.

The leaders began the discussion of the new topics by pointing out that ignoring (extinction) can be used to decrease nondestructive problem behaviors and presented the criteria for effective ignoring (see Kindy, 1978). It was emphasized that ignoring should always be used along with a reinforcement program for a positive behavior. Some mothers commented that they had tried ignoring in the past but eventually found themselves yelling because they were unable "to take it any longer." Leaders modeled the effective use of ignoring through role plays and gave parents suggestions to help them ignore their children's inappropriate behavior. For example, parents were told to leave the room, get involved in an activity, or make coping statements to themselves (e.g., "I know that ignoring is difficult, but I want to eliminate this behavior so it is important that I stick to it. I know I can do it."). Leaders stressed the importance of decreasing "bootlegged reinforcement" by enlisting the help of other family members. The parents were instructed to train the other family members in ignoring through instruction and role play and to reinforce their use of the procedure. Members were given further practice with this technique by additional behavioral rehearsal and an oral exercise. The leaders had members divide into subgroups and discuss how the prepared examples met the criteria for effective ignoring. The exercise included such examples as the following:

> Sally, age 8, was getting on the nerves of her parents and four brothers because she continued to repeat questions that they had answered several times already. Usually when Sally asked the same question more than two times she would get a response like, "Can't you listen?" or "I've already told you that, dummy!" Her parents took her to a doctor who assured them that Sally could hear perfectly well. Sally has been repeating questions more and more recently and her family has been getting more and more aggravated with her.
>
> A social worker suggested to Sally's parents that they ignore the questions after the second time, if they are sure she heard and understood them. They have been doing so, but Sally has not stopped asking the questions. They also told their sons to ignore the questions but there is some problem with that. When Sally asks the repeated questions of her brothers they tell her, "I'm just going to ignore you" and then turn their backs to her. Yet Sally just keeps asking the questions more and more until her brothers just cannot stand it and either yell at her to "Shut up!" or go to complain to their parents.

The leaders next defined punishment and highlighted the problems frequently associated with punishment (as described in Unit Eight of *Parents Are Teachers*) and gave examples of the problems.

Some members expressed concern about the presentation on the problems with using spankings saying, "You mean I can't use spanking any more?" "I know if my kids get really bad that I'll spank them. It's the only thing that works when they are like that." The leaders explained that they were not saying that the parents cannot use spanking. They were pointing out the possible effects of frequent spankings on the relationships between them and their children and were suggesting that the parents try some alternative methods which have been shown to be effective with a number of undesirable behaviors. The leaders also suggested that the parents who wanted more information about the use of punishment read ahead to Unit Eight of *Parents Are Teachers.*

Time-out from reinforcement was introduced as a mild nonstimulative punishment procedure which is less likely to have the adverse emotional side effects of the more stimulative forms of punishment (e.g., spanking). Utilizing the Time-Out Criteria Handout (see Kindy, 1978), the leaders explained the criteria for the effective delivery of time-out and modeled the appropriate use in role plays. Participants discussed the remaining vignettes in the exercise and rehearsed the time-out procedure. Parents encountered several difficulties in the use of time-out. For example, parents gave lengthy explanations of the rule infraction and frequently forgot to praise the child role player for being quiet in the time-out location. As with ignoring, leaders stressed the importance of using reinforcement to increase an incompatible behavior in conjunction with the time-out procedure.

Finally, the leaders asked each group member to report on the successes and problems she had in monitoring her child's behavior during the previous week. Members were prompted to praise successes and offer suggestions to deal with problems after each member's presentation.

Intersession assignments were to: (1) continue monitoring the child behavior; (2) continue recording the phrases and statements of praise that parents make to their children; (3) read Unit Three in *Parents Are Teachers*; (4) complete the reinforcement survey schedule (see Rose, 1977, pp. 96-97); (5) call buddy.

After the session, Chris told the leaders that she was considering dropping the group. She said that since she was the only parent with education beyond high school, she felt out of place and bored with the slow pace. Previously the leaders had noted that Chris had more frequently spoken with them than with other members before and after the group and during the break. In order to increase the attractiveness of the group for Chris, and avoid problematic subgrouping with the leaders, the leaders praised Chris for her rapid learning of the material and suggested that she begin assuming some leadership functions in future sessions by helping other members who were slower learners. Chris agreed to this plan and the leaders planned with her to help with a part of each of the following sessions. For example, she helped Shirley develop a token economy in session four and helped Sally construct a graph in session five.

Session Four

In session four, the primary concepts introduced were principles of rule setting, token economies, and contingency contracting. The primary skills taught were developing appropriate rules, designing a token economy, and writing an effective contingency contract.

In reviewing the process data from the first three sessions, the leaders noted that Rosemary's frequency of interaction was 50 to 75 percent less than the mean rate for all members. This data confirmed their subjective opinion that Rosemary was not participating much in the group discussions. Concerned with the negative effects her lack of participation may have on her learning and the attractiveness of the group to her, the leaders decided to treat the behavior as an interactional group problem. At the beginning of this session, the leaders reported that one member had indicated on her evaluation that she would like members to participate more equally in the discussions. After presenting the data on individual rates of participation, the leaders pointed out that the frequency of individual interactions is maintained by the way in which other members respond to the interaction and is therefore a group problem. The leaders asked the members to suggest ways to help each other participate more equally. Shirley, one of the more verbal members, suggested that members could reinforce each other for participating, especially reinforcing those that have not participated much, such as Rosemary and Mary. All members agreed to this plan and, at the leader's suggestion, developed a list of nonverbal (i.e., smiles, eye contact, head nodding) and verbal (i.e., "That's a good idea;" "I'm glad you said that;" "What do you plan to do about that problem?") reinforcement. This intervention increased Rosemary's participation in subsequent meetings from 25 to 50 percent. Several members reported in their evaluations that this procedure helped them function better as a group since it gave them a structured way in which they could help each other during the session. In addition, the majority of members gave a higher rating to the usefulness of the session and their desire to return the following week.

The leaders introduced the concept of rule setting by distributing a checklist for rule setting (see Kindy, 1978). The leaders explained that rules provide both parent and child with a predictable environment. Predictability provides the child with structure and security and is a way of showing love or caring. After reviewing the criteria for rule setting, several examples were given which dealt with such behaviors as getting dressed before breakfast, changing school clothes before going out to play, making the bed before leaving for school, and mowing the lawn after lunch. Following the program format, the leader discussed the first example in detail, explaining how it met the stated criteria. Parents were asked to critique the remaining examples with the leader serving as prompter and consultant. Leaders modeled appropriate ways to present rules to children and then had subgroups of parents rehearse the rule-setting procedure.

The principles of a token economy were presented. Leaders explained that tokens (stars, points, bottle caps, money) were a useful means of rewarding simple behaviors that occur frequently becuase tokens are concrete, visible, and easy to dispense. Leaders pointed out that token economies could be designed to change a number of behaviors in one child or in the entire family and could be used to change a wide range of behaviors such as self-care skills (brushing teeth), household chores, communication skills (speaking in a conversational tone of voice, making feeling statements), and self-control skills (completing homework).

Leaders outlined the steps in developing a token economy and provided written examples. Members met in subgroups and practiced designing a token economy from sample data.

In preparation for designing the first treatment program, leaders gave a lecture on contingency contracting and provided several examples of well-formulated contracts. Using the monitoring data and information from the reinforcement survey schedule, parents developed a change plan for increasing one child behavior. (If a token economy was used, parents planned to increase several child behaviors at once.) In writing the contract the parents adhered to the following guidelines: (1) specify tasks as well as consequences; (2) itemize each task so that each task has its own consequence; (3) use both positive and negative consequences; (4) use Premack's Principle if possible; (5) involve significant others; and (6) put the contract in writing.

The discussion on contracting led to a presentation of the ways in which parents could introduce the program or contract to their children. The group leaders modeled examples of appropriate introductions which were then rehearsed by the members. For example, "Alice, I'm very pleased with how you continue helping your little sister. Now I think you're ready to do something about your not putting your things away, like your bike and books from school. My nagging or yelling at you doesn't work and neither of us likes that anyway. I have an idea that will help both of us—help me stop nagging and help you learn to put your bike and books away. This is the way it works . . ." (explain specific recording and reward system).

Members again met in subgroups and rehearsed with each other the way in which they planned to present to their children the change plans they had developed. Other members of the subgroup gave suggestions for improvement and the presentations were rehearsed to success. Throughout this subgrouping, leaders directed all questions back to other group members and praised all problem-solving statements.

Intersession assignments were to: (1) implement the change plan designed in session; (2) continue monitoring the target behavior; (3) read Unit Four in *Parents Are Teachers*; (4) call buddy.

Session Five

In session five, the primary concepts introduced were shaping, modeling, and cueing. The new skills taught were methods for teaching new behaviors and graphing.

On the evaluations for session four, one member stated that she did not like the buddy system because her buddy contacts were "always depressing." She said that her buddy was always complaining about her children and her boyfriend and that no matter how "nice and understanding" she tried to be and no matter how many suggestions she made to help solve the problems, her buddy would not "take any advice" but went right on complaining about the same things. Furthermore, she was not getting any help from her buddy because her buddy never asked about her programs or problems. In order to facilitate the pair becoming more mutually helpful, the leaders began the meeting by reviewing the purposes of the buddy system and role playing a negative model of a buddy contact in which one member was reinforcing off-task behavior and not giving the other member feedback on her program. The leaders then asked the parents to discuss ways in which this buddy contact could be improved and then asked two members to demonstrate the same buddy contact incorporating the suggestions the group had made. On the evaluations for this and subsequent sessions, several members indicated that they found this review of the buddy system helpful since their buddy contacts had not been as useful as they could have been. (In more recent parent groups, the leaders have had the members give a brief report on their buddy contact at the beginning of each of the three sessions following the introduction of the procedure. This report helps identify problems early and foreshadows appropriate use of the contacts.)

Shaping, modeling, and cueing were described as key concepts in teaching new behaviors. For each concept, leaders presented a handout (see Kindy, 1978), gave a theoretical rationale, gave examples of its use, and asked parents to provide examples of the concept from their own experience.

After teaching the three concepts, leaders asked members to meet in subgroups, to select one problem behavior of their child, and to describe in writing how they would employ one of the three procedures discussed. After the participants had developed a plan, each member explained the program that she had developed to the group for feedback and suggestions for improvement. The primary difficulties encountered by the parents were that the steps in the shaping procedure were too large, that members felt "silly" demonstrating the behavior they wanted their child to imitate, and that members gave lengthy and confusing instructions to the role played child in the modeling procedure.

Leaders briefly discussed making a graph, provided model graphs, and had members develop graphs in session for the child behaviors they monitored. To encourage member participation and leadership, members who had difficulty were helped by other members.

Finally, parents presented the current results of their home management program. The leaders encouraged group members to reinforce success and suggested specific program changes to help solve the problems that arose during the first week of treatment.

Intersession assignments were to: (1) continue implementing the home management change plan; (2) continue monitoring the target behavior; (3) graph data on all behaviors monitored from baseline to present; (4) read Unit Six in *Parents Are Teachers*; (5) call buddy.

Session Six

In session six, the primary concepts introduced were reinforcing inappropriate behavior through "negative" attention and response cost. The new skills taught were response cost procedures and stop-the-world.

At this point in the development of the group, the leaders wanted parents to increase autonomous in-group problem solving. In the first five sessions, members had emitted few problem-solving statements independent of leader promptings (e.g., "Do you think Sally's description is specific enough?" "What are other ways to handle this situation?"). Since an increasing portion of the remaining sessions were to be devoted to solving problems that arose in the home management programs and since transfer of learning outside the therapeutic setting is enhanced by providing clients with a cognitive problem solving paradigm (Goldstein, Heller, and Sechrest, 1966, pp. 240-50), the leaders instituted a token reinforcement procedure to increase autonomous problem solving. Baseline data taken during the three problem-solving sections of session five were presented at the beginning of the group along with the rationale for increasing autonomous problem solving. In order to specify the desired behavior, the leaders outlined six components of problem solving:

1. specify the problem in operational terms;
2. collect information and data;
3. develop alternative solutions;
4. evaluate the alternatives and narrow them down;
5. implement one alternative;
6. evaluate the results and extend or revise the plan (D'Zurilla and Goldfried, 1971).

Leaders gave examples of each of these components. An autonomous problem-solving statement was defined as any statement made by a member which was a component of the problem-solving process and did not follow a leader's prompting. Each time a member performed the desired behavior, one of the leaders would throw a poker chip into a large can. The poker chip reinforced the member for making a problem-solving statement and cued other members to do the same. Problem-solving statements were monitored only during problem-solving portions of the agenda. At the beginning of each session, members would agree on a goal level of autonomous problem-solving statements per minute based on the previous week's performance. If the group attained this goal, at the following session the leaders would bring in a "special treat" (e.g., coffee cake) for them to have at the break; if the group did not attain the goal, they could not have any coffee at the break (these contingencies were negotiated with the members). As can be seen from Figure 3-1, the group procedure increased the frequency of autonomous problem-solving statements during the remaining sessions.

The leaders next identified and discussed "the criticism trap", a common parent-child interactional pattern in which inappropriate behavior is reinforced by "negative attention" (e.g., yelling, criticizing). Using model role plays, leaders demonstrated ways of avoiding "the criticism trap" by increasing the use of positive methods of child management. Several members commented that

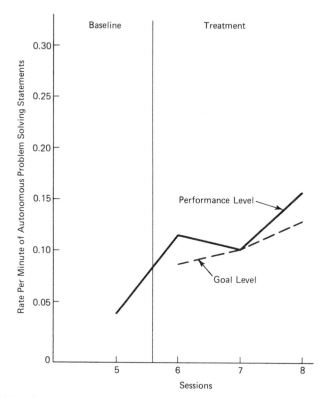

FIGURE 3-1 Frequency of Autonomous Problem Solving Statements by Group Members

through the course of training, they had become aware of how often and the variety of ways (e.g., yelling, nagging, spanking, saying "I don't want you to . . ." rather than "I want you to . . .") they had relied on negative means to manage their children. Members were then given examples of "the criticism trap" and were asked to demonstrate in role plays how to avoid the "traps."

Leaders introduced two new procedures designed to decrease inappropriate behavior: response cost and stop-the-world. The procedures were modeled by the leaders and then rehearsed by group members. Leaders explained that these procedures along with ignoring, rule setting, and time-out were used to decrease problematic behaviors when the use of a reinforcement for incompatible behaviors was not strong enough to achieve a change in the behavior. (Leaders pointed out that the current program to increase the frequency with which the meeting was finished on time was a combination of reinforcement and response cost procedures.)

After the ongoing home management programs were reviewed, parents were asked to design a monitoring plan for their second behavior. To facilitate autonomous parent problem solving and mutual sharing of knowledge, the leaders served as consultants, giving suggestions only when necessary.

Intersession assignments were to: (1) continue implementing the home management change plan including any modifications made in session; (2) continue monitoring and graphing the targeted behavior and begin to monitor and graph the newly selected behavior; (3) read Units Eight and Nine in *Parents Are Teachers*; (4) call buddy.

Session Seven

In session seven, the leaders introduced the principle of maintenance of behavior change. The teaching of communication skills which was planned for this session was eliminated from the agenda to allow more time for the home management part of the session and to review the skills already covered. This change in the program format was a result of members' comments on the weekly evaluations that the pace of the program was "too fast" for them.

At the beginning of this session, leaders presented ways in which parents could maintain newly learned behaviors while modifying the highly structured program to a more "natural" one. Parents were told that once the child had performed the new behavior successfully, they should begin slowly fading the tangible reinforcement (tokens, toys) and structure (keeping data, charts) by expecting more behavior for the same reinforcement, by delaying the reinforcement for longer time periods, by delivering the reward at random intervals or after random performances of the behavior, and by pairing the tangible reinforcement with praise and then gradually dropping the tangibles (Brockway, 1974). Emphasis was placed on "going slowly" during the fading. Parents were told to keep data during this phase so they could evaluate the effects of their maintenance of change procedures. As a model for fading reinforcement, leaders began fading the reinforcers for their own finishing on time as described in session three.

On the weekly evaluation forms, several members requested a review of negative reinforcement and the time-out from reinforcement procedure. The leaders provided a brief explanation of negative reinforcement and gave several examples of negative reinforcement (e.g., fastening seat belt to stop buzzer). To assess their understanding of this concept, the members were asked to write down the appropriate responses to several prepared examples which were taken from Brockway (1974). Members were asked to assume the leadership in critiquing each other's answers in order to provide them with additional participation and problem-solving opportunities.

In reviewing time-out, parents described difficulties that they experienced in the use of this procedure. For example, one mother stated that she could not keep her child in the time-out room; and another mother did not know what to do when her child made a mess in the time-out place. After appropriate solutions were offered, the leaders asked Chris, who was skilled in using time-out, to demonstrate time-out incorporating the suggestions. The members who had experienced difficulty with the procedure next rehearsed time-out until they were successful.

The last part of the session was devoted to developing a home management plan for the second target behavior. In order to continue to encourage autonomous problem solving, the leaders had the members work together in pairs to develop plans based on the data collected and then report to the group on the plans for further feedback. The leaders did not participate in the subgroups except to answer questions that the buddy could not solve.

Intersession assignments were to: (1) continue implementing the first home management change plan; (2) start fading procedures if appropriate; (3) implement a home management plan for the second target behavior; (4) monitor and graph both behaviors; (5) read Unit Ten in *Parents Are Teachers*; (6) call buddy.

Session Eight

In session eight, all concepts and skills introduced and practiced during the previous group sessions were briefly reviewed through the use of a film "Who Did What to Whom?" (Mager, 1972). The film consists of a number of short vignettes illustrating behavioral principles and techniques. The leaders stopped the film after each vignette and asked the group to identify the principles and techniques that were demonstrated and the likely effect on future behavior. Parents commented that the film was an interesting and humorous way to review and that they enjoyed being able to correctly identify the principles in the vignettes. One member suggested the film be used at the first meeting as an introduction to the program which would replace the introductory lecture that was "too long" and abstract.

To facilitate transfer of change outside the group, the leaders conducted a discussion on ways of dealing with the school system and teachers. The discussion covered such topics as parent and child rights, school and community resources available to help with school problems, and procedures to use in approaching teachers before and when problems arose. Several members commented that they often felt "very defensive" at teacher-parent conferences and because of this discomfort one mother had stopped attending these conferences. Other members also acknowledged that they had difficulty asserting themselves with school personnel (asking teachers to send notes home, requesting special tutorial help, asking to be called immediately when a problem arose). Leaders presented several suggestions to aid parents in developing constructive relationships with teachers. These suggestions included:

1. Contact the teacher at the beginning of the school year to introduce yourself and to let the teacher know you are interested in your child's education.
2. Talk about your child in a positive, yet realistic manner to avoid "labelling" your child.
3. Ask for positive feedback concerning your child ("What does she do well?" "What improvement have you seen since our last conference?").
4. Acknowledge teacher identified problems ("You seem frustrated by his sloppy penmanship.").
5. Reinforce teacher efforts by praise and home follow-through.
6. Request the help you feel your child needs.
7. Utilize school or social service personnel to obtain services for your child and/or to act as your advocate if you have a complaint that can not be handled through the teacher.

To emphasize the desirability of generalizing the basic principles learned throughout the program, parents were requested to write an appropriate plan for each situation and then to demonstrate through role play several basic procedures. Parents provided feedback to each other using the criteria on the appropriate check list. The assignment (see Kindy, 1978) provided the group members with an opportunity to demonstrate their knowledge of child management techniques and provided the leaders with a way of assessing the parents' cognitive and behavioral learning.

Parents briefly discussed their two home programs and completed a treatment summary form for the first program (see home management section). The leaders outlined follow-up arrangements that were available (maintaining contacts with buddies, getting in touch with resource persons, and reading additional material). Parents were given the names of several county social workers who were knowledgeable about behavior modification techniques and who had agreed to act as resource persons when the group ended. (Several of these workers had participated in the initial home observations.) Arrangements were made to have four booster sessions over a period of three months during which concepts and techniques would be reviewed and plans would be made to deal with any current child management problem. The agenda for the first booster session was developed by the members of the group. Finally, members completed a final evaluation form which gave overall feedback on the content, group procedures, structure, and leadership of the group. Members indicated that positive reinforcement, token reinforcement and time-out were the most useful techniques in dealing with their children's behavioral problems. Parents listed negative reinforcement, modeling, and fading as the concepts or techniques with which they still needed help. In learning the behavioral approach, parents found the following methods to be the most helpful: lecture by leaders, monitoring of behavior, review of evaluation and observer data, home programs, reading *Parents Are Teachers*, and group discussion of parents' experience.

All members rated the group as "very useful" or "useful" and stated that they had recommended this type of group to other parents.

HOME MANAGEMENT PROGRAMS

Group members treated a total of 22 behaviors. All members who completed the training program reported at least partial success in treating a minimum of one behavior.

Case Summary 1

Shirley was a 47-year-old divorced mother of 10 children, 6 of whom were living at home during the course of the training program. Shirley worked part-time as a bookkeeper. Shirley defined and treated the following behaviors for all her children.

Behavior: (1) making beds in morning;
             (2) completing assigned chore in morning.

Treatment: Shirley and all 6 of the children living at home (ages range from 7 to 19 years) participated in the home management token system. Each family member received praise and a check mark on a chart posted on the refrigerator when he or she finished making the bed or completed another assigned job (e.g., taking out trash, doing dishes) before noontime. Shirley recorded the check marks at the beginning of the treatment program. The older children took over the monitoring responsibilities in the later phases of treatment. The reward system varied according to age and individual preferences. The tokens (check marks) could be traded in for such items as money, going out to eat, use of the car and special events. Written reminders in the form of riddles were employed in the initial phase of treatment.

Results: Shirley achieved the desired results (80 percent completion of bedmaking and chores per week) with all family members, including herself, during the first two weeks of treatment using the token system. These levels were maintained throughout the course of the eight-week training program. At the two-month follow-up meeting Shirley reported continued success with all but her 18-year-old son.

Case Summary 2

Rosemary was a 25-year-old divorced mother of one. She was an unemployed high school graduate. Rosemary successfully treated two behaviors of her two-year-old son, Peter.

Behavior: (1) climbing in window;
            (2) appropriate play (e.g., playing with toys on floor or in own room, helping or reading with Mom; absence of window climbing).

Treatment: Peter received one cent for every half hour of appropriate play (no window climbing) accompanied with verbal praise. After Rosemary delivered one cent to the child, they would both walk to his room so that he could place the money in his bank. Cuing was used to interrupt the dangerous behavior of window climbing. When Peter approached the window or was climbing on the window, Rosemary said "down" to which Peter responded appropriately.

Rosemary monitored another behavior, playing with television knobs, for a one-week period. The baseline data revealed that the behavior occurred at a low rate so that no other intervention was initiated.

Results: The window climbing behavior decreased from a baseline frequency of 30 per week to 3 occurrences per week after five weeks of treatment (see Figure 3-2). The behavior was maintained at this level at follow-up.

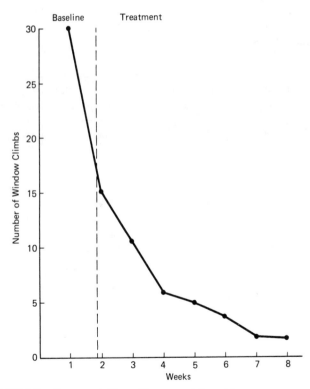

FIGURE 3-2   Rosemary's Home Management Program

Case Summary 3

Mary was a 34-year-old divorced mother of two. She had completed the eighth grade and was employed as a babysitter. She worked on the following behavior for her son John, age seven.

> *Behavior:*   (1) wetting bed at night (nocturnal enuresis). Medical workup was negative.
>
> *Treatment:* John selected a favorite breakfast food on mornings that he was dry and received verbal praise from his mother. John also received a check mark on a chart that was kept by his mother. On mornings that he was wet, John was instructed to remove the sheets from his bed. During treatment Mary tried limiting liquid intake in the evenings and waking John at midnight. Mary reported that she was unable to implement these changes on a consistent basis as John would obtain liquids on his own and frequently could not be awoken to make the trip to the bathroom.
>
> *Results:* Baseline data indicated that John was dry 3.5 mornings per week. By the end of the training program he was dry 5 nights per week.

Case Summary 4

Sally was a 22-year-old married mother of two. She had completed the tenth grade and was not employed at the time of the group. Sally's attendance in the parent group was court ordered. Sally dropped out of the program after the sixth meeting as her children were placed in foster care because of her husband's alleged abuse of the children. Although Sally's participation was mandatory, her involvement in the sessions was enthusiastic. She worked on the following behavior for her two children:

> *Behavior:*   (1) nocturnal enuresis of five-year-old, Steve;
>   (2) nocturnal and diurnal enuresis of three-year-old Angela.
>
> *Treatment:* Children received pennies or pieces of candy and verbal praise for dry mornings and dry pants during the day. Accidents were ignored.
>
> *Results:* No data was available as Sally terminated the group early and subsequently moved from the area.

Case Summary 5

Chris was a 26-year-old divorced mother of two. She completed two years of college and was employed as a computer programmer. Her children were returned from foster care to her care after the fourth week of training. She worked on the following behaviors for both her children.

Behavior: (1) compliance to commands;
              (2) sitting down when told "no";
              (3) crying when put to bed at night.

Treatment: Jessica, age two, received a small piece of fruit or candy and time with Mom for compliance to her commands (Jessica was allowed two reminders). The older child, Jason, age four, was used as a model for compliance behaviors. Jason was praised for compliance in his sister's presence. Ignoring was used to decrease Jessica's night crying and sitting down when told "no."

Results: Compliance to commands increased from a baseline rate of 30 percent to 70 percent after two weeks of treatment. Night-time crying decreased from 30 minutes of crying on the first night of treatment to less than 30 seconds on the fourth night. The night crying was maintained at this level for three weeks. Night crying drastically increased after this time period when Chris was ill and a grandmother cared for the children for several days and did not apply the behavioral program. The crying was again brought under control when the mother resumed the program.

RESULTS

Process Measures

Assignment completion.   The rate of assignment completion was used as a measure of group productivity. In the present training program, the mean rate of assignment completion for all members across all sessions was 96 percent, indicating a high rate of productivity.

Group attendance and promptness.   Data was collected on attendance and promptness as process measures of productivity and group attractiveness. The mean rate of attendance for all members across all sessions was 85 percent, and the mean rate of promptness for those members present was 92 percent (across all sessions).

Weekly evaluations.   The weekly evaluations were used as indicators of parent satisfaction with group content, process, and leadership. Member responses revealed a high degree of satisfaction with the program. On a 1 to 10 scale (10 being high), the mean score for all members across all sessions was 9 on session "usefulness" and 9.4 on the same scale on members' desire to return next week.

Outcome Measures

Knowledge questionnaire.   The knowledge questionnaire (Brockway, 1974) was given to assess the parents' knowledge of learning theory principles, terminology, and child management techniques. Questionnaires were blind scored by the observers. All members who completed the training program showed a gain of at least 30 percent on the pre-post knowledge exam; the maximum increase was 65 percent.

Walker Problem Behavior Identification Checklist. The Walker Problem Behavior Identification Checklist (Walker, 1970) was administered at the beginning and again at the end of training to evaluate changes in parental attitudes regarding the targeted child. Several mothers completed forms for a child other than the initially selected child on the posttraining form so that comparisons on the Walker Problem Behavior Identification Checklist were not possible.

DISCUSSION

This paper described a group training program designed to teach parenting skills to AFDC parents. Intended for parents of both problem and nonproblem children between the ages of 2 and 12, the program provided parents with a learning theory framework; taught them behavioral child management skills such as social reinforcement, cueing, time-out from reinforcement, extinction, and contingency contracting; and trained them in treatment planning and problem-solving skills so that they could continue to effectively modify their children's behaviors in the future. The program evolved from a series of parent training groups carried out as a part of the Interpersonal Skill Training and Research Project (see chapter 1) at the School of Social Work, University of Wisconsin-Madison. Feedback from parents and observations from trained observers in the earlier groups were important in developing the present model. Although this particular program was developed for AFDC parents, similar ones have been successfully applied to other parent populations including middle class and foster parents.

In the current group, five AFDC parents participated in weekly two hour sessions over eight consecutive weeks. All parents reported at least partial success in treating one or more behaviors. No failures were reported. The behaviors treated included enuresis, crying, performance of household chores, and compliance. All members increased their scores on the written pre-post knowledge exam by 30 to 65 percent. A number of group treatment procedures successfully modified a variety of group problems including attendance, promptness, group cohesiveness, frequency of member participation, and frequency of autonomous problem solving.

The parent-reported data on the home management programs and the difference scores for the written knowledge test are more positive than the results reported for other homogeneous AFDC parent training groups (e.g., Rose, 1974).

A number of changes in the group format proposed here could be made to enhance its effectiveness in training other AFDC parent groups. During the group and in the final evaluations, members reported that they felt that they were given too much material and that the pace of the group was too fast. The review in sessions seven and eight was not adequate to deal with this problem. Because of the limited educational background of many AFDC parents, it may be necessary to extend the eight session model to ten or twelve sessions, introducing no more than two new concepts or skills each session and allowing ample time to review the concepts or skills.

Although several procedures were employed during the training to enhance the maintenance of the newly learned child management skills (e.g., the buddy system, the shift in leadership functions, the preparations for dealing with new problems in an unsympathetic environment, the scheduled follow-up sessions), more attention needs to be given to long-term maintenance planning. The principle of overlearning new behaviors may be especially important to the AFDC population. Since child management is but one of the multiple problems that face the typical AFDC parent, it is possible that they will revert to the old, well-learned aversive child management techniques they practiced before training (e.g., negative reinforcement and stimulatory punishment) unless their use of the newly learned positive techniques is periodically reinforced over an extended period of time. In the current group, the leaders provided the parents with a list of county social workers who had agreed to function as resource persons to help maintain the new skills, yet the extent to which an AFDC parent would seek out a social worker for help in preventing child management problems, much less the ability of the social worker to respond to such requests, remains an unresolved question. In future groups, leaders could arrange to have agency social workers visit parents on a regular basis to monitor progress in existing home management programs, help develop new programs for new behavioral problems as they occur, and observe the generalization of parenting skills to nontargeted behaviors and children. Ideally, the agency worker should have been a coleader of the training group. Future groups could also enhance transfer of learning of child management skills by conducting a maintenance group periodically with parents assuming most or all of the leadership responsibilities or by offering an "advanced group" or periodic "booster sessions."

The initial two-hour home observation was the only direct observation of parent and child behavior in the natural environment. Consequently the leaders had to rely on parent-reported data for the home management programs to assess change in child or parent behavior. The reliability of such data is open to question (see Johnson and Bolstad, 1973). In addition, relying on parent-reported data made it difficult to determine the degree to which the parent skills had generalized to other nontargeted behaviors and children (an important transfer of learning question). Finally, the data reported for the present group were insufficient to evaluate maintenance of appropriate child management skills over an extended period of time.

The purpose of this paper was to describe a model program for training AFDC parents in the verbal and behavioral skills necessary to manage effectively their children's behaviors, including the use of group procedures designed to increase the productivity of a homogeneous group. Despite the limitations of the outcome data, the individual and group procedures described offer the clinician means to conduct training groups to help the AFDC parent cope with one of her or his most prevalent problems.

REFERENCES

Becker, W. C. *Parents are teachers: A child management program.* Champaign, Ill.: Research Press, 1971.

Berkowitz, B. and A. Graziano. Training parents as behavior therapists: A review. *Behavior Research and Therapy*, 1972, *4*, 297-317.

Brockway, B. *Training in child management: A family approach.* Dubuque, Iowa: Kendall-Hunt, 1974.

Brown, D. B. *Behavior modification in child, school, and family.* Champaign, Ill.: Research Press, 1972.

Cone, J. D. and E. W. Sloop. Parents as agents of change. In A. Jacobs and W. W. Spradlin (eds.), *The group as agent of change.* New York: Behavioral Publications, 1974.

D'Zurilla, T. J. and M. R. Goldfried. Problem solving and behavior modification. *Journal of Abnormal Psychology*, 1971, *78*, 107-26.

Gardner, J. M. Teaching behavior modification to nonprofessionals. *Journal of Applied Behavioral Analysis*, 1972, *5*, 517-21.

Goldstein, A. P., K. Heller, and L. B. Sechrest. *Psychotherapy and the psychology of behavior change.* New York: John Wiley, 1966.

Howard, O. Teaching a class of parents as reinforcement therapists to treat their own children. Paper presented at the meeting of the Southwestern Psychological Association, Louisville, Kentucky, 1970.

Johnson, S. M. and O. D. Bolstad. Methodological issues in natural observation: Some problems and solutions for field research. In L. A. Hamerlynck, L. C. Handy, and E. J. Mash (eds.), *Behavior change: Methodology, concepts, and practice.* Champaign, Ill.: Research Press, 1973.

Kadushin, A. *Child welfare services.* New York: Macmillan, 1974.

Kindy, P. Criteria checklists for evaluating effective applications of behavioral procedures by parents. Interpersonal skill training and research project, U. of Wisconsin, Madison, 1978.

Kovitz, K. E. Comparing group and individual methods for training parents in child management techniques. In E. J. Mash, L. D. Handy, and L. A. Hamerlynck (eds.), *Behavior modification approaches to parenting.* New York: Brunner-Mazel, 1976.

Lindsley, O. An experiment with parents handling behavior at home. *Johnstone Bulletin*, 1966, *9*, 27-36.

Mager, R. F. *Who did what to whom?*, Champaign, Ill.: Research Press, 1972.

Patterson, G. R., R. S. Ray, D. A. Shaw, and J. A. Cobb. Manual for coding of family interactions, 1969. Available from: ASIS National Auxiliary Publications Service, c/o CMM Information Services, Inc., 909 Third Avenue, New York, New York 10022. Document Number 01234.

Phillips, E. L., E. A. Phillips, D. L. Fixsen, and M. M. Wolf. *The teaching-family handbook*. Lawrence: University of Kansas Printing Service, 1974.

Rose, S. D. A behavioral approach to the group treatment of parents. *Social Work*, 1969, *14*, 21-29.

Rose, S. D. Group therapy: A behavioral approach. Englewood Cliffs: Prentice-Hall, 1977.

————. *Treating children in groups*. San Francisco: Jossey-Bass, 1972.

————. Group training of parents as behavior modifiers. *Social Work*, 1974, *19*, 156-62.

Shack, J. R. and L. W. Barnett. *An annotated and indexed bibliography of behavior management with children*. Chicago: Loyola University of Chicago, 1973.

Tams, V. and S. Eyberg. A group treatment program for parents. In E. J. Mash, L. C. Handy, and L. A. Hamerlynck (eds.), *Behavior modification approaches to parenting*. New York: Brunner-Mazel, 1976.

Walker, H. M. *Walker Problem Behavior Identification Checklist*. Los Angeles: Western Psychological Services, 1970.

PHILLIPS KINDY, JR. and PATRICIA M. PATTERSON

4

behavioral-cognitive therapy in a group for the prevention of obesity

INTRODUCTION

Obesity is one of the most prevalent health problems in the United States. Affecting up to one-quarter of American adults (Stuart and Davis, 1972), obesity is associated with a variety of physical illnesses and psychological problems (Robbins and Hall, 1970). Until recently, the outcomes of outpatient treatment for obesity were discouraging:

> Most obese persons will not remain in treatment. Of those that will remain in treatment, most will not lose weight, and of those who do lose weight, most will regain it (Stunkard, 1958, p 79).

Since Stuart's pioneering paper "Behavioral Control of Overeating" (1967), there has been a rapidly increasing number of studies applying behavioral techniques to the treatment of obesity and comparing these techniques to other treatment modalities. Several recent reviews have concluded that behavior therapy appears to be superior to all other methods for managing mild to moderate obesity in the short term (Stunkard, 1972; Abramson, 1973; Hall and Hall, 1974; Bellack, 1975; Franks and Wilson, 1975; Stunkard and Mahoney, 1976).

The effectiveness of behavioral treatment for morbid obesity has not yet been demonstrated.

Although few studies examined the relative contribution of specific behavioral techniques, some generalizations can be made about the efficacy of specific behavioral techniques applied to weight control. Antecedent stimulus control procedures are the most well investigated and, in combination with other treatment techniques, have been shown to be most effective (Bellack, 1975). Teaching patients self-control procedures has been found effective in obesity control and enhances long-term maintenance of weight loss efforts after treatment termination, since the patient becomes his own therapist (Abramson, 1973; Balfour, 1974; Hall and Hall, 1974; Stunkard and Mahoney, 1976; Hall et al., 1977).

Stunkard and Mahoney (1976) outlined the following components for a maximally effective program based on their analysis of frequent components of successful behavior programs:

1. A simple and portable self-monitoring system that emphasizes actual behaviors *rather than weight* (e.g., eating habits, exercise, food relevant thoughts, etc.).

2. Basic information on nutrition with an emphasis on the development of sound long-term eating patterns which permit weight control without jeopardizing essential nutrient intake (i.e., no crash dieting, no totally restricted foods, etc.).

3. Instruction in exercise management outlining the physiological assets of exercise and encouraging increases in daily energy output (activity patterns) which are more likely to be maintained than effortful calesthenics.

4. Diet instruction in the many facets of simulus control as a means of regulating food intake.

5. Initial provision of therapist or group support with the magnitude and frequency of this reinforcement gradually withdrawn as the individual continues progressing.

6. Training of spouses and other family members in social reinforcement strategy in order to maintain program induced improvements.

7. Training in the modification of self-defeating thought patterns and unrealistic performance standards.

8. Training in the development of broad problem solving skills and the establishment of self-regulating incentive systems (e.g., tangible self-reward, self-praise) to enhance maintenance (pp. 67-68).

An alternative approach to obesity control is to train patients in the self-control skills necessary to prevent them from becoming obese rather than treating them only when they are obese. Surprisingly little attention has been given to utilizing behavioral methods to prevent obesity.

Many studies of the behavioral treatment of obesity have taken place in a group context (e.g., Wollersheim, 1970). Most of these do not report the use of group treatment procedures to help achieve training goals. Those studies that do describe their use of the group process do not do so in sufficient detail to be of use to the clinician (Rose, 1977).

The purpose of this chapter is to describe a prevention oriented approach to the behavioral control of obesity in a group context. The chapter describes a comprehensive group training program applied to seven marginally obese female patients at a primary care clinic. The use of individual treatment techniques to modify patient behavior and the use of group treatment techniques to modify group attributes are discussed in sufficient detail to enable the clinician to employ them in designing and implementing future programs.

THE SETTING

Recent developments in the field of internal medicine have resulted in the development of a primary care specialty and a team approach to medical practice. Internists trained in primary care are generalists working together with a multidisciplinary health care team in an outpatient clinical setting. The team provides continuous, coordinated, and comprehensive health care to a limited number of patients. With its emphasis on preventative medicine and on the personal and social context of illness, the primary health care clinic allows optimal opportunity for the comprehensive, long-term treatment of obesity.

One of the most frequently encountered problems at the Adult Medicine Clinic has been obesity, a problem that increases the patient's health risks and exacerbates health care problems. Several patients had complained to the clinic personnel that they had exhausted all community resources (e.g., mental health center, Weight Watchers, TOPS) in their efforts to lose weight without any significant weight loss. In response to this patient-identified need for an alternate service, the medical counselors developed a weight loss program for obese patients in conjunction with physicians, nurses, and the hospital outpatient dietician. Although some patients were seen individually, most patients were referred to weight loss groups because it was believed that for most patients the group process would enhance weight loss efforts. The main purpose of the groups was to teach members cognitive/behavioral self-control skills which would enable them to change effectively those eating and exercise-related behaviors which had contributed to their obese conditions. Each group met for 10 sessions over a 14-week period. An ongoing bimonthly group maintenance clinic was offered free of charge to all group members.

Recently the Adult Medicine Clinic has added a prevention oriented weight loss group, teaching marginally obese patients (15 to 20 percent over their ideal weight as determined by the Metropolitan Life Insurance Company Tables, i.e., about 10 to 30 pounds over their ideal weight) the skills necessary to achieve and maintain their ideal weight. In keeping with the clinic's concern with preventative medicine, this service was offered in response to patients requesting services to help them control their weight before they became obese. In the absence of controlled studies demonstrating the long-term efficacy of behavioral treatment of obesity (Wilson, 1976), using cognitive/behavioral group methods to prevent obesity may be a more effective means for long-term obesity control.

GROUP ORGANIZATION AND ASSESSMENT

Patients were recruited for the group in two ways: (1) Health professionals in the Adult Medicine Clinic and in other medical services in the University of Wisconsin Hospitals were given an information sheet describing the group, its purposes, and its content and were given an approximate date for the first session. They were asked to refer patients who were 10 to 30 pounds overweight who indicated dissatisfaction with their weight or who needed to lose weight for medical reasons. (2) A sign was posted in the clinic waiting room advertising all groups offered by the clinic. Patients who were interested in one of the groups were directed to ask the clinic receptionists for an information sheet describing the group. If the patient was interested in the group or wanted more information about the group, he/she was asked to return a portion of the information sheet to the receptionists so that a counselor could contact him/her. (In subsequent groups, leaders have generated a larger number of referrals by putting information about upcoming groups in the hospital weekly newspaper.)

Shortly after a patient returned the form indicating interest in the group, a counselor contacted the patient to answer any further questions about the group. Then, if he/she was still interested, the patient was sent the pregroup questionnaire, a modification of the "Stanford Eating Disorders Clinic Questionnaire" (Agras et al., 1976). The purpose of the questionnaire was to: (1) obtain medical, demographic, and sociological information on each patient for clinical and research purposes; (2) consider any health problem which may have to be followed during weight loss or may contraindicate participation in the group; (3) help assess patient motivation in weight loss efforts (Agras et al. state that returning the completed questionnaire has significant screening value for patient attrition); (4) assess the patient's anxiety about participating in the weight loss program.

After receiving the completed questionnaire, the counselor scheduled a pregroup interview with a patient to review the information on the questionnaire, discuss any medical or psychological abnormalities reported by the patient, answer any further questions the patient may have about the group, and weigh the patient. At this time the patient was told that he was admitted to the group. After 10 patients had been admitted to the group another 5 patients were put on a waiting list in case of pregroup attrition. If there was no attrition, then the wait-listed patients were admitted to a subsequent group. The exact day and time of the group was also set during the interview according to what was most convenient for the majority of the group members.

One week before the group began, each member had an additional brief meeting with one of the group leaders. (Although the members of the current group met individually, members in subsequent groups met with the leaders as a group for this second interview.) The purpose of this interview was to obtain further assessment information, to collect a refundable deposit from the members, and to distribute materials for assignments to be completed by the first session. Members were reweighed in order to determine whether their weight loss began when they were admitted to the group or when they had begun learning self-control skills in the group. Using this second pregroup weight, leaders calculated the reduction coefficient for each member in order to determine the weight reduction index at various stages of treatment (Feinstein, 1959). This index provides a standardized way of measuring success in weight reduction, taking into account initial weight, amount overweight, ideal weight, and pounds lost.

During the interview members were asked to complete the "Weight Loss Checklist," a 26-item list of stimulus situations frequently associated with overeating. Members were to indicate the frequency with which they ate in these situations by rating each item on a one to three scale. In addition, each member was given copies of the "Food Diary" (Ferguson, 1976) to monitor food intake and various associated stimuli for the four days before the group began. (Four days is hardly an adequate baseline but, despite the contingencies set, members in previous groups have consistently failed to complete more than four days of monitoring on this type of form.) The checklist and the pregroup monitoring provided baseline data regarding food intake, helped identify stimulus control patterns associated with appropriate and inappropriate eating, and helped orient members to the treatment approach. At this time, members were lent a copy of the "text" for the group, *Permanent Weight Control* (Mahoney and Mahoney, 1976), and given an initial reading assignment to be completed by the second meeting.

Finally, each member made a $20.00 refundable deposit. Deposits have been shown to decrease attrition in weight loss groups (Hagen, Foreyt, and Durham, 1976) and to increase promptness and assignment completion in groups (Rose, 1977). Refunding the deposit in increasing increments has been found to help maintain attendance during the course of the group (Horan et al., 1975). The deposit for the current group was refunded in increasing increments contingent upon attendance, promptness, and assignment completion. While being weighted in at the beginning of each session, the member received his/her refund for that week according to the following schedule: 25 percent for attendance, 25 percent for promptness, and 50 percent for assignment completion.

GROUP COMPOSITION

Of the 11 patients who expressed interest in the group, eight women scheduled pregroup interviews and subsequently enrolled in the group. One patient was not able to meet at the time most convenient for the rest of the patients; the other two could not afford the group fees. All group members had referred themselves upon reading the sign in the waiting room or upon hearing of the group from friends who were clinic patients. None of the group members showed a significant weight change between the two initial weigh-ins.

Four of the group members were married, three were single, and one was widowed. Two women had children living with them. Age ranged from 21 years to 71 years (mean age, 30.8 years). All had earned bachelor degrees in college and three had or were currently pursuing postgraduate degrees. All women stated that looking better and feeling more physically fit were their major reasons for losing weight. Only two women had been told by their doctors that losing weight would be beneficial for their health. The others felt that the pressure to lose weight came from themselves. All had tried unsuccessfully to lose weight previously, except one who had never attempted to lose weight. Three had lost weight for one year and then regained it. All were able to identify problem eating patterns and priorities which might interfere with weight loss efforts.

GROUP FORMAT AND
GENERAL GROUP PROCEDURE

In planning for the current group the leaders assumed that patients with 10 to 30 pounds to lose would need from six to eight sessions to successfully learn the self-control skills necessary to lose weight and maintain the loss, in contrast to those with over 30 pounds to lose, who would need more sessions. The present group was originally designed to meet for six two-hour sessions on six consecutive weeks with a one-month follow-up session. At the request of the members the structure was modified to six training sessions with two follow-up sessions at three- and four-week intervals. In order to efficiently teach members the verbal and behavioral self-control skills in a relatively short-term program, the training sequence for new skills in each session was structured to: (1) provide a cognitive framework for the new skill by teaching principles underlying the skill; (2) provide positive and negative models of the application of the skill;

(3) provide extensive practice in the skill by means of written exercises, in-session behavioral rehearsal, and behavioral assignments to be carried out in the natural environment. Each session was structured in the following way:

1. As the members came in one of the leaders weighed them individually, checked their assignments, and refunded the portion of the deposit they had earned for attendance, promptness, and assignment completion. In order to make the refund maximally reinforcing, members were encouraged to spend the refunded deposit on "something special" rather than "just putting it back into the general fund." Weekly weights were plotted on a graph with a criteria line of one-pound-a-week loss as an additional means to motivate patients to behavioral changes resulting in weight loss (Fisher et al., 1976).

2. At the beginning of the group session, leaders (a) distributed the session agenda indicating behavioral goals, treatment procedures to be discussed, and assignments; (b) reviewed salient points from the previous week's evaluation; and (c) asked for any questions about readings, assignments, or previous sessions. In reviewing the evaluations the leaders reinforced members for their evaluative comments of the group process by demonstrating the ways in which they had incorporated feedback into the program or discussing comments in the evaluations with the members in order to resolve the member-identified problems. Many of the group process problems were discussed at this time (see session summaries below).

3. In the larger group or in the two subgroups, the leaders facilitated member discussion and evaluations of the results of the home assignments using self-control skills taught in previous sessions. At this time leaders encouraged group problem solving around individual member's programs.

Group problem solving was used whenever a member identified a problem she was having with her self-control program. Problem solving for each other gave members practice in general problem-solving skills, enabling them to be more effective in self-control of weight-related behaviors in the future. When a member identified a problem, other members would help her generate a number of alternative action plans while leaders wrote these alternatives on the blackboard. Especially in later sessions, leaders asked questions and made statements that encouraged members to generate alternatives for each other rather than suggesting alternatives themselves. The individual then evaluated the alternatives and selected those which were most likely to lead to the desired outcome. She implemented the plan during the week and reported on how well it worked during the following session. As the group learned more self-control techniques, they suggested a greater variety of alternatives allowing the member to develop a more comprehensive plan. For example, one member expressed a concern about eating and drinking when she was depressed. After a number of suggestions from the group, the member decided not to get so upset about being occasionally mildly depressed by telling herself, "It's O.K. to be somewhat depressed once in a while and it's O.K. to have *one* drink to numb me a little." If she felt like having something to eat or more than one drink, she then began to implement any of several strategies to deal with the depressing situation immediately rather than just "riding it through" (e.g., participate in a pleasant activity, identify and alter depression-eliciting cognitions). She would also be sure to monitor her eating and drinking when depressed. Alternatively, she could participate in an alternative activity (e.g., relaxing or meditating, watching T.V., or some other "numbing" activity) or "blow off steam" by running or punching a pillow. If she felt the urge to eat, she would build in a five-minute delay before eating.

4. Leaders provided a conceptual framework for the area of self-control to be learned during the session by making a brief didactic presentation (5 to 10 minutes) highlighting the salient concepts in the assigned reading and expanding upon them. The didactic presentation included positive and negative models of relevant self-control behaviors which the leaders presented to the members for evaluation and discussions according to the conceptual criteria they had presented. The didactic material was summarized in handouts distributed for later reference.

In addition, during the group the leaders developed self-control programs for themselves and shared the results of their programs to model new concepts and procedures. In order to serve as models, the leaders kept their programs one step ahead of the members' programs. Thus, leaders had already developed a self-control contract to use as a model when they introduced the technique to the group. (The leaders did not use their program as a perfect model; indeed at times they intentionally built-in "mistakes," e.g., forgetting to monitor, in order to demonstrate realistic goal setting, realistic expectations of a self-control program, and methods to cope with "failures.") One leader developed a program to lose weight, the other developed a program to decrease consumption of beer.

5. In the earlier sessions, members divided into two subgroups and were given written or verbal exercises to rehearse the new self-control behavior. They then took turns presenting the data relevant to these behaviors which had been collected during the previous week as an assignment for the present session. With the help of the group, each member developed change plans to be implemented during the next week for that area of self-control. Group problem solving was an integral part of this process.

6. In order to encourage independent planning and problem solving toward the end of the group, in later sessions the process described in step five was modified as follows: Members rehearsed the new skill area evaluating models and practicing example provided by the leaders. Members were then given an assignment to develop a plan during the week to implement this new self-control behavior, get midweek feedback on the plan from their buddy, and then present the plan they developed at the next group session for group feedback before they actually implemented the plan during the following week. Using this procedure, members could continue to benefit from group feedback while developing skills in autonomous problem solving.

7. At the end of each session members were given assignments to carry

out the change plan developed in the session as well as change plans previously developed in other self-control areas. Members were also given reading and monitoring assignments in self-control areas to be taught in the next session. Leaders often modeled the assignment and often structured the assignments to include using the buddy for specific midweek feedback.

Based on feedback from previous group members, the leaders' clinical judgment, and anecdotal evidence from other investigators, the self-control skills were introduced in the following order:

1. Skills were introduced from the least to the most invasive, e.g., self-monitoring was introduced before self-control contracts. By introducing less invasive procedures first, it was assumed that members were more likely to comply with the procedures; furthermore, the less invasive procedures were often sufficient to change and maintain behavior and can be more easily maintained over an extended time period.
2. Those skills which were prerequisites for more complex skills were taught first, e.g., goal setting was taught before stimulus control procedures.
3. Cognitive skills were taught before overt behavioral skills. Introducing cognitive restructuring before contingency contracting helps the patient modify her self-defeating belief system which may be necessary before the patient can use operant techniques most effectively (Wilson, 1976).
4. Self-control skills were taught before environmental control skills., e.g., self-monitoring and self-reinforcement were taught before developing assertive skills to use in the social environment.
5. Weight-related self-control behaviors were taught before exercise-related skills to avoid the introduction of too many demands for change at one time.

The order in which skills were introduced in the eight sessions was: self-monitoring with food exchanges, problem solving and goal setting, cognitive restructuring and self-reinforcement, stimulus control, exercise, use of social environment, consequation control and self-control contracts, relaxation, and maintenance procedures.

Let us now examine the specific content of each of the eight sessions.

SUMMARY OF GROUP SESSIONS

Session One

The goals were that each member would be able by the end of the first session to:

1. state the first name of each group member;
2. state the purpose and describe the format of the group;
3. describe the buddy system and state the name and phone number of her buddy;
4. describe the reason for the food exchange system and demonstrate how to use it;
5. demonstrate how to use the exchange monitoring form;
6. state the assignments for the next week.

After the initial weigh-ins and deposit refund, the leaders began the group meeting by asking the members to divide up into pairs, interview each other, and introduce their partner to the group. The leaders modeled the procedure by introducing each other and then explained that, while listening to the introductions, members should be considering which member they would like to choose for their buddy later in the session.

The leaders next presented a brief overview of the group including: (1) the group's focus on problem solving and self-control skills to change behaviors that result in losing weight and maintaining weight loss; (2) a summary of skills which would be taught in each session; and (3) the general format for each session. In order to clarify expectations and responsibility, members were given a group contract to read, modify, and countersign with the leaders. Each member kept a copy of her contract; the leaders kept the other copy.

In order to place the immediate focus on behavior patterns and reinforce members for completing the monitoring assignments, the leaders asked members to form subgroups and report on personal eating patterns they identified and on any problems they encountered in monitoring. The problems reported included: forgetting to monitor until evening; changing eating patterns with monitoring; not knowing exact quantities or contents of foods when eating at a restaurant; not being able to identify mood when eating.

Members were verbally reinforced for monitoring and analysis of behavior patterns. On the session evaluations, several members noted that the process of sharing their problematic behavior patterns gave the group "an open, sharing atmosphere." In discussing these comments in session two, members indicated that the process made the group more attractive to them and helped desensitize them to some of the anxieties about losing weight by providing them with evidence contrary to the thought that they were the only ones who had such "terrible" eating behaviors.

During the next portion of the meeting, the clinic's nutritionist provided the members with information on basic nutritional principles and taught them to monitor their food intake using a flexible food exchange system (American Diabetes Association, 1950). Stressing the medical and psychological problems associated with poor nutrition, she began with a brief presentation on the necessity of learning nutritionally sound eating patterns during a long-term

FIGURE 4-1 Weight Loss Group Contract

1. Members understand that the program is a three part plan including environmental control, reduction of calorie intake, and exercise.
2. Weight loss can result only if members carry out the plans developed in the group to change eating and exercise patterns. To this end, members will contract to follow the plans during the week.
3. Leaders will educate and guide the members in making weight loss plans. As the meetings progress, members will be expected to take more and more responsibility for planning and carrying out the individual programs as well as group sessions.
4. Each member will determine the life style changes she/he will make in order to lose weight.
5. Since attendance at group meetings is very important for the success of the treatment programs, members are expected to be present at all scheduled meetings.
6. If a member is unable to attend a meeting, she/he is to: (a) inform the group leader before the meeting date; (b) continue any assignment agreed to at the previous meeting, including contacting her/his buddy during the week.
7. Since there will be a full agenda for each session, members are expected to arrive and be ready to work on time. Each session will start on time.
8. Members understand that the leaders will help them plan for maintenance of weight loss after the group terminates.
9. This contract can be amended by mutual consent of the group members.
10. Call leaders if you cannot solve problems that come up during the week with the help of your buddy.

_____   _____

(member)   (leader)

weight loss plan in order to remain in good health and enhance maintenance of the weight lost. Using an audio tape/slide program, food models, and handouts, the nutritionist instructed members in the food exchange categories and portions. After presenting two typical meals in terms of food exchanges, she asked members to describe the types and quantities of foods of two or three meals they had monitored during the previous four days and then guided the group in determining the number of each type of exchange represented in the meal.

About half way through the nutritionist's presentation, the group took a 10-minute break. During the break the nutritionist made individual appointments with each member for the following week to develop an individualized food exchange diet based on the member's food preferences, eating habits, exercise level, and previous weight loss history. To increase the attractiveness of the group, leaders provided low calorie refreshments (coffee, tea, celery, carrots, etc.). On the evaluations some members said that serving food during the weight loss group seemed to be inappropriate. In discussing the comments at the second session, members agreed to have only liquid refreshments available during the break.

After the break the nutritionist instructed members in the use of a monitoring system for food intake on the individual exchange diets (an adaptation of the Stuart and Davis', 1972, system). She demonstrated the use of a monitoring system with sample menus and then had members practice monitoring with the menus they had converted into food exchanges before the break. At the end of this presentation, one of the leaders noted that although the members said they understood the monitoring system, some members looked confused while practicing with the examples. In order to assure that all members understood this important self-control procedure, the leader asked the members to turn to their neighbors and briefly explain the monitoring procedure and then have the neighbors explain it to them. After doing this, members had several additional questions about monitoring.

The remainder of the session was devoted to establishing a buddy system. Leaders explained that members were to choose a "buddy" from the group with whom she would work as a support team during the 10 weeks the group met. Each buddy team was expected to make at least one intersession contact during which they would discuss each others' progress in their behavior-change efforts, reinforce successes, help develop solutions to problems, and answer each other's questions on the material covered in the group or in the readings. If a member could not solve a problem with the aid of her buddy during the week, she was to call one of the leaders for help. (During the group, leaders received no such calls since buddies were able to answer all questions without the help of a leader.) Leaders emphasized that the buddies ought to make the contacts enjoyable rather than strictly "business calls." After role playing a model buddy telephone contact, the leaders asked the members to choose a buddy, exchange telephone numbers, and arrange a specific time to call or meet during the following week. As suggested by a member from a previous group, buddies were given the last 15 minutes of group time to become better acquainted with each other in order to function more efficiently as a team. Some teams stayed in the meeting room while others sat outside or went across the street for a cup of coffee. At the beginning of the next three sessions, leaders monitored buddy contacts by asking for a brief report on the content and usefulness of each team's contact.

Before the group split into pairs, the leaders asked members to fill out anonymously a weekly session evaluation. Given at the end of each group session, the evaluation asked the following questions:

1. What did you like most about this session?
2. What things about the session did you like least?

3. What did we talk about that you did not understand and would like to talk more about?

4. What can you suggest about the group (what we did, the leaders, suggestions for future sessions, or anything else)?

5. Rate how useful you think the session was in helping you to lose weight (1 to 10 scale).

6. Rate your current motivation to lose weight (1 to 10 scale).

7. Rate your current ability to control your weight (1 to 10 scale).

Intersession assignments were:

1. Before seeing the nutritionist: (a) read pages 91-107 (Mahoney and Mahoney, 1976); and (b) make up a list of foods you wish to include in your diet and note the time of day that you would want something to eat.

2. Read pages 1-68 (Mahoney andMahoney, 1976).

3. Use the information in your readings to develop a criticism of the claims made in the "fad diet" ad we provided. You need not write your criticism out but you may wish to make notes so that you can present it briefly in the group. If you prefer not to criticize the ad we provided, you could clip another one out of a magazine and criticize it.

4. Using the food exchange system, calculate the number of calories you consumed over the previous four days.

5. Using the food exchange system and the exchange monitoring form, monitor daily food intake.

6. Call buddy.

7. Bring in all assignments.

Session Two

The goals for the second session were that each member would be able by the end of the session to:

1. state the monitoring results of her buddy;

2. state three criticisms of one of the fad diets another member presented;

3. state at least three guidelines for goal setting;

4. state the positive feedback procedure for giving members feedback on their programs.

On the evaluation for the first session, two members indicated that they were bothered by one member who was overly talkative. In order to develop a cohesive group and keep group discussion on-task without stigmatizing one member, the leaders decided to use instructional control to modify indirectly the talkative member's behavior so that her comments would at least be on-task. In reviewing the evaluations, the leaders did not mention the comments about the talkative member. However, in introducing the section of the agenda in which each member reported on her monitoring, they modeled and discussed "how to give feedback in a group." In order to cue members to use the feedback procedure and to reinforce them for using it during the reports on monitoring, leaders asked each member to give a poker chip to another member when the other member had given her specific positive feedback or followed negative feedback with a suggestion for specific alternatives or a piece of specific positive feedback. Although two members thought that the procedure was unnecessary or "silly," the rest seemed to enjoy giving and receiving tokens for appropriate feedback and one member indicated on her evaluation that she liked seeing immediate effects of behavior change demonstrated in the group.

However, according to the leaders' subjective impression and members' feedback on evaluations in session three, providing a model for feedback was not sufficient to decrease the frequency of the offending member's talking or increase her on-task talking. In the fourth session the leaders asked the group to suggest ways to insure that each member got her share of the group discussion time. The group decided that the discussion of each member's change plan should be timed and that each member would take a turn being the timekeeper. Although the timing did decrease the inordinate amount of talking by the offending member, many of her comments continued to be off-task.

During the reports on monitoring food intake, leaders encouraged members to monitor their food just before they ate it. The leaders pointed out that premonitoring intake was a simple means to preplan a meal or snack and could help limit food intake (Bellack, Rozensky, and Schwartz, 1974).

After reporting and problem solving around monitoring food intake, members critiqued the "fad diets" they had reviewed during the week. The exercise gave the group practice evaluating dietary programs from medical and psychological perspectives presented in the week's reading and in the previous session. (In other groups, members have been given quizzes to determine their understanding of the material.) Leaders first asked members to "brainstorm" on criteria for evaluating diets (e.g., nutritionally balanced, deals with eating behavior, and does not involve radical life system changes). Then members broke into subgroups of people who had reviewed the same diet. Each subgroup consolidated their critiques of the diet and then presented the diet and their critique to the remainder of the group for discussion.

The remainder of the session was devoted to learning and practicing problem-solving and goal-setting skills. Leaders gave a five-minute lecture on the skills as a supplement to the reading assignment in Mahoney and Mahoney (1976). Problem solving and goal setting were presented as complex cognitive skills that are necessary components of successful self-control programs. Using the Mahoney and Mahoney (1976) mnemonic S-C-I-E-N-C-E paradigm, the leaders outlined the constituents of problem solving as described in D'Zurilla and Goldfried (1971), stressing problem definition, generation of alternatives, and evaluation. Although members were not given any exercises or assignments to practice problem solving, leaders introduced examples of each new self-control skill by going through the problem-solving paradigm. Leaders also guided members through the components of problem solving, identifying the components of the process each time the group or an individual would bring up a problem. For example, during the section on developing plans to alter stimulus cues, one member said that she was having a problem snacking on baked goods about 4:00 PM. As often happens when the group began to suggest alternative ways to deal with the problem, the member stated reasons why each

FIGURE 4-2   Goal Setting

Goals are statements of desirable future levels, frequencies, or intensities of behaviors. Goals should be specific, reasonable, and flexible.

Specific

1.   Describes *behavior* not process (e.g., not losing weight but changing habits);
2.   Stated in operational terms (observable/measurable);
3.   Answers who, what, where, when, how often;
4.   Evaluation criteria clear (when goal will be achieved, under what conditions, how will behavior be judged if it's performed correctly).

Realistic and Flexible

1.   Examine all component behaviors (e.g., rather than say, "I eat too much and therefore must cut down on eating," identify component eating behaviors, such as eating in front of TV, midday snacking, eating when not hungry, eating when angry).
2.   Take small steps toward final goal (avoid perfectionism, can you really see yourself doing that behavior as you project into the future, would you give the same goal to a friend, are you assuring yourself success in the first step?)
3.   Based on current performance (don't try to run if you haven't learned to crawl, don't expect too much of yourself if you have not been doing the goal behavior much, even if you think that you *should* be able to do it).

Examples or Goals

1.   To avoid additional food intake at night, I will rehearse singing between 8:00 and 9:00 PM; I will make that a regular activity three times per week (Tuesday, Friday, and Sunday).
2.   I will decrease my daily weigh-ins to three times per week (8:00 AM, M, W, F).
3.   Every day I will begin to walk down three flights of stairs at least once.

of the alternatives would not work. At that point, the leader pointed out that in generating alternatives, it is better to consider all possible alternatives before evaluating and discarding any one of them. Subsequently, the member found a combination of alternatives that proved to be an effective solution.

After presenting the criteria for goal setting and discussing positive and negative models of goal setting, the leader gave members examples of goal statements made by members in previous groups. Members were asked to critique the goal statements according to the criteria. Members then split into pairs and helped each other develop a goal statement for an eating behavior to be implemented during the next week. For example, one member who habitually snacked about 8:30 PM developed the following goals: "to avoid additional food intake at night, I will rehearse singing between 8:00 and 9:00 PM on Tuesday, Friday, and Sunday." Members then formed two subgroups and presented their goal statements for additional feedback on how well they met the criteria. One member who wanted to begin a regular exercise program set a goal to exercise every day for 30 minutes. When other members pointed out that the goal was not specific enough nor was it based on her present level of exercise, she changed it to read, "At 8:00 PM on Monday, Wednesday, and Friday I will walk one mile with my husband." In order to evaluate goal attainments each member devised a plan to monitor the behavior in terms of which the goal had been defined.

In order to prepare members for monitoring self-defeating cognitions during the next week, the leaders modeled their own self-defeating cognitions that they were in the process of modifying in their own self-control program as well as other self-defeating cognitions identified by previous group members.

Intersession assignments were:

1. Reread pages 30-68.
2. Continue monitoring intake.
3. Call buddy.
4. Implement and monitor the behavior change in your goal statement.
5. Identify two examples of recurrent negative food monologues described in chapter 6 (Mahoney and Mahoney, 1976).
6. Bring in all assignments.

Session Three

The goals for the third session were that each member would be able by the end of the session to:

1. state the rationale for substituting positive for negative monologues;
2. state the negative self-monologue of her buddy and a positive alternative;
3. demonstrate how to graph caloric intake.

During the individual weigh-in, one member said that she was getting very discouraged because she was not losing weight. In order to encourage the member and to stress the primary importance of behavior change, the leader responsible for the weigh-in pointed out to her that although she had not begun to lose weight she had begun to change her eating habits and by doing so would eventually lose weight. The leader stressed the necessity of focusing on changing eating and exercise patterns to effect slow but permanent weight loss. In addition, the leader checked on the accuracy of the member's monitoring by asking her (1) if she was monitoring her food at the time of eating rather than by memory at a later time; (2) if she was measuring and weighing her food to assure accurate portions; (3) if she was including all foods she was eating, e.g., the fats used in frying. The member said she was monitoring consistently but had not really weighed her meat exchange or measured out the fat exchanges. Furthermore, she realized she had not been including salad dressing in her monitoring. The leader encouraged the member to change these behaviors and to note the effect it had on her weight loss. During the following week, the member reported that she had been underestimating her food servings and with accurate measurements she had begun to lose weight.

After reviewing questions on the reading in the previous session, the leaders asked members to form subgroups and individually present their successes achieving the goal they set at the previous session. During the review the leaders stressed the necessity for flexibility in goal setting. For example, some members had set a calorie intake goal level they thought to be reasonable for seven days, yet had found that they had not maintained the level for one or two days during the week. They reported feeling guilty and discouraged at their inability to maintain the intake level they had set, which for most was higher than the level suggested by the dietician (they were shaping themselves to the goal level set by the dietician). One member, in particular, reported that she was beginning to think about food so much that she was becoming extremely anxious trying to maintain the goal level she had set and "had to overeat one day" in order to alleviate the anxiety. Consequently she felt extremely guilty and regarded herself as "a hopeless case." The leaders pointed out that the goals of these members were probably too large for the initial step and suggested that they either set a higher caloric intake goal and then shape themselves to lower and lower levels, or allow themselves one or two "free days" when they could have as many calories as they would like but would continue to monitor as before. Some of the members reported that the idea of a "free day" was most beneficial to help reduce their feelings of "cognitive claustrophobia" (Mahoney and Mahoney, 1976, pp. 50-54) in setting intake goal levels.

The review of the goal setting assignment led naturally into a discussion of the way in which cognitions affect behavior. The leaders gave a brief presentation of some fundamental concepts of rational emotive therapy (Ellis and

Harper, 1975; Maultsby, 1975) to supplement the readings in Mahoney and Mahoney (1976). The concepts included the etiology of emotions, distinguishing "facts" from interpretations about those facts, criteria to determine the functional usefulness of interpretations of facts, and methods to generate alternative interpretations of those same facts. In addition, leaders briefly introduced the technique of thought stopping as a means to control the food related thoughts (Wolpe, 1973).

Members then broke into subgroups and individually presented "negative monologues" they had identified during the previous week and the places and times the negative monologues occurred most frequently. After each member stated her "negative monologue," the leader asked her which was the most important/troublesome one and then asked the subgroup to discuss ways in which the monologue might interfere with weight loss efforts. If the member had not developed an alternative "positive" monologue to replace the "negative" one, the leader asked the subgroup to generate an alternative monologue using the problem-solving "brainstorming" techniques (D'Zurilla and Goldfried, 1971). After listing all suggested alternative monologues the member would evaluate each alternative and select those which she believed would be most effective in helping control inappropriate eating behavior and negative emotions which are antecedent to inappropriate eating behavior. During the subsequent weeks, the member was to use the situation in which the negative monologues had frequently occurred as a cue to detect those monologues. Once she detected them, she was to use thought stopping to stop it and then use the selected alternatives to "reinterpret" the situation. The leaders stressed the importance of using the alternative monologues consistently during the initial week when the members were likely to experience some cognitive dissonance in changing the thought patterns (Maultsby, 1975).

For example, one member reported that whenever she felt rushed at work or at home she would tell herself, "I feel really tense. If I could only eat some chocolate I would feel better. I won't eat anything tomorrow to make up for it." As the group brainstormed alternative monologues, the leader listed them on the blackboard. Alternatives included ones to prevent the anxiety (e.g., "Slow down you can't do everything at once, it is not that important if this gets done right away"); ones to "challenge" the negative monologues (e.g., "Not eating tomorrow is unrealistic," "I can take care of myself best one day at a time"); and ones to instruct herself to cope with her anxiety in a better way if she has not been able to prevent it (e.g., "What else can I do to relax?" "I will take some time for myself today"). The member selected some of each of these suggested alternatives since she thought each type of monologue would be helpful to control the anxiety that often times was antecedent to eating chocolate. Since she frequently looked at her watch when she began to feel rushed, she put a small mark on her watch crystal as a cue to check for negative monologues and anxiety and to utilize the "coping" monologues developed in the group.

In one of the subgroups, one member said that she did not think that she had any negative monologues since she had not been able to detect any during the previous weeks. Since the leader had noted in previous sessions that this member often spoke negatively about her ability to control her weight, she pointed out that detecting the negative monologues was frequently difficult to do and asked the group if they could help this member identify at least one problematic monologue. Some members gave her more examples of their own monologues which they thought could be similar to hers; others suggested that some of the things she had said about her ability to lose weight might be important negative monologues for her. The member agreed that her statements about her ability were probably one of the reasons she did not feel very motivated and decided to monitor those thoughts during the next week.

At the end of the session, the leaders gave members a handout on drawing a graph, explained how they would draw a graph of caloric intake, and provided model graphs they had made for their own programs. In addition to the line representing daily intake levels, members were asked to draw two criteria lines across the graph representing the goal intake level determined by the dietician and the intake level at which she would maintain weight. Members of previous groups had found that these two lines had helped them decrease negative monologues when they ate more than their goal level but less than their maintenance level. When they ate within this range they could look at the graph and tell themselves, "Well, at least I am not gaining weight." In order to insure that all members had the skills to draw a graph, leaders asked buddies to help each other set up the ordinate, abscissa and criteria lines for the graph of their caloric intake. During this time the leaders walked around the room answering any questions about graphing that arose.

In explaining the assignment, the leaders gave the members a handout with examples of situational control hierarchies developed by previous group members to use as models for the hierarchies they were to develop during the following week.

Intersession assignments were:

1. Read pages 108-27.
2. Continue monitoring intake.
3. Graph all intake data to date.
4. Call buddy.
5. Implement the positive monologues you have developed.
6. Using the data to date (food diary, exchange monitoring, weight loss checklist) develop a hierarchy of situations, times, emotions, etc. when you are most likely to eat inappropriately. Make the hierarchy from the easiest to the most difficult situation, emotion, etc. to control.
7. Bring in all assignments.

The goals for the fourth session were that each member would by the end of this session be able to:

1. state at least one success and one problem another member had in replacing negative with positive monologues;
2. give two examples of how environmental cues affect weight loss;
3. state three environmental cueing procedures for weight loss;
4. state two ways in which she can become less efficient in expending physical energy.

In checking assignment completion, one member said that she was not able to complete graphing her data or make her hierarchy because she had had a number of house guests and had not been able to find the time. Although assignment completion was not as much a problem in this group as it had been in other groups, the leader responded to this "excuse making" behavior in the usual manner—ignoring the excuses and noncompletion while reinforcing the member for the assignments she had completed. In refunding the member's deposit the leader again ignored the noncompletion by merely praising the member for attendance and promptness while handing her the portion of the deposit earned.

On the previous session's evaluation, some members indicated that they would like to spend less time in subgroups because they wanted to hear what the members of the other subgroups were doing. Discussing these comments at the beginning of the session, the leaders said that they had broken into subgroups frequently in order to maximize the time each member had to develop and report on her individual change plan. If they cut down on this time, members would have less time to discuss their individual plans. In order to consciously model its use and enhance group problem solving, the leaders guided them through the various stages of the problem-solving paradigm to solve the issue. The group decided to combine two suggested alternatives: (1) vary the members and leaders that compose each subgroup; (2) form subgroups when developing plans based on new material but report the results of their plans during the previous week and modify their plans in a larger group.

The leaders implemented the new group procedure immediately by asking each member to report briefly to the larger group on the successes and problems she had in using her "positive monologues." Some members said that the positive monologues were quite helpful in controlling eating since learning ways to change their thoughts and feelings gave them a sense of control over themselves and helped to decrease their guilty feelings about the inappropriate eating behaviors. Other members had difficulty implementing the cognitive procedures. For one member who found that she would get so involved in a situation that she would forget the new procedure, the group developed a more effective cueing mechanism. For another member who complained that when she tried to use the positive monologues in the actual situation she did not believe them, the leader and some of the members pointed out that the belief she held now was merely a subjective interpretation of the same reality and that she would have to consistently use the new interpretation in order to begin to believe it in the actual situation.

In discussing stimulus control eating behaviors the leaders used the term "environmental cues" which members in previous groups found less confusing than other terminology. The leaders introduced stimulus control by giving a five-minute talk on basic principles of operant conditioning ("the A-B-Cs of behavior") and providing a handout with examples of cue elimination, cue suppression, and cue strengthening (Stuart and Davis, 1972). Picking an example from their own self-control programs and using Mahoney's S-C-I-E-N-C-E problem-solving paradigm, the leaders modeled the various steps in developing a stimulus control program.

FIGURE 4-3   S-C-I-E-N-C-E and Problematic Eating Behaviors—Leader's Model

1. Specify the category: Hierarchy of inappropriate eating situations:

1. snacking while preparing dinner, especially after working all day;
2. overeating at dinnertime;
3. eating at bedtime;
4. eating when problem resolved or task completed.

2. Collect data using food diary (e.g., for number 1 above):

3. Identify patterns:

Snacked while preparing dinner *most* when:

1. no lunch or lunch while working;
2. food available in sight, while preparing dinner, e.g., cheese, raisins, crackers, etc.;
3. very tired but do not sit down at all before starting dinner (also resenting husband sitting);
4. stomach feels empty, i.e., "rubs."

4. Examine options: Options considered:

*1. always eat adequate lunch;
*2. never eat while working, i.e., writing up notes;
3. change food available while cooking, e.g., celery, green pepper, or make one cup of hot instant soup (low calorie);

FIGURE 4-3   Continued

	*4.	eat dinner out four to five days per week and be relieved of preparation when tired or rushed;
	5.	use relaxation procedure before cooking;
	6.	put on cheerful music before cooking;
	7.	lie down 20 minutes before cooking.

5. Narrow options and experiment:

*Items with * were not considered feasible at this time due to pressures at work or due to friction it would cause at home.

6. Compare data:

Options 3, 5, 6, and 7 were tried. Comparing data, controlled snacking while preparing dinner most consistently when using the following alternatives:

1. lie down 20 minutes before cooking;
2. take hot soup before cooking.

7. Extend, revise, and replace:

Revised original plans:

1. lie down *on bed*, without reading, 20 minutes;
2. ask husband to put on cheerful record that pleases both of us while I cook;
3. drink hot soup or eat green pepper, celery, etc.;
4. reevaluate plans every two weeks.

Members then formed subgroups and reported on the hierarchy of situational cues they had developed. In order to enhance initial success in stimulus control of eating behavior, the leader asked each member to select a situation that was low on the hierarchy (i.e., relatively easy to change), and with the help of the group develop a change plan to modify the problematic eating behavior using the principles of stimulus control. In addition, each member was to specify a means of monitoring behavior change. For example, one member developed the following hierarchy of stimulus situations:

1. eating after work (4:00 to 5:00 PM);
2. eating at a restaurant;
3. eating as a dinner guest;
4. eating late at night;

5.   eating when my schedule is interrupted by an unexpected event;
6.   eating when physically uncomfortable;
7.   eating when bored or tired;
8.   eating rapidly;
9.   eating when anxious or afraid or frustrated;
10. eating out of self-pity.

The member said that she would like to develop a plan to decrease eating late at night. Although this was the fourth item on her hierarchy, she reported that over the past three weeks she had been able to control the first three patterns on her hierarchy by monitoring her food intake on a regular basis. With the help of the group the member developed a number of different alternative plans and from these alternatives selected the following means of changing her night eating behavior:

1.   save allowable foods from the day for a late night snack;
2.   premonitor eating after supper;
3.   substitute another activity such as walking or relaxing or taking a hot bath in place of eating; and
4.   have low calorie foods available for late night snacking.

For the next two weeks the member monitored her late night eating and her use of the change plans by means of a checklist which she filled out just before she went to bed at night. During this period of time she was quite successful at changing this inappropriate eating pattern, eating foods that she saved from her food exchange diet plans for that day or low calorie "free" foods as specified in her change plan on only two out of fourteen days. Of the plans developed to help change this eating pattern she most frequently used premonitoring and substituting other activities. During these two weeks she added three additional stimulus control procedures which she used quite frequently, eating with chop sticks, measuring all foods before eating them, and eating in one place. During the seventh and eighth sessions this member developed plans for other inappropriate eating patterns further in her hierarchy: eating when her schedule is interrupted by an unexpected event, eating when bored or tired, and eating rapidly. At that time she reported that eating late at night was no longer a problematic pattern.

The remainder of the session was devoted to preparing members to plan for ways in which they could increase their general activity level. Using Ferguson's (1976) energy balance equation (energy in = energy used + storage), the leaders emphasized that by increasing the amount of energy used in performing normal daily activities, members would be able to lose weight more rapidly and maintain the weight loss more readily. While they recommended a regular exercise program such as the aerobics program (Cooper, 1970) or programs offered at local health clubs because of their conditioning effect on muscular and cardiovascular systems, the leaders stressed that in order to get long-term benefit for weight control, it was more important for members to set realistic and reasonable goals for themselves to increase their activity level. They pointed out that although brief periods of intense exercise are beneficial for physical conditioning, increasing the amount of energy expended in activities throughout the day is likely to result in a greater number of calories expended. The leaders passed out a handout with a number of suggestions on how to increase general activity levels (e.g., taking stairs instead of elevators, parking a car at the far end of the parking lot, meeting the bus at the next stop down the line) and asked the members to brainstorm on additional ways of increasing their activity level. The leaders presented four methods of monitoring activity level: counting calories expended by means of a chart (Ferguson, 1976); approximating the number of calories expended by means of a formula (Stuart and Davis, 1972); a simple frequency count; and a simple duration count. Since the frequency and duration counts were easy to use and since members in previous groups had been discouraged by how few calories were expended in any one daily activity, the leaders recommended that the members adopt one of the latter two monitoring methods. For the last 10 minutes of the session, members regrouped into pairs and helped each other begin to develop a plan for increasing their activity level. Members were instructed to check each other for reasonable, realistic, and flexible goals in order to find pleasant ways for themselves to make increased activity a long-term habit.

Intersession assignments were:

1. Read pages 69-91.
2. Continue monitoring and graphing daily intake.
3. Call buddy.
4. Implement and monitor cueing procedures developed in group.
5. Continue to implement the positive monologues that you have developed.
6. Finish developing a reasonable plan to increase your general activity level, checking this plan with your buddy during your weekly contact; bring in this plan in writing.
7. Bring in at least one example of how you have used family/friends to help in weight loss efforts and at least one problem you have had with family/friends interfering with weight loss efforts. These will be shared in the group and solutions developed for problems.
8. Bring in all assignments.

Session Five

The goals for the fifth session were that each member would by the end of the session be able to:

1. state two ways in which she can rearrange her social environment to facilitate weight loss efforts;
2. demonstrate procedures for reinforcing friends/family for their cooperation in weight loss efforts;
3. demonstrate how to develop a self-control contract according to the criteria presented in the group;
4. state two guidelines for planning for maintaining weight loss efforts during the break.

On the evaluation of session four, one member stated that she was not clear about the differences between environmental cues and negative monologues. Rather than answering this question themselves, the leaders chose to give the group members leadership responsibilities by asking them to respond to the question. One member explained that the monologues were thoughts while the environmental cues were situations, times or events which preceded good or bad eating habits. Another member said that she had found that some of her own negative monologues also functioned as "internal cues" to some of her "bad" eating habits. The leaders verbally reinforced these members for helping to answer the questions and asked the group whether they had any additional questions about monologues, environmental cues, or any other concepts that had previously been discussed.

Three members had indicated on the evaluations that they felt that there was too much material being presented and that the sessions were going too fast for them to understand and utilize all the concepts and techniques presented. Some members said that they had read ahead in the book to the chapter on relaxation and would like to have a chance to learn relaxation with the help of the leaders (the leaders had not originally planned to train members in relaxation because of the limited number of sessions). In discussing this problem, the group decided that they would like to extend the number of sessions to eight sessions and negotiated with the leaders to teach them relaxation during the following session. The eight-session format has since been adopted for all subsequent groups.

In order to monitor progress in behavior change plans developed during the first four sessions and to allow members to reinforce each other for their successes, the leaders asked each member to give a brief report on the results of plans that they had developed and implemented to date. Following this report the leaders asked each member to present her individually developed plan to increase activity levels. The group members were asked to critique each other's plans for specificity of behavior and monitoring methods as well as reasonableness and flexibility of goals. Because of their previous practice with group problem solving, members were readily able to identify problems in each other's plans and offer suggestions for alternatives with little prompting from the leaders. For example, one member stated that she would increase her activity level by doing three minutes of calesthenics, by walking home from work twice a week, and by following the aerobics jogging program. In asking questions to determine how realistic these goals were, the group discovered that she was doing 5 sit-ups and 5 "hip rolls" each day and felt that she should be much more active. Several members pointed out that she was trying to increase her activity level too rapidly and would be better off developing some plans which fit more closely into her current daily activities so that she would increase regular exercises more gradually. With the help of the group this member developed the following plan: 8 sit ups and 10 "hip rolls" daily; walk the distance of three bus stops twice each week; walk during lunch hour twice each week; place all canned goods in the basement in order to increase the number of trips up and down the stairs. All these behaviors were to be monitored by a simple frequency count.

The leaders introduced the topics of using the social environment to help lose weight by giving a brief presentation supplementing the readings in Mahoney and Mahoney (1976). The presentation covered two general areas: assertive behavior and social reinforcement. Using concepts from the assertive training literature (e.g., Lange and Jakubowski, 1976), the leaders stressed the necessity of asserting oneself in social situations frequently associated with inappropriate eating and outlined various means to do so. Using concepts from operant theory on reciprocal influence in personal interaction (e.g., Watson and Tharp, 1972), the leaders pointed out ways in which behavioral consequences influence one's actions and demonstrated ways in which members could reinforce others for helpful responses and ignore others to extinguish unhelpful responses. The leaders illustrated these concepts by drawing on their own experiences and members were assigned to bring in examples of ways in which family and friends had been helpful as monitors, mediators, or cue providers.

After the general introduction, members formed subgroups and individually presented problems they were having with their social environments. The leader asked each member to select one problem she would most like to discuss and role play in the group. The remainder of this section of the agenda was conducted as a typical assertive training session. Each subgroup member in turn role played her problem, received feedback and suggestions for change in her own behavior to improve the situation, and role played the situations repeatedly until she performed in a manner with which she was satisfied. At the end of the role-playing sequence, the group member would have a specific plan of action to be implemented during the following week. Members were assisted in giving feedback by a checklist of "assertive behaviors" (e.g., eye contact, tone of voice, "I" statements). Frequently the leader would ask other members to model the suggestions that they made to the member and then asked the member to imitate the aspects of the model she found most useful for herself.

For example, one member said that whenever she went home to visit, her mother would spend much time cooking very high calorie meals and would say such things as, "I guess you just don't appreciate everything that I have done for you," if she did not eat large portions of the meal. The member said that she tried to explain to her mother that she was trying to go on a diet to lose weight but that she had been unsuccessful since her mother would say such things as, "What are you on a diet for, you don't need to lose weight!" The member said that since she was an only child, her mother, a widow of four years, was "trying to show her love by cooking" and that she felt obligated to eat the food. Another member said that she had run into a similar problem with her grandmother. She said that she had dealt with this by explaining the food exchange system in detail to her grandmother and consciously reinforcing her when she did nonfood related things that showed affection (e.g., sewing her a blouse). The leader asked this second member to model for the first member how she explained the food exchange system to her grandmother and how she reinforced her for these alternate behaviors. The first member then rehearsed explaining the food exchange system to her mother and reinforcing her mother for alternate behaviors until she felt comfortable enough to try it out the next time she visited home. In addition, with the help of the group she developed other things that she could do to help control the situation (e.g., putting low calorie foods in the refrigerator, planning specific activities to do during the day with her mother in order to get her out of the kitchen and show affection toward her).

Problems that other members had with the social environment included the following: husband saying he loves me as I am; husband making numerous negative comments about my weight loss efforts while he is gaining weight; husband ignoring all of my weight loss efforts; husband and children expecting me to cook a full meal and making negative comments if I eat something different; in-laws insisting that I eat foods that do not fit my daily exchanges; feeling obligated to eat baked goods that my best friend says she "made just for me;" sharing cooking and eating in a cooperative living situation where others make high calorie meals with large portions; a coworker making daily trips to the donut shop during coffee break and acting "hurt" if I do not eat one of the donuts she brings back; business associates and clients expecting me to have an alcoholic drink at informal business meetings in a cocktail lounge; living alone with no friends or neighbors to help with my weight loss efforts.

To help members develop specific plans to maintain the behavior changes during the three-week break between the sixth and seventh sessions and to enhance the likelihood that they would follow the plans without the weekly group contact, the leaders completed this session by presenting the fundamental concepts of contingency management and methods of developing self-control contracts. Expanding on the presentation on operant conditioning in session four, the leaders used examples from their own program and from programs of previous group members to demonstrate how contingencies control behavior. They then introduced self-control contracting by providing the members with a handout that had a model contract developed by a member of one of the previous groups, a contract form on which to write their own contracts, and a checklist of contract conditions and rules for consequences (Mahoney and Thoresen, 1974, p. 54). In reviewing the model contract, the leaders pointed out how it met each of the criteria for contingency contracting on the handout. Then they presented the group with two additional contracts and asked them to critique them according to the criteria. With little leader prompting, the members were readily able to identify the strengths and weaknesses of the model contracts. The leaders instructed members to make realistic plans and include only those plans and techniques that they thought would be most useful for their individual case when making their self-control contracts during the next week.

Intersession assignments were:

1. Read pages 147-61.
2. Continue monitoring and graphing daily intake.
3. Call your buddy.
4. Continue to implement the positive monologues and the cueing procedure.
5. Implement the plan to use your social environment to help lose weight as role played in the session.
6. Implement your plan to increase activity level.
7. Develop a self-control contract plan to maintain your weight loss efforts during the three-week break. Check the plan with your buddy, use the duplicate contract form provided and bring in this plan, in writing.
8. Bring in all assignments.

Session Six

The goals for the sixth session were that each member would by the end of the session be able to:

1. state the ways in which at least two of the members used their social environment successfully over the past week;
2. demonstrate how to use progressive relaxation;
3. state at least two ways to use relaxation to help control weight;
4. state her self-control contract for the break;
5. state her buddy's self-control contract during the break.

After reviewing the evaluations and responding to questions on readings and last week's session, the leaders asked each member for a brief report on successes and problems in the social interactions role played in the previous session. After each member's report, the group enthusiastically reinforced the successes and briefly discussed and role played possible solutions to the problems.

Most of the session was devoted to giving members preliminary training exercises in progressive relaxation, using the standardized format as reported in Bernstein and Borkovec (1973). Supplementing the readings in Mahoney and Mahoney (1976), the leaders discussed ways to use relaxation to control inappropriate eating: relaxing during stressful times to decrease anxiety which may lead to overeating, and relaxing in situations in which they have overeaten in the past as an alternate response to anxiety, frustrations, anger, etc. In addition, the leaders asked the group to brainstorm a list of other alternate responses to stress that members could use (e.g., going for a walk, taking a hot bath). After presenting a brief overview of relaxation, the leaders modeled and had the group practice tensing each of the 16 muscle areas. Members then laid down on floor mats and, following one of the leader's instructions, practiced the entire relaxation process. The leaders noted that most members relaxed fairly successfully for the first trial.

The leaders asked members to practice relaxation for 15 to 20 minutes each day during the three-week break and to record their relaxation levels on a 1 to 10 scale before and after practice. The leaders emphasized relaxation was a skill and members would have to practice it a number of times before they could expect to achieve a state of deep relaxation. Leaders said that during the follow-up group they would be willing to give members more practice with relaxation or refer them for additional individual or group relaxation training if they so chose.

The last 30 minutes of the session were spent reviewing and critiquing the self-control contracts for the three-week break. As with other individually developed plans, the leader asked each member to present the contract that she had developed and then asked the group to critique the contract according to the criteria presented in the previous session. Modified contracts were then signed by the members and cosigned by their buddies. Although most of the contracts adhered to the criteria, some of them needed to have the behaviors and consequences stated more specifically while others needed to be itemized so that each behavior was associated with a specific consequence. With the help of the group one member rewrote her contract as follows:

I hereby agree to perform the following behaviors:

1. monitor food intake daily;
2. keep consumption below 1,200 calories on weekdays and 1,700 on weekends;
3. jog three times a week for 10 minutes;
4. weigh myself only once per week and while weighing myself replace monologues such as "I am not losing fast enough" with monologues such as "focus on the patterns not the pounds."

When I have completed the above I will be rewarded by:

1. wearing my new negligée to bed;
2. taking a bubble bath in the evening;
3. taking one dollar each time I jog from the miscellaneous budget fund to spend as I please;
4. earning tokens toward a special soap to be bought at a local store (three tokens = one bar of soap).

If I do not complete the above stated behaviors I will walk up and down my apartment stairs four times for each behavior not completed. I will call my buddy at 8:00 PM Thursday to tell her of my progress each week. This contract will be renegotiated after three weeks.

Intersession assignments were:

1. Read pages 151-64.
2. Continue monitoring and graphing calorie intake.
3. Carry out self-control contract during the break.
4. Practice relaxation 15 to 20 minutes each day, monitor your relaxation level before and after relaxing.
5. Contact buddy weekly.
6. Bring in all assignments.

Sessions Seven and Eight

Goals for these sessions were that each member would by the end of each session be able to:

1. state her plans to maintain weight loss efforts;
2. state the plans of her buddy to maintain weight loss efforts;
3. state at least one problem and one success experienced by other group members in their weight loss efforts.

Held after intervals of three and four weeks respectively, sessions seven and eight were primarily devoted to reviewing members' behavior change programs, and developing long-term maintenance plans. In order to encourage problem solving during these groups the leaders functioned as consultants and facilitators, supplying some information but spending the majority of the time encouraging and reinforcing members for solving each other's problems. During these two sessions members had much time to discuss specific successes and problems they had in their individual programs and to review and discuss material presented in the first six sessions.

Typical of the problems encountered during the break between sessions were the following: One member found that she was telling herself that she was "home free" now that the group was no longer meeting on a weekly basis. She therefore stopped monitoring as consistently as she had been during the group and found that many of her old behavior patterns were returning. In addition, she found that she was losing weight in the wrong places, i.e., her bust measurement had decreased in size but her thigh measurements had stayed essentially the same. In addition, her in-laws had come to visit and since she had not developed any specific plan to deal with the event, she found that while entertaining them she had ceased to think about any of the behavior change efforts of which she had been so conscious before. Another member found that between the seventh and eighth sessions while preparing for a solo public performance, she reverted to past patterns and yet felt worse about it than she had before the group because she was very much aware of what she was doing. She said that she panicked because she found herself disregarding all of the things that she had learned. In the middle of the month she decided that she would change her habits back again and failed because she did not develop any specific plan and tried to change too many behaviors at once. In addition, this member said that she had begun to feel complacent because she had never been at a lower weight in the last 10 years and had gotten several compliments from other people.

In developing plans to deal with such problematic situations, leaders encouraged members to develop a number of different ways of dealing with each situation. By having a variety of means to cope with each problematic situation, the member can select the means that will be most effective for any one given situation in "cafeteria style" as Meichenbaum and Turk (1976) have found useful in management of chronic pain. For example, the member who became anxious over returning to some of her old eating and exercise patterns developed the following list of ways of coping with this type of situation in the future:

1. plan ahead for stressful events when they can be predicted;
2. during stressful events, plan to eat at a calorie level that will maintain weight rather than to continue to lose;
3. develop a specific self-control contract making sure to reinforce self for all appropriate behaviors and build in a response cost for all inappropriate behaviors;
4. call buddy for help and advice;
5. monitor negative, anxiety-producing monologues and develop positive monologues to replace them;
6. practice relaxation whenever feeling anxious about weight loss efforts, especially if the anxiety is likely to lead to inappropriate eating;
7. before eating any food that was not preplanned, build in a delay by participating in an alternate activity, e.g., writing a letter, walking around the block.

Another member was concerned about her eating pattern while visiting her mother and her sister. She developed the following plan.

1. identify negative monologues (e.g., "I can't turn down food my mother tells me to eat") and substitute suggested alternatives (e.g., "I can say no to my mother when she offers me food.");
2. as role played in the group, ask her family not to say to her "Can you eat this, can you eat that?" when she explained to them that she is trying to lose weight;
3. bring along low-calorie foods;
4. premonitor all eating;
5. monitor the number of times she goes to the refrigerator and the number of times she takes food out of the refrigerator;
6. monitor night eating;
7. if she becomes frustrated with her family, go up to her room and practice relaxation.

At the end of session seven, leaders prepared members for developing long-term maintenance plans by presenting and discussing principles of transfer of change and maintenance of change. Using their own long-term maintenance plans as models, the leaders demonstrated the ways in which these principles can be put into practice in order to maintain weight loss efforts. During session eight each member's maintenance plan was reviewed and critiqued by the group. In addition, plans were made to join the ongoing maintenance group, to continue buddy contact, to participate in clinic weigh-ins, or to develop plans to work with families or friends (perhaps a mutual effort) to control weight.

One member's long-term maintenance plan included:

1. weigh twice a week;
2. stick with plan even if no weight loss;
3. monitor and graph daily eating;
4. monitor and graph exercise (reevaluated periodically);
5. practice relaxation daily;
6. carry a picture of me both heavy and light as a motivator;
7. limit myself to a six-pack of beer a week.

Another member developed the following long-term maintenance plan:

1. premonitor all food intake;
2. graph intake;
3. weigh weekly and graph;
4. make a weekly buddy contact;
5. participate in one hour of tennis, walking, or calesthenics five days a week;

6. preplan meals;
7. preplan for special occasions;
8. keep low calorie foods in refrigerator;
9. do not buy junk food;
10. keep wardrobe in repair, do not allow self to wear baggy clothes;
11. avoid TV eating by keeping busy at night especially in the winter, i.e., reading, sewing, etc.;
12. allow one free eating day per month;
13. develop a special plan for holidays;
14. maintain contract and revise periodically;
15. participate in the maintenance group once a month.

At the end of the eighth session members were given a 20-item final evaluation to complete and return in a self-addressed, stamped envelope. On the final evaluations members indicated that they found the following techniques most useful: monitoring and graphing, stimulus control, cognitive restructuring, and role-playing assertive responses. Members indicated that they would like more help learning the following techniques: exercise program, cognitive restructuring, assertive responses. For follow-up help, members most frequently requested: calling the group leader occasionally, periodic weigh-ins, periodic follow-up groups. The majority of members indicated that the length of each session was satisfactory as was the size of the group, but they would like more group sessions. Most members indicated that they liked the group as it was with two leaders; found the $20 deposit effective in encouraging attendance, promptness, and assignment completion; and found the two breaks between the last three sessions somewhat useful to help learn how to maintain weight loss efforts. Members found the following group procedures most useful: reading Mahoney and Mahoney, monitoring behavior, discussing individual problems, reporting individual programs, behavioral assignments, and buddy contacts. Members indicated that session goals were attained most of the time. Five of the seven members had recommended the group to others with weight problems and two members indicated that they would be interested in assisting leaders to conduct future groups.

Group Maintenance Clinic

In order to enhance long-term maintenance of weight loss efforts, the leaders organized a ongoing group maintenance clinic to provide members with "booster" sessions (Stunkard and Mahoney, 1976). Held at bimonthly intervals, these hour-long group sessions were offered free of charge to all members including the prevention-oriented group. The agenda for each session was determined by the members. The majority of the sessions were devoted to members reporting on their behavior change plans, reinforcing each other for successes, and helping each other solve problems as they arose. As in the seventh and eighth sessions, leaders functioned primarily as consultants and facilitators. At the request of the group, leaders periodically reviewed or gave further instruction in the concepts and skills taught during the original six sessions. Members attended the maintenance clinic at variable individual frequencies.

RESULTS

Process Measures

Assignment completion. For six sessions, assignment completion for all members present was 100 percent. In order to obtain a 100 percent score each member had to complete all of the assignments for that week, including monitoring and graphing daily caloric intake, making at least one buddy contact, a reading assignment, and practice on the behavioral skill taught the previous week. In the two sessions where assignment completion was not 100 percent (88 percent) the same member did not complete her assignments.

Attendance. Initially the group consisted of eight members. After the third meeting one member dropped out stating she did not have the time to complete assignments. This woman did not attend any meetings other than the first. Excluding her, members were absent in four other sessions. Overall attendance was 88 percent for seven sessions. Fifty-six percent of the group members were present at the eighth session. Two of the four absent members in the final session were on vacation; one was out of town for the summer.

Promptness. Two members were late to the first session. Excluding the member who attended only the first session, only one additional instance of tardiness occurred for the rest of the sessions. Overall promptness was 93 percent for eight sessions.

Subjective ratings. (satisfaction, motivation, and ability to control weight). On the session evaluations group members were asked to rate on a 1 to 10 scale their satisfaction with the meeting, motivation to lose weight, and ability to control their weight. The overall level of satisfaction for seven sessions was 8.5 with a range from 8.0 to 9.1. Ability to control weight scores ranged from 6 to 8.8 with a mean of 8.0 over the six treatment sessions. Scores of motivation ranged from 8.8 to 9.5 with a mean of 9.0.

Deposit refund. All members initially deposited $20 to be returned contingent on attendance, promptness, and assignment completion. Four members earned the entire $20 back. The other three earned back $17, $18 and $19 respectively.

Weight loss.   At the end of six treatment sessions group members had lost a mean of 7 pounds (range: 4 to 12 pounds). At the seventh session members lost a mean of 9.18 pounds (range: 4.5 to 21.5 pounds), and at the eighth session members had lost 13.5 pounds (range: 6.75 to 21.5 pounds). Only one person gained any weight back during the treatment period.

Group leaders set an arbitrary criteria of one pound per week as "successful" weight loss. Five of the seven members lost six pounds in the first six weeks. Three weeks later, at the seventh session four of the seven members had lost nine pounds over the nine weeks since treatment began. At the eighth session, four weeks following the seventh session (thirteen weeks since treatment began), two of the four members attending the meeting had lost thirteen pounds or one pound per week.

Weight reduction index.   Weight reduction index was calculated for all members for weight lost at sixth, seventh, and eighth sessions. Feinstein (1959) sets an arbitrary criteria of an index of 60 for individual success in weight reduction. At the end of treatment, three members (43 percent) had exceeded this criteria. One member had just met this criteria. One member had an index of 57.16, and the other three members ranged from 16.88 to 37.62.

Behavior change.   All members were required to graph daily caloric intake. As expected, those members who consistently stayed between the level of caloric intake necessary to maintain weight and the level of caloric intake set by the dietician lost weight. Since members chose their own behaviors to modify and developed their own monitoring systems, the only data common to all group members was calorie intake.

DISCUSSION

This chapter describes a comprehensive group training program for the prevention of obesity designed for and implemented in an adult primary care medical setting. Intended for patients 15 to 20 percent over their ideal weight, the program used a number of individual and group procedures to provide patients with a cognitive-behavioral learning framework; to train them in self-management skills such as self-monitoring, problem solving, goal setting, self-reinforcement, cognitive restructuring, stimulus control, use of social environment, consequation control, and relaxation; and train them in autonomous problem-solving skills so that they could continue to modify their problematic behavior patterns after the group terminated. The program described is a part of the group treatment services developed by the health care team at the Adult Medicine Clinic at the University of Wisconsin Hospitals. Offered in response to patient request for such services, the prevention-oriented group is a modification of the ongoing group program for mild to moderately obese patients. Originally developed from the literature on behavioral procedures in weight loss, feedback and evaluation by patients participating in previous groups were important influences in the evolution of the current group format.

Although the data presented do not allow evaluation of the long-term efficacy of the program, it is hoped that the detailed description of individual and group procedures will aid clinicians in designing future prevention-oriented obesity control groups.

REFERENCES

Abramson, E. E. A review of behavioral approaches to weight control. *Behavior Research and Therapy*, 1973, *11*, 547-56.

Agras, W. S., U. M. Ferguson, C. Greaves, B. Qualls, C. S. W. Rand, J. Ruby, A. J. Stunkard, C. B. Taylor, J. Werne, and C. Wright. A clinical and research questionnaire for obese patients. In B. J. Williams, S. Martin, and J. P. Foreyt (eds.), *Obesity: Behavioral approaches to dietary management.* New York: Brunner-Mazel, 1976.

American Diabetes Association, Inc. *Meal planning with exchange lists.* New York: 1950.

Balfour, J. G. A comparison of the effects of external control and self control on the modification and maintenance of weight. *Journal of Abnormal Psychology*, 1974, *83*, 404-10.

Bellack, A. S. Behavior therapy for weight reduction. *Addictive Behaviors*, 1975, *1*, 73-82.

Bellack, A. S., R. Rozensky, and J. Schwartz. A comparison of two forms of self-monitoring in a behavioral weight reduction program. *Behavior Therapy*, 1974, *5*, 523-30.

Bernstein, D. A. and T. D. Borkovec. *Progressive relaxation training: A manual for the helping professions.* Champaign, Ill.: Research Press, 1973.

Cooper, K. H. *The new aerobics.* New York: Bantam Books, 1970.

D'Zurilla, T. J. and M. R. Goldfried. Problem solving and behavior modification. *Journal of Abnormal Psychology*, 1971, *78*, 107-26.

Ellis, A. and R. Harper. *A new guide to rational living.* No. Hollywood, Calif.: Wilshire Book Company, 1975.

Feinstein, A. R. The measurement of success in weight reduction. *Journal of Chronic Diseases*, 1959, *10*, 439-56.

Ferguson, J. M. *Habits not diets: The real way to weight control.* Palo Alto, Calif.: Bull Publishing, 1976.

Fisher, E. B. Jr., L. Green, C. Frieling, J. Levenkron, and F. L. Porter. Self-monitoring of progress in weight-reduction: A preliminary report. *Journal of Behavior Therapy and Experimental Psychiatry*, 1976, 7, 363-65.

Franks, C. M. and G. T. Wilson. *Annual review of behavior therapy: Theory and practice*, vol. 3. New York: Brunner-Mazel, 1975.

Franzini, L. R. and W. B. Grimes. Skinfold measures as the criterion of change in weight control studies. *Behavior Therapy*, 1976, 7, 256-60.

Goldstein, A. P., K. Heller, and L. B. Sechrest. *Psychotherapy and the psychology of behavior change*. New York: John Wiley, 1966.

Hagen, R. L., J. P. Foreyt, and T. W. Durham. The dropout problem: Reducing attrition in obesity research. *Behavior Therapy*, 1976, 7, 463-71.

Hall, S. M. and R. G. Hall. Outcome and methodological considerations in behavioral treatment of obesity. *Behavior Therapy*, 1974, 5, 352-64.

————, B. L. Borden, and R. W. Hanson. Follow-up strategies in the behavioral treatment of overweight. *Behavior Research and Therapy*, 1975, 13, 167-72.

————, G. DeBoer, and P. O'Kuletch. Self and external management compared with psychotherapy in the control of obesity. *Behavior Research and Therapy*, 1977, 15, 89-95.

Horan, J. J., S. B. Baker, A. M. Hoffman, and R. W. Shute. Weight loss through variation in the coverant control paradigm. *Journal of Consulting and Clinical Psychology*, 1975, 43, 68-72.

Lange, A. J. and P. Jakubowski. *Responsible assertive behavior: Cognitive/behavioral procedures for trainers*. Champaign, Ill.: Research Press, 1976.

Mahoney, M. J. and K. Mahoney. *Permanent weight control: A total solution to the dieter's dilemma*. New York: Norton, 1976.

Mahoney, M. J. and C. E. Thoresen. *Self-control: Power to the person*. Monterey, Calif.: Brooks-Cole, 1974.

Maultsby, M. C. *Help yourself to happiness through rational self-counseling*. New York: Institute for Rational Living, 1975.

Meichenbaum, D. and D. Turk. The cognitive-behavioral management of anxiety, anger, and pain. In P. O. Davidson (ed.), *The behavioral management of anxiety, depression and pain*. New York: Brunner-Mazel, 1976.

Robbins, L. C. and J. H. Hall. *How to practice prospective medicine*. Indianapolis: Methodist Hospital of Indiana, 1970.

Rose, S. D. *Group therapy: A behavioral approach*. Englewood Cliffs, N.J.: Prentice-Hall, 1977.

Stuart, R. B. Behavioral control of overeating. *Behavior Research and Therapy*, 1967, 5, 357-65.

———— and B. Davis. *Slim chance in a fat world: Behavioral control of obesity*. Champaign, Ill.: Research Press, 1972.

Stunkard, A. J. The management of obesity. *New York State Journal of Medicine*, 1958, 58, 79-87.

————. New therapies for the eating disorders. *Archives of General Psychiatry*, 1972, *26*, 391-98.

———— and M. J. Mahoney. Behavioral treatment of the eating disorders. In H. Leitenberg (ed.), *Handbook of behavioral modification and behavior therapy*. Englewood Cliffs, N.J.: Prentice-Hall, 1976.

Watson, D. L. and R. G. Tharp. *Self-directed behavior: Self-modification for personal adjustment*. Monterey, Calif.: Brooks-Cole, 1972.

Wilson, G. T. Obesity, binge eating, and behavioral therapy: Some clinical observations. *Behavior Therapy*, 1976, 7, 700-701.

Wollersheim, J. P. Effectiveness of group therapy based on learning principles in the treatment of overweight women. *Journal of Abnormal Psychology*, 1970, *76*, 462-74.

Wolpe, J. *The practice of behavior therapy*, 2nd ed., Elmsford, N.Y.: Pergamon Press, 1973.

JEFF COURT and SHELDON ROSE
with KEVIN MURPHY and LINDA PARICIO

5

use of group activities and reinforcement in training first- to third-grade children in classroom behaviors

INTRODUCTION

As a part of the Interpersonal Skill Training and Research Project, a children's social skills group program was initiated at an elementary school located in Madison, Wisconsin. The program was designed to increase the frequency of appropriate attending and social skill behaviors among first-, second-, and third-grade students. The leaders followed a format described in detail by Rose (1972). Four girls and eight boys participated in the project. All of the children were enrolled in the school's "open classroom" program. As members of this program, the children spent most of their day in a "mainstream" classroom. However, at other times, the children left this classroom to participate in auxiliary classes such as art, music, library, and gym. Each class was taught by a different instructor.

Data gathered from assessment instruments (see below) indicated that the children, although manifesting few problems in their "mainstream" classroom, presented a variety of them in the auxiliary classrooms. These problems included "nonattending" behaviors, such as staring into open space and physically moving about the classroom at inappropriate times (e.g., while teacher was reading a story). Disruptive behaviors, such as inappropriate shouting, talking with a classmate in order to draw him/her off task, and physical aggression (e.g., shoving, hitting, etc.) were also observed. The four girls seldom participated during classroom discussions and they appeared to interact socially only among themselves.

ASSESSMENT AND MEASUREMENT

In order to obtain data on each of the children recommended for the group, the referring teachers were interviewed and asked to fill in a behavior checklist; the children were interviewed; the group workers observed the children in the classroom; and trained observers used a formal observation schedule for observing the children throughout and following the treatment period.

Social Skills Checklist

A social skills checklist developed for use in school settings was completed by each teacher on all 12 children. The checklist (see below) was designed to rate the frequency (always, frequently, occasionally, never) of behaviors in the following skill areas: initiating and conversation skills with peers, feedback skills, parallel play skills, cooperation and game skills, and miscellaneous skills (e.g., works independently, follows directions). In targeting child behavior problems, therapists sought to isolate similarities and gross discrepancies among teacher ratings.

Nonstructured Observations

Using an adaptation of a previously developed scale, group workers observed the children in all five classroom settings over a two-week period. Observers attempted to rate the frequency and quality of social skill behavior observed (Lateu, 1974).

Systematic Observation

Using an adaptation on another previously developed observational system (Wodarsky et al., 1973), trained observers monitored child behaviors in both the "mainstream" classroom as well as auxiliary classrooms. Data were collected in each class setting on a weekly basis.

Observers took data in random five-minute time samples on each child. At the outset of each 10-second interval, the observer recorded the category (disruptive, nonattending, or attending) of behavior exhibited by the child. The behavioral categories were defined as follows:

Name _____

SOCIAL SKILLS CHECKLIST

Feedback Skills	Never	Occasionally	Frequently	Always	Comments
1. Thanks others.					
2. Praises others.					
3. Criticizes others correctly.					
4. Accepts praise from others.					
5. Accepts criticism from others.					
6. Accepts winning gracefully.					

FIGURE 5-1   Sample Portion from Social Skills Checklist

QUALITATIVE RATINGS

Date _____
Time _____

Didn't Occur	0
Poor	1 2
Average	3
Excellent	4 5

Names	I. Separation	II. Free time (WA)	Plays alone	Plays parallel	Plays w/others	Leader in group (PIN)	Plays with equipment	Maintains independence from others (TIC)	Continuity of activity (AT or DK)	Looks at ease (P/A)	Other	Other	Notes

FIGURE 5-2 Sample Portion of Qualitative Observation System

155

I.   Disruptive behavior
   A.   Verbalizations
      1.   Talking to another child
         a.   During individual work time
         b.   Inappropriately during group activity
      2.   Speaking out loud without directing the conversation to anyone
      3.   Miscellaneous: name calling, crying, swearing, loud laughter, screaming, etc.
   B.   Gross motor behaviors: Out of seat or position during group activity or individual work time.
   C.   Object interference: A child plays with some object that interferes with his/her own or another child's participation in the group, e.g., taps a pencil on the table or slams things on furniture.
   D.   Physical contacts: Physical contact by one child which disrupts another child's participation in an activity such as hitting, kicking, shoving, throwing objects, etc.

II. Nonattending to task
   A.   Staring into space
   B.   Playing with objects
   C.   Engaged in separate activity but not disruptive

III. Attending to task (behavior directed toward completion of an individual or group task or toward participation in the group activity)
   A.   Appropriate verbalizations
      1.   Cooperative or task oriented
      2.   Asking for directions
      3.   Volunteering ideas during discussions
      4.   Initiating conversation at appropriate time
      5.   Maintaining conversation at appropriate time
   B.   Physical activity necessary for task completion or game participation
   C.   Ignoring distractions
   D.   Appropriate eye contact with task
   E.   Following teacher directions

Reliability checks were made by the trained observers in order to help insure accurate data. Agreement averaged 82 percent over 14 sessions.

Preliminary Assessment and Treatment Goals

Following this assessment process, data on each child were examined. Appropriate social skill behaviors, as well as problematic classroom behaviors, were identified. Targeted behaviors then became the focus of planned group intervention. A brief description of each child based on assessment data is included below.

Jeff: Jeff interacted appropriately with peers in a variety of settings and on several occasions. Nevertheless, Jeff frequently failed to attend to task. It seemed that he often missed directions completely and experienced difficulty in maintaining attention during classroom activities. Alternatively, he would stare at other classroom stimuli, talk to classmates, and occasionally walk away to engage in some isolated activity (looking at books, playing with the window shade, etc.). A neurological examination, completed just after the beginning of the group, suggested that Jeff's attending problem was primarily related to an organic learning disability.

Tim: Tim interacted in a socially appropriate manner with most of his classmates and teachers. He usually followed directions and contributed to class discussions. Classmates recognized Tim as a leader, often imitating his behavior and following his suggestions. As a result of this influence, Tim's occasional attempts at socializing with friends during learning activities contributed to significant classroom disruption. Targeted behaviors included: increased attending during class activities, increased sharing, and taking turns with less assertive students.

Rich: Rich appeared to be ignored and disliked by his classmates. At times, he demonstrated that he could interact in a socially acceptable manner. More often, however, he interrupted others by talking loudly or making noises. He frequently initiated physical aggression toward classmates and during teacher-directed activities he would often sit under tables. Targeted behaviors included: increased attending during self-directed activities and increased demonstration of leadership behaviors (modeling for others, assisting classmates with tasks and initiating shared activities).

Patti: Patti demonstrated many appropriate social skills but often interacted only with other girls. She followed directions and usually answered questions correctly. She spoke very softly and made few verbal contributions to group discussions. Occasionally she would look around the room or fidget with her shoelaces during teacher-directed activities. Targeted behaviors included: increased attending skills and increased assertive skills (increased verbal responses, increased eye contact, and increased voice volume).

John: John was well liked by his classmates. He usually interacted in a socially appropriate manner during free time. During classroom activities, he often talked and giggled with other students. He frequently interrupted others, initiating physical aggression. During teacher-directed group activities he occasionally crawled across the floor on his hands and knees. When John attended appropriately, he demonstrated many nonassertive behaviors such as low voice volume, infrequent eye contact, and slouched posture. Targeted behaviors included: increased frequency of appropriate verbal responses, increased eye contact, increased voice volume, and sitting up straight.

George: George was a good student. He generally followed directions, completed assignments, and verbally contributed to class discussions. He was well liked by teachers and classmates. He helped other students with assignments and frequently volunteered to assist Ann, a classmate who suffered frequent epileptic seizures. George occasionally responded to distractions presented by friends. When interrupted, he would stop working and begin socializing. George did not like to lose during games. When this happened, he would criticize teammates and accuse the opposing team of cheating. Targeted behaviors included: appropriately ignoring distractions and appropriate winning and losing behaviors.

Beth: Beth demonstrated appropriate social interaction but primarily with other girls. During assessment observations, she was never observed to make a contribution to any group discussion. She spoke in a very quiet tone of voice. Beth frequently fidgeted with objects or appeared to daydream during group activities and independent work time. Targeted behaviors included: increased attending skills, increased voice volume, and increased frequency of verbal participation.

Sue: Although Sue contributed verbally to class discussions, she also spoke in a very quiet voice. She exhibited many appropriate social skills but lacked assertiveness in interactions with boys. She attended appropriately most of the time, although she had difficulty in ignoring distractions during individual and group tasks. Targeted behaviors included: increased attending, increased voice volume, increased frequency of verbal responses, and increased initiation of interactions.

Dave: Dave followed directions well and contributed eagerly to class discussions. He was often the first to volunteer for demonstrations and classroom tasks. He interacted socially with most of his classmates and appeared to be well liked. Although Dave seldom initiated off-task behavior, he frequently imitated others in socializing at inappropriate times. Targeted behaviors included: allowing others to go first, sharing, and ignoring distractions.

Ann: Ann attended well to tasks within the limits of a seizure disorder. She volunteered consistently during class and worked independently with occasional supervision. Ann was socially isolated from her classmates, largely for reasons related to her physical disability. As a result of her illness, Ann attempted to avoid overexcitement during activities. She received individual help from the learning disabilities teacher, and therefore left the primary classroom several hours each day. Finally, some of the other students avoided Ann because they appeared to be frightened by her seizures. Targeted behaviors included: increased attending during individual and group tasks, increased eye contact, initiating and maintaining contacts with classmates, sharing, giving and receiving praise.

Mike: Mike engaged regularly in social interactions with other classmates. During individual work time, Mike was frequently observed to be daydreaming or socializing. He appeared to be easily distracted from his work, and occasionally he copied assignments from other classmates. Targeted behaviors included: increased attending during individual and group work time, completing his own assignments and contributing to class discussions.

GROUP ORGANIZATION

The twelve children were divided into two groups of six and two group leaders were assigned to each group. Two of the group leaders were graduate social work students, one was an undergraduate social work student, and one was a graduate student in school psychology. The composition of each group was determined on the basis of sex (i.e., two girls and four boys in each group), individually targeted behavior problems (i.e., a balance between children demonstrating aggressive behaviors and those who were isolated or withdrawn, and positive behavioral skills which could be used in modeling procedures).

Fourteen group meetings, all one hour in length, were held. Groups met twice a week for the first four weeks and once a week during the final six weeks. One extra meeting was held with just the girls in an effort to work on assertive behaviors such as speaking louder and using more eye contact.

For purposes of organizing this presentation, three phases of treatment have been identified: early, middle, and final. The early phase covered the first through fourth meeting; the middle phase covered the fifth through tenth, and the final phase covered the last four meetings. Although there was some overlapping of activities between phases, each was sufficiently distinct to warrant separate consideration.

The major treatment procedures used were verbal and token reinforcement and games and other group activities. How these activities and the use of tokens were incorporated into the various phases of group treatment is described below.

Early Phase

Initially, many of the group activities were aimed at developing group attractiveness and cohesiveness. Activities such as films, games ("Simon Says" and "Giant Steps"), and drawing with background music proved to be quite attractive. The groups each chose a name and symbol; the implicit competitiveness between the two groups seemed to contribute to the group cohesiveness. For example, members of both groups stated that their group's name and symbol were the best. Even during activities where the two groups operated separately, children asked, "Are we earning more points than the other group?"

At the second meeting a token economy was introduced. Members earned tokens for specific behaviors during group meetings and for completion of behavioral assignments outside of the group. They cashed their tokens in at the end of each meeting for a variety of small candies, toys, and other objects such as pencils and crayons.

Games such as "Simon Says," "Giant Steps," and the "Olympics," in addition to increasing group attractiveness, were used as a means of increasing social interaction. Children were given tokens for exhibiting specific behaviors, such as following the rules, praising and encouraging others. Response cost was implemented as they lost tokens for behaviors such as pushing or shoving, teasing, or bickering. Group contingencies were sometimes used (if the entire group played appropriately, all earned a reward) to encourage cooperative behavior. The following illustration provides an example of a typical early group session agenda.

Children's Social Skills Group Session Two Agenda

I.   Brief introductions in pairs, then introduce partner to group
    A.   Name.
    B.   Discuss favorite activity in school.

II.   Introduce token system and store

III. Assignment check (members show assignment card and tell buddies favorite game)

IV.   Draw a picture about the group name
    A.   Draw pictures.
    B.   Discuss pictures and possible group symbol.

V.   Praise exercise on pictures
    A.   Leaders model praise examples.
    B.   Members practice.
    C.   Play back members with tape recorder.

VI.   Game "Simon Says"
    A.   Leaders explain rules.
    B.   Group contingency reward for following the rules.

VII. Assignment
    A.   Leaders explain and model.
    B.   Group members model.
    C.   Assign partners.

VIII. Spend tokens

IX.   Evaluation

In the fourth session, children and group leaders discussed individual learning goals for each child. These goals were defined behaviorally and then conceptualized for the children through group discussions. Children received tokens for displaying these behaviors during group meetings as well as outside the group, through completion of behavioral assignments. Later, through group discussions, the concept of peer monitoring was introduced. The children were taught to cue each other to perform learning goal behaviors and to praise each other for performance. While the children seemed to understand this concept, as evidenced by their ability to cue and praise each other during group meetings, since no observations were made of these behaviors, we do not know whether they actually did either of these behaviors outside the group meetings.

Middle Phase

During the middle group sessions, modeling and behavior rehearsal were used to teach specific skills, such as praise, active listening (paraphrasing), and self-reinforcement. The behavior was first explained and modeled by the leaders, then the children were reinforced for practicing it. The following is an example of a typical middle session agenda.

Children's Social Skills Group Session Six Agenda

I.   Review of assignments
      A.   Reinforce for bringing cards.
      B.   Reinforce for having teacher's signature.
      C.   Reinforce for writing or drawing the behavior if it was exhibited by the child.

II.   Music exercise
      A.   Tokens given for on-task behavior.
      B.   Tokens contingent upon seeing the movie.

III. Movie about farm animals (tokens given for correct answers)

IV.   Kite project
      A.   Leaders reinforce members for praising.
      B.   Leaders reinforce members for sharing.

V.   Discuss purpose of group
      A.   Leaders review specific behavior each member is working on.

VI.   Assignment
      A.   Tell someone who is not in the two groups what you are working on and have that person sign the assignment card.
      B.   Exhibit the behavior (optional).

VII. Evaluations

VIII. Cash in tokens at store

For example, in teaching self-reinforcement, group leaders explained that teachers, friends, parents, and other important people in their lives can't see all of the good things that children do for others. So it's important to say something to yourself (praise, statement) in order to give yourself credit for the good thing you do (e.g., I'm in the classroom after everyone has gone home and no one is around. I find a friend's pencil and put it in his cubbyhole. I could say to myself, "That was a nice thing to do. Now his pencil won't get lost or stolen"). The group members then described a unique situation and practiced a self-reinforcement statement out loud. Finally they were instructed to close their eyes and imagine a situation and reinforce themselves silently.

Closely related procedures were employed in an effort to improve the assertiveness (especially voice volume and clarity) of the four female group members. For portions of two meetings, the girls and two group leaders met separately to engage in several assertion training exercises.

One exercise aimed at increasing voice volume and eye contact involved sitting in a circle and tossing a yarn ball. Each member would throw the ball to another member. However, before throwing the ball, the group member had to shout a word or phrase that related to her favorite TV program. Group leaders modeled the exercise initially and praised group members for all instances of appropriate voice volume and eye contact.

A blindfold was used during the next exercise. One of the girls was blindfolded while another found a hiding place in the room. The remaining group members would shout directions to the girl who was blindfolded until she was able to find the group member in hiding. Group leaders occasionally coached the girls by whispering the appropriate directions. The girls received praise from the leaders for shouting clear and loud directions.

A final voice volume exercise involved the use of a tape recorder. During this procedure, the girls were reinforced with tokens for speaking into the tape recorder in an effort to make the volume needle register at an appropriate level. Following appropriate responses, the tape was played back to the group members and group leaders praised successful attempts.

Simulation exercises, as well as group discussions, were major components of late middle and final group meetings. These exercises were designed to approximate the usual learning activities of various auxiliary classes. During these exercises, both groups were brought together and group members were reinforced with tokens for behaviors appropriate to that activity. Response cost was also used as a consequence for inappropriate behaviors. Most of the exercises were videotaped and played back to the group members. In order to facilitate conceptualization of their learning, the tape was frequently stopped and group members were asked to explain why they had earned or lost tokens.

Working on a kite was used as an approximation of art class activities. Here, the children sat in their small groups at two tables and worked together using art materials (crayons, paper, scissors, etc.) to design a kite. Behaviors such as sharing, praising, and staying on task were reinforced by the leaders with tokens and praise.

In simulated library and music classes, story-reading exercises and sing-along exercises were used respectively. Children received tokens for specific behaviors appropriate to each setting (attending, singing along, participating in the correct activity at the correct time, staying on task without disruptions).

The children also practiced attending to individual work. In the simulated regular classroom exercises, children were given worksheets and were reinforced intermittently with tokens for keeping their eyes on their own sheets and staying on task. In simulating classroom activities, leaders attempted to pay close attention to detail by using actual art materials, musical instruments, library room materials, etc.

During all phases of group programming the use of behavioral assignments was a very important procedure. Assignments to perform behaviors outside the group were an important means of transferring behaviors learned in the group to the actual environmental situation. Behavioral assignments were closely coordinated with the learning goals of each group session. An assignment was given following every meeting, completion of which was reinforced at the subsequent meeting. Assignment completion was monitored by use of index cards on which the children either recorded what they had done or which an observer (such as a group leader or teacher) signed. The cards were kept in a special folder in the children's regular classroom.

Initially, simple assignments were given to establish a pattern of completing all homework. Assignments were then used as a means to get the children to practice their individual behaviors in their regular classroom.

Final Phase

In the final phase of the programming, assignment cards were used to monitor the children's performance of specified behaviors in their library, music, and art classes (as mentioned above). In each of these settings the children initially received and lost points for specified behaviors, which were dispensed by one of the group leaders who observed the class. (Points earned were cashed in at the "store" at the next meeting.) Then, the group leader's signature on the children's cards, earned by an overall good performance and worth a lump amount of points, was substituted for specific points plus and minus. All points and signatures were paired with verbal praise. Then the teachers signed the cards with coaching from the group leaders on giving feedback and praise to the children on their behavior. Eventually, the teachers signed the cards without a group leader present.

In addition to the primary transferring of learning to the natural environment by means of behavioral assignments (Goldstein, Heller, and Sechrest, 1966, pp. 212-259), other transfer techniques were implemented. These included the fading of token reinforcement during group sessions and the conceptualization of learning through group discussion.

During the final stage of group programming, the prices of the store items were gradually increased while the amount of tokens earned by children was decreased. Simultaneously, group leaders increased their use of verbal praise for appropriate behaviors. By the twelfth session, the store was greatly reduced in size with all edibles removed. Activity reinforcers such as games and drawing, which were used in the regular classroom, became more readily available in an attempt to simulate their real (school) world as nearly as possible. The children were then given a choice of spending their points in the store or trading all their points for one of the three activities (two different games or coloring with crayons). For the final two sessions (13 and 14), points were eliminated entirely. The children were required to earn three out of four possible signatures in their special classes during the week to be able to play a game at the end of the group meeting. The reasons for fading the tokens were discussed with the children.

Children's Social Skills Group Session Ten Agenda

GOALS

I.   By the end of this session, group members will have practiced attending behaviors and appropriate social skills in a simulated music class setting.

II.   By the end of this session, group members will have demonstrated an understanding of their individual target behaviors through their verbal participation in a group discussion and problem-solving exercise.

AGENDA

I.   Assignment check and discussion
   A.   Check assignment cards
   B.   Discuss the purpose of "getting points in the classroom"
   C.   Discuss the eventual fading of tokens and store

II.   Music simulation exercise (token reinforcement for appropriate behaviors)
   A.   High note-low note exercise
   B.   Singing and body movement exercise

III. Review individual behaviors
   A.   Discussion
   B.   Group problem solving

IV.   Classroom simulation (group members do worksheets)
   A.   Discussion of purpose
   B.   Practice

V.   Assignment

VI.   Evaluation

VII.   Store

Continued discussion and practice of self-reinforcement occurred spontaneously during group discussions. During discussions, children would comment on positive changes in their own classroom behavior. At times, they would note that teachers did not always praise them for newly exhibited good behaviors. For example, Tim reported that he was now singing along appropriately in music. Previously, when the music teacher turned her back, he would stop singing and make faces at friends. Since Tim had never been caught, the music teacher could not know that his behavior had improved. Group leaders explained, however, that he could still give himself credit for improving. Tim was asked to create a self-praise statement. Group members contributed by offering suggestions. Tim was then asked to say the statement out loud several times until his voice volume and tone sounded appropriately assertive. Group members helped by modeling for him. Finally, Tim and the other group members were asked to practice reciting the statement covertly as they imagined a scene from their music class.

The changes the children perceived in their behavior, what they had learned during group, and why these changes were desirable was also discussed several times in the last phase of the program. Most of the children were able to restate these ideas in their own words and contribute to these discussions. The amount of time spent in group discussion was increased during the final programming stage, while games and other activities decreased. Finally, the children and group leaders discussed the changes the children perceived in their behavior, what they had learned during the group, and why these changes were desirable.

RESULTS

Data provided by assessment procedures suggested that the development of attending skill behaviors was an appropriate program goal for all 12 children. The children also exhibited a variety of disruptive and nonattending behaviors ranging from passively staring into space to hitting peers or crawling under furniture during class activities. Nevertheless, in all cases the positive alternative to these were appropriate attending behaviors. While other social skills (i.e., sharing, taking turns, praising, assertiveness, etc.) were also taught, data gathered by trained observers measured progress in the development of attending skills for each child across classroom settings.

The weekly percentage of time spent in attending, nonattending, and

TABLE 5-1   Each Child's Percentage of Behavior Change from Week 1 to Week 11 for All Three Measured Categories

Child	Percent of Attending Increase	Percent of Nonattending Decrease	Percent of Disruptive Behavior Decrease
Jeff	+55	- 34	- 21
Tim	+48	- 12	- 36
Rich	+41	- 22	- 19
Patti	+32	- 21	- 11
John	+22	- 2	- 21
George	+16	- 10	- 6
Beth	+16	- 9	- 7
Sue	+13	- 2	- 14
Dave	+12	- 2	- 13
Ann	+11	- 6	- 5
Mike	+ 2	- 2	- 4

disruptive behaviors in art, music, gym, library, individual mainstream class activities, and group activities in the mainstream classroom was recorded during the 12 weeks, the percentage increase or decrease for the three measured categories of behavior was computed for each child. These scores are shown in Table 5-1.

As indicated in Table 5-1, the total weekly percentage of attending behavior increased during the program. Jeff's increase was the most striking with a 55 percent increase in attending between the first and last week. After the group's inception, Jeff was given a neurological examination and was diagnosed as having a learning disability. Since the classroom teacher and his parents were aware of his diagnosis and suggestions were made for working with Jeff, this may have had an effect on Jeff's increased performance reported here.

Tim's improvement was also impressive as indicated by a 48 percent increase in attending as well as a 36 percent decrease in disruptive behaviors.

Conversely, Mike's percentages show only slight percentage changes over the course of the program. It should be noted however that Mike's percentage of attending behavior remained relatively high throughout the program and he was the only child to reach the 100 percent mark during the program. From week 1 to week 11, the average weekly percentage of time spent in appropriate attending behavior increased nearly 27 percent. Time spent in nonattending and disruptive behaviors decreased by 9.75 percent and 14 percent respectively.

DISCUSSION

The data indicate overall increases in attending and decreases in nonattending and disruptive behaviors. The children's self-reports and the subjective reports of the special subject teachers also indicated a substantial increase in attending and decrease in nonattending behaviors. It appears then that the group program did result in the targeted positive behavioral changes.

In the development of this children's social skill training program, many problems were encountered which impinged on the accuracy of the data collection. The leaders of the groups and the observers had a one-week spring break during the third week of the program during which no data was taken and there were no group meetings. Following vacations, we noted a surge of maladaptive behavior among all children in the class. In the sixth week of the program, the regular classroom teacher was ill for the entire week during which time there was a substitute student teacher. Having a new substitute teacher for such a long period of time also seemed to result in a decrease of the children's appropriate behaviors and an increase in their inappropriate classroom behaviors.

Although the observation system appeared to be reliable, some variation in application did occur. Not all children received the same number of observations. During each hourly visit to the classroom, the observers randomly chose the child to be observed for each five-minute period. Therefore, with a limited number of observers and a short period during which the observation could be made, often not all the 12 children in the program were observed. This resulted in variability in observation frequency. A further consideration in the amount of data taken is the fact that on occasion children were not in class because of illness or any number of other reasons. At other times observers were not able to observe due to an illness or transportation difficulty.

The structured use of time during group sessions also presented difficulties. In some of the early group sessions the one-hour time period was not well structured. This resulted in confusion, especially in regard to leader transitions between planned activities. Later as programming became more creative and structured, too many activities were scheduled. In trying to complete them all, children were returned to class 10 minutes late. This problem was partially resolved through leader experience as well as the practice of timing individual activities and then closely adhering to time limits. One further solution for future group programs would be to plan a session agenda with an over abundance of activities. Activities of varying time lengths should be included. Then certain critical activities could be marked and completed with the other exercises being used to fill the remaining time gaps. This would allow for more leader flexibility and still provide the session with adequate structure.

The time constraints of a 10-week program contributed to one final overall problem. Although program goals called for training in both the areas of attending and social skill behaviors, this project emphasized the former at the expense of the latter. Time did not allow for extensive training in both areas. Furthermore, early assessment indicated that the frequency of attending skill behaviors was greatly divergent among this group of children. Thus it would not have been appropriate to place program emphasis on more advanced social skills until all of the children had demonstrated an ability to attend adequately. A separate social skill training group oriented toward increasing attending behavior may have been advisable for the children who were socially withdrawn prior to their entry into a group.

In spite of these problems, the program not only demonstrated modest behavioral gains among the children, but also won favor within the school system in which this pilot group was organized. Since this group was completed, over 40 others (including the one reported in Chapter 6) have been initiated using a similar format. These groups have been carried out not only by members of the ISPR project, but also by regular social work and counseling staff in the school system.

REFERENCES

Laten, S. An Observation System for Children, University of Wisconsin, School of Social Work, 1974. Unpublished paper.

Rose, S. D. *Treating Children in Groups.* San Francisco: Jossey-Bass, 1972.

Wodarski, J. S., G. M. Rubeiz, and A. R. Feldman. Social Group Work with Anti-social Children, *American Journal of Orthopsychiatry, 43,* 2, (1973), 250-251.

SHELDON D. ROSE and ALISON ROESSLE

6

social skill training in a group for fourth-and fifth-grade boys

INTRODUCTION

Because of problems in a classroom, five boys, aged 9 to 11, grades four and five, were referred by their classroom teachers for involvement in a social skills group sponsored by the Interpersonal Skill Training and Research Project of the School of Social Work (University of Wisconsin-Madison). The leaders were graduate students in that program.

Following a two-week pretreatment assessment, the group met for 10 weeks, twice a week for half-hour sessions. In the initial phase, sessions 1 through 4, the focus was on increasing group attractiveness and in shaping problem solving, discussion skills, and the completion of behavioral assignments; the boys were also trained in simple observation techniques. The middle phase, sessions 5 through 16, consisted of programs and interventions designed to modify specific individual social behaviors and to modify group patterns of interaction. The final phase, sessions 16 through 19, stressed primarily the transfer and maintenance of behavior change and preparation for termination.

ASSESSMENT

The assessment procedures utilized for the member description included: (1) the initial interview with the classroom teachers; (2) the Walker Problem Behavior Identification Checklist (Walker, 1970); (3) teacher specification of two problem areas; (4) systematic in-class observations by trained observers; (5) calls to the parents, explaining the group and eliciting any feedback about their children; and (6) data collection during group meetings.

Background data on each child was gathered by asking the teachers to specify any nonbehavioral or physiological problem which may influence the child's behavior. The Walker Checklist was filled in by both the teachers and the parents.

As a final rudimentary assessment, the occurrence and nonoccurrence (coded by a yes or no—see below) of two problem behaviors was observed three days a week, twice each day, AM and PM, by each teacher for each group member. The initial identification of the problem behaviors was done by the teacher and then the coleaders met with the teacher to define the behaviors in specifically observable terms. For instance, one teacher identified a problem of one of the children, "he needs a chance to do things with a group of boys ... he's rather shy and sometimes has difficulty expressing himself." This broad description was broken down as follows: (1) cooperative behavior in a group discussion, defined as contributing information or opinions. Has Ike cooperated in a group discussion with at least one response directed to the whole group during class time? (2) Participate in a group activity, defined as playing a game with at least one other person, approaching and talking to someone on the playground. Has Ike played cooperatively at least once during free time periods or other informal group activities?

FIGURE 6-1   Recording Outline

Name____Ike_____ Week___3-16 to 3-20_____

BEHAVIOR:____Cooperation_____

	M	T	W	TH	F
AM	Yes	Yes	Yes	No	Yes
PM	No	Yes	No	Yes	Yes

Utilizing the Childrens Behavior Code (Rose 1977) systematic observations were made in the classroom and in gym class, first by the two coleaders and then by trained observers. The observers were trained using vidotapes and were instructed not to make any verbal or nonverbal contact with the children (Barrish et al., 1969; O'Leary et al., 1969; Wodarski et al., 1974). The instruments used were a stopwatch and a recording sheet. Reliability was assessed with a second observer recording behaviors simultaneously with the regular observer. The interobserver reliability was 85.2 percent.

The group leaders and a trained observer collected data on the group intervention. The observer was trained by the leader for one hour, by reviewing the definitions with examples of the responses followed by practice on a videotape. Ongoing data on the group was obtained not only through continued systematic observations in the classroom and in the group meetings, but also through parent-teacher reports on results of behavioral assignments for the group members, a self-report diary system, role plays, problem-focused discussion, a group score card or tally sheet of ongoing ingroup interactions, and charts of behaviors monitored by the group members. The charts were kept on the attendance and group productivity (number of completed behavioral assignments). A thermometer registering points earned toward a group contingency (a field trip) was also used.

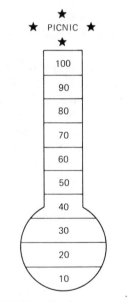

FIGURE 6-2   The Group Thermometer

MEMBER DESCRIPTION

Skip, age 11, fifth grade, was referred to the group by his teacher who felt he needed to learn how to get along better with his peer group and learn some social communication skills. This need for better peer relations was exhibited, according to the teacher, by the fact that Skip had only one friend, Darryl, another group member. The Walker Checklist indicated acting out and distractability as problem areas. In the classroom and gym the observer data indicated few physical disruptions, but frequent verbal disruptions which the teacher identified as "acting silly to attract attention." These outbursts were met unsystematically with ignoring and scolding from the teacher. Skip also had difficulty attending to activities especially in gym. His inattention was demonstrated by his gazing off into space or talking to himself. Skip's mother reported that he easily became angry when teased and expressed this anger by either storming off or screaming at people. He rarely abused them physically. Skip helped care for his younger brothers (ages 1 and 2) and according to his mother has been kind to them. This kindness or sharing was also demonstrated during a group meeting when Skip, on his own accord, shared his cookies with each of the members. Skip enjoyed chemistry, was interested in fish life, and was good in science and reading, all of which appear to have had reinforcing value for him. The two individual target behaviors for Skip to change were to increase his friendly behavior with his classmates, defined as interacting positively, working with or playing with his peers, and decreasing his inappropriate attention getting behavior such as "bugging" and teasing. The first goal was to increase his positive interactions, since this would be incompatible with his acting silly and could be positively reinforced.

Darryl, age 9, fourth grade, was referred to the group by the classroom teacher because of "undercover" acting out. The Walker Checklist indicated a high frequency of acting out and distractability. These "undercover" behaviors include pinching, kicking, and taking of school supplies. According to the teacher she received from one to three complaints pertaining to these behaviors daily. The teacher also reported that Darryl was unable or unwilling to accept responsibility for his behaviors, as evidenced by Darryl insisting "it's the other guy's fault." Darryl's mother reported sassy talking back and noncompliance to her requests. She felt this general bad attitude may have been due partially to the fact that she and her husband had been separated for a year, and that Darryl had changed schools and was the only child. Darryl was a good reader and enjoyed sports, which probably could serve as reinforcers. The two target behaviors for Darryl were to increase cooperative group interaction and decrease inappropriate behaviors such as pinching, hitting, and taking of supplies.

Ike, age 9, fourth grade, was referred to the group by his teacher because he acted withdrawn in the classroom, as indicated by the Walker. Classroom observation data indicated that he seldom participated in group discussion or other interactions with his peers. During class discussion Ike did not contribute, did not raise his hand or offer information, and lacked eye contact with the speaker. He seemed to be nonassertive in the class and in social free play situations, since he rarely approached peers. According to Ike's father, he was reinforced for not "bugging" his sister (only gets points if he does not "bug" her all day) and minding his parents. Ike was in most instances unassertive. Classroom observations and teacher reports of the Walker data revealed no evidence of acting out behavior and he did attend to the teacher. Ike collected stamps and beer cans, and liked baseball, soccer, and scatter dodge. He could possibly be used as a model for other group members who have to increase attending behaviors and decrease their acting out behaviors. Ike's individual treatment goal was to participate in group discussion.

Cal, age 10, fifth grade, was referred to the group mainly because of acting out behavior. He was large in stature and pushed the smaller children around. Gym and classroom observations revealed high frequency of positive interactions but also physical disruptions. The Walker data suggested that acting out (hitting, bumping, slapping, etc.) was a problem followed by immaturity and distractibility. Cal's mother labeled him as immature, but did not elaborate. The teacher identified lack of attending as another difficulty; he rarely got his materials ready promptly, he sharpened his pencil when unnecessary, and frequently walked around the room. The teacher felt his inattention to tasks such as map work was partially due to Cal's lack of fine motor skills, thus making it hard for him to write small enough for map work. It was observed in the group that he was good in math when he very rapidly did some calculations; he enjoyed all sports, especially hockey and baseball, again all potential areas of reinforcers. Cal's individual treatment goals were to increase the duration and frequency of attending to his written tasks and to decrease his acting out behavior of hitting, kicking, pushing, etc.

Stan, age 10, fourth grade, was referred to the group because he hit others as his reaction to anger. His immediate response to any behavior which annoyed him (e.g., accidentally being bumped) was hitting. The classroom observations also indicated a high degree of nonattending behavior, as evidenced by lack of eye contact with the board, book, or movie; an absence of note taking, and a playing with the contents of his desk. The teacher report also included treating the teacher disrespectfully. For example, if he was "fiddling" with his desk and asked not to, he would usually not comply with the request and often talked back. Stan was interested in ice boating and building balsam wood models. Stan's individual treatment goals included decreasing the frequency of acting out and increasing the frequency of carrying out responsibilities in his academic work.

GROUP ATTRACTION AND CONTRACT

During the first meetings it was crucial that the group be made as attractive as possible. A familiar meeting place was arranged, the school social worker's room, which had a pleasant work area with enough room for moving around.

As each child entered the meeting room for the first meeting, he was given a cookie paired with, "Hey, I'm glad you came." Once all the members were seated around the table, they were each given a token for coming in and sitting right down. They were instructed to put their token in their special token bank in front of them (empty cans) and promised that they would get more throughout the meeting. They would later be able to trade the tokens in for "neat things."

During the first meeting, the members worked on composing the following group contract:

We, the members of Silver Hawks, promise to come to each meeting and to come on time. We also promise to do some work and do some fun things.

The leaders of Silver Hawks promise to bring neat things that aren't too expensive to earn and to have things to do.

Leader Signature	Group Member Signature
Ben Smythe	*Cal*
Alice Crome	*Ike*
	Stan
	Darryl
	Skip

REINFORCEMENT

In the initial phase of treatment, frequent opportunity for reinforcement was created. The boys were awarded tokens which could earn them valued prizes (e.g., match box cars = 30 tokens) when they saved enough. At first, the children had an opportunity to sample potential reinforcers such as special games without having to earn them. Later the privileges to play the popular games had to be earned by behavioral achievements. In order to discover other reinforcers the children in the first meeting were instructed to interview each other in dyads to discover the other's favorite food, favorite game, what they would buy in a store with 50 cents, etc.

Reinforcement was available for completion of behavioral assignments which were behaviors to be completed in classroom, playground, home, or neighborhood. Self, buddy, and teacher monitoring of the assignments were used. A contingency contract was employed for each assignment, that is a written statement of a desired behavior to be performed and the tokens or other reinforcers to be received if the behavior is performed. Cal, who was working on completing written work, had the following assignment.

If I (Cal) begin my math assignment on time three times this week, have the teacher initial my card, and return the card next week in group, then I will earn five tokens. If I do not begin my assignment on time three days, but get the teacher's initials and return the card, I will earn three tokens. If I forget the card, but bring it in the following week, complete, I will earn two tokens.

_____Cal_____ Member

_____Ben_____ Leader

Skip who was working on being friendly had the following assignment:

If I make a new friend this week, then I can invite him to come to the group. And my new friend will be able to earn tokens during our meeting to be added to the thermometer.

_____Skip_____ Member

_____Alice_____ Leader

Each individual received tokens not only for the completion of behavioral assignments but also for desired ingroup behaviors such as participation at certain times during the meeting and also for honest praise of one of the other members. Tokens purchased various individual rewards. But as the individual reinforcers were faded in later meetings, group contingencies were introduced, for example, a field trip to the university and a picnic at a local park. These field trips were earned by saving up tokens by the entire group.

GAMES AND VIDEOTAPING

In addition to serving as reinforcers, various games helped to keep the group attractive and to shape the skills necessary for role playing. Observation skills and situation description training were also practiced informally during games such as "hot/cold," "detective," and pantomime. The hot/cold game was used to teach successive approximation to attending to subtle cues. One group member would leave the room while the other members chose an object in the room. When the member returned to the room, the closer he neared the object the louder the members clapped and, conversely, the farther he departed from the object the softer the members clapped until the given child located the object.

The detective and pantomime games were used to provide practice in observing and detecting minor differences or synthesizing a pattern of responses.

The detective game had one or two detectives and three or four tricksters. The detectives carefully investigated the tricksters' clothing and then left the room while the tricksters changed their appearance, parted their hair on the opposite side, untucked their shirt, untied their shoes, took off their socks, etc. The returning detectives had to solve the mystery.

During the pantomime game, one or two members would act out a scene (gardening, playing hockey, getting into a fight) without using any sounds. The first person to guess the scene correctly became the next pantomimist.

Other games were played primarily for fun such as the rug race, although it did require a degree of cooperation. The group divided into two teams. Each team would position themselves on a throw rug or old blanket on their hands and knees and try to move themselves across the floor to the finish line while the other team members were the timers.

Games gave way to more complex activities such as a group production of a videotape. This served both as an opportunity for cooperative and complex social behaviors and an educational device. The group planned and rehearsed the program for the videotaping. The script was designed to portray a normal session and served as an opportunity for the members to review some of the purposes of the Silver Hawks and their individual targets for change. Each member had a chance to perform either as a leader for the review of assignments or role plays or as an actor for a role play.

The videotape vividly demonstrated to the parents and the teachers the actual processes of the group. Viewing the videotape gave the parents and teachers a basis for discussing the group with the leaders. The leaders used the tape as a model for the reinforcement procedures used in the group: praise, touch, and talk. The parents and teachers were encouraged to practice these techniques and use them with the children.

ROLE PLAYS

Once the boys had developed accurate observation skills, they worked on role plays. Information obtained during the problem-solving phase supplied the material for the role plays. Subjects revolved around attending in class, conflict resolution, and making new friends.

After reporting that he volunteered during the class meeting, Ike demonstrated his success by role playing. Cal played the role of class president and led a simulated class discussion. Ike was then able to practice the steps he was working on to increase his class participation. He thought of a news item to share, raised his hand, waited to be recognized, and then said in a loud, clear voice that he had heard about a robbery at the local jeweler. After the role play, the members gave Ike some positive feedback, related to his voice tone, eye contact, and whether he met his goal of participating in the class discussion. After the members offered positive feedback, they offered alternative responses such as talking a little slower. At this point Ike re-rehearsed the role play, remembering to talk more slowly.

Stan reported that he got into a fight with another classmate over a ball on the playground. He chose Skip to play the other classmate, and the two boys role played the scene, this time with Stan practicing how he could have avoided the fight. Stan had the ball and the other boy came over to get it. "Hey, I want to use the ball now." "Nope, I'm not done with it yet. Go get another one." "No, you said I could use this one halfway through recess and it's time." "Well, I'm in the middle of a four-square game. Would you like to join the game?" "Well, okay, I guess so." "Good, you can go first. Here's the ball."

Darryl reported that he had been friendly to a disabled child by playing with him outside. The group decided it would be helpful to see this role played, so Darryl chose Skip to be the disabled boy. Darryl invited Skip to play in the sand box with him and then helped him walk over. When recess was over, Darryl helped Skip back into school. The group decided Darryl might practice using more words while in the sandbox. The two boys re-rehearsed the scene, this time talking about what to build in the sand and how to do it.

PROBLEM SOLVING

Learning how to use the steps in problem solving was one of the most important goals in the social skills group. A combination of problem-solving and behavioral techniques was used so that the individual progressed from "brainstorming" and selecting workable responses to rehearsing the new behaviors. In the initial phase brainstorming centered around obtaining responses to the question, "What can you do when you get angry?". Many possible responses were offered with the most frequent being "ignore, count to ten, remove self from the situation, and reason with the person."

One group session was devoted to cognitive restructuring and the acquisition of skills to cope with anger. First they discussed if it was possible to feel yourself getting angry. Then, they looked at what they say to themselves when angry. Third, problem solving was carried out around alternative statements. And finally they developed a brief cognitive script (see Meichenbaum, 1977, for a detailed description of this procedure) as a coaching device for when they did get angry.

"Who can describe how they feel when they start to get angry: Okay, Ben give it a try."

"Well I can really tell when I'm getting mad. It feels just like a volcano erupting. I feel all bubbly inside and get hotter and hotter."

"Great description. I can really get an idea of how you feel inside. Anybody have other feelings? All right. What do you guys say to yourself when you are mad? Stan, you've got some ideas."

"Yeah, I say stuff like I could smash him. I can't believe he did such a stupid thing. Man I can hardly wait to show how I feel. I could just kill him!"

"Wow, those sure are angry words. I wonder if you could come up with some other things to say to yourself when you get so mad?"

After a few minutes of brainstorming, the group developed the following script.

Ok. Calm down. Don't get so mad. Yeah, he did a stupid thing, but I don't have to hit him. Try to calm down. One, two, three, ten. Good, stay as calm as you can. Don't worry if you still feel mad. If I catch myself saying I could just smack that guy STOP IT!!! Now is a good time to think of some other things to do. I could tell the teacher, talk to the kid and tell him I didn't like what he did, practice keeping my cool, or leave. Great, now just choose one and try it.

Each member was encouraged to change the basic script to fit his own situation and vocabulary. They all received a copy of their own script and during the next several sessions, time was devoted to overt rehearsal and later covert rehearsal of these coping statements.

TREATMENT PLANS

Although each child was working on a specific individual behavior, the general plan for each was the same. Each boy chose two people in his class (nongroup members) who did a good job on the behavior on which the member needed work (e.g., Skip was trying to be more friendly so he chose two people who were especially friendly in his class). The next two assignments consisted of observing a specific situation involving the person they were observing, and describing what happened. And the final set of assignments was concerned with the child performing the target behavior in the classroom. Each was told that to earn tokens from that point on he would have to work at increasing the frequency of his target behaviors. The leaders modeled how to monitor one's own behavior and how to request the teacher's signature. Then each child role played how he or she using an index card, would monitor his or her own behavior.

Skip's behavioral assignment of observing someone in class was described on an index card as follows: "observe the person you chose who acts friendly to people. Describe one situation when he acted friendly. (1) What happened? (2) Who was involved? (3) How was the person friendly (name three ways)." The behavioral assignment designed to practice was worded, "Did you do anything with your classmates (other than Darryl) today? With whom? What happened?" There was also a place on the card for the teacher's initials. The initial reinforcement was contingent on receiving two "yesses" over a five-day period as to the occurrence of the desired target behavior. Two occurrences permitted some initial success, but was slightly better than earlier performances.

For Skip's second behavior, not acting silly (remaining task-centered in informal activities), his assignment was to describe one time a day when he did not act silly and explain what he did instead. The teacher's initials were required for the assignment to be complete.

Darryl's observation assignment and in-class assignment of being friendly and not acting silly was the same as Skip's.

Ike's observation assignment was to "observe the person you chose who does a good job of participating in group discussion. Describe one situation. (1) What happened? (2) Who was involved? (3) How did the person participate? (4) What did he say?" His in-class assignment was "Describe one time when you participated in a group discussion. What was happening? How did you participate? What did you say?" The teacher initialed his card.

Cal's observation assignment was to "observe the person you chose who does a good job of doing his written assignments. Describe one situation when he did work on his assignment. (1) What was the subject? (2) Did he get his materials ready promptly? (3) Did he look at his paper? (4) Did he write?" For the second assignment, the discriminative stimuli were not as specific. "Name three things he did to help you know he was working." For Cal's classroom behavior, the assignment stated: "Did you begin your written work on time and start to write for the assignment? List three things you did." Since Cal's baseline was zero, initially any approximation to attending resulted in positive reinforcement. In the twelfth session, the second target behavior was presented: keeping his cool. "Did you keep your cool today?" The teacher initialed his answer. At this point his assignment of attending to his written tasks was increased to complete the task. The following excerpt is an example of how Cal was prepared to carry out his assignment. This is similar to the way in which all the children were prepared.

"Okay, now we will all help Cal practice paying attention to his math assignment. From Cal's homework cards which he monitored himself and Mrs. P has checked, I can tell Cal is improving and really trying to get his assignments started on time in class and work on them. That's terrific Cal; I like your hard work. If it's okay with you, I'd like to try a role play where we play we're all in math class and someone will try to bug you while you are trying to work. Does that sound okay with you? Good, then who wants to be the teacher? And we need two other people to play the pests. You guys have to try to distract Cal. The rules are that first you can only do little things to try to bother him, nothing really big, maybe whisper or laugh. Then after Cal tries really hard to keep at his work and we time how long Cal can concentrate, I'll tell you guys to really bug Cal!

You can do anything to bug him except do not hurt him. Cal, you have to try your hardest to keep at your work. Can you remember the ideas we've been practicing to deal with people who really bug you? Yes, those are all good ideas. Now, let's see if you can act them out. For the other people, including the teacher, you play consultants and observe how everyone does the role play. Can you tell me four things you will watch for. Okay. Terrific. Everyone ready? Here we are in math class."

Stan's observation assignment was to observe a person in class who "keeps his cool," and describe one situation where he kept his cool when he could have gotten into a fight. You will have to find a situation where the person could have started a fight but did not. (1) What happened? (2) Who was involved? (3) What did the person do and say to keep his cool? Name three things." Stan's in-class monitoring assignment was, "Did you keep your cool today, instead of fighting? When? What happened? What did you do?" Stan's second target behavior was to complete his written work on time. "Did you complete a written assignment today on time? What subject? List three things you did to help you finish the assignment on time."

GROUP INTERVENTION

Two group problems became apparent in the fourth session. The first was a disparate distribution of participation among the members; the second involved a low frequency of praise statements emitted by all of the members. In order for a group to function effectively, it was assumed that it would be desirable to have a relatively even distribution of participation; otherwise, some members fail either to obtain feedback or to have an opportunity to talk about their program or problem. Positive statements or praise are necessary to build relationships of the members with each other as well as relationships with persons outside the group. For these reasons, both problems were addressed during the fifth through eighth meetings along with the other programs mentioned earlier.

In order to evaluate the effectiveness of the intervention baseline, data on participation of each member and on positive praise statements were collected during two half-hour sessions by observers who recorded for samples of five minutes on, 30 seconds off. Observers continued to record their observations on both variables until the end of the experiment.

Intervention involved primarily the distribution of tokens for every participation up to five in a period of five minutes. After a person received five, one would be removed for each time he participated. Social reinforcement was paired with the giving of tokens. The intervention began with the following introduction:

Ben and I both think that all of you are doing a fine job of following the Silver Hawk's contract. We also think you're trying really hard to talk one at a time and listen to what the others have to say and I think it's paying off since there have been some good ideas expressed. I have noticed one behavior which I think the group could work on as a whole. I have been observing the group discussion as I think some of you noticed. When I was making marks on the index card, I was recording each time someone spoke. This is the information I obtained (refer to blackboard with tally). What do you think this information means? Do you think this kind of group is a place for people to talk the same amount? I think you all have good ideas to offer and I enjoy hearing everyone speak. Can anyone think of a plan we might use to get Ike and Darryl to talk some more and help keep the rest of us a bit more quiet? (At this point one of the members, Skip, suggested trying to keep his talking time down near five times in five minutes.) Now as a method of practicing to keep each person's communication even with the other members, I've got a plan similar to the idea Skip offered. For the next five minutes, each time a person talks he will receive a token until he has earned five tokens. Then everytime after that when he talks, he will lose a token. We will try this a couple of times during the rest of this meeting. Can you think of any ways you can help remind each other, maybe a buddy system?

The five-minute game not only resulted in more even participation during the game, it generated equal participation in the rest of the meeting.

The next group intervention began with a similar introduction, followed by presenting the data for praise statements (zero baseline). They all knew what praise meant and the main thrust of the discussion was to elicit from the members (1) ways that the leaders have reinforced, and (2) which of their behaviors deserves positive reinforcement (a good idea, a new idea, follow group rules, a good role play, good listener, etc.). How the members liked to receive compliments was discussed; ideas such as using the person's name, looking at the person, and meaning what you say were suggested. Next the leaders modeled two ways of giving a compliment, a negative and a positive model, and the group discussed what they observed. The group then broke up into two subgroups and each leader worked with the smaller group in practicing to give each other compliments. The boys were told that henceforth whenever they gave a compliment they would earn a token. The feedback procedure after the role plays offered a perfect time to implement this phase. The members were also asked to practice giving each other and their friends compliments outside of the group.

Both group programs were quite popular and were continued until session 18 when they were terminated. In order to clarify why they would be ended, the following explanation was given.

We feel you are all doing a great job of taking turns and are giving each other very meaningful compliments. We changed the five-minute talking game so you each had to keep track of your own talking time and at the end of the five-minute period, if you talked four or five times, you earned one token. Now we'd like to see you keep it up, without any tokens for the talking game or the "raise the praise" game. Do you think you can keep working just as hard without the tokens? You know, soon Ben and I won't be around to give you tokens, but you will be around each other and can give each other praising statements.

TERMINATION

Not only was it necessary to end the experiment on the group problems as the group began to approach the last weeks of the school year, it was also necessary to prepare the members for leaving the group and to help them to function without its support. For this purpose a number of exercises were used. In order to prepare them for situations not already encountered in the group but which could readily occur, the members were asked to read the following situations:

> Your family suddenly has to move to a new neighborhood and you must change schools. At your new school, on your first day, the teacher asks you to introduce yourself and tell something about yourself.
>
> It is a beautiful warm sunny day outside and the teacher says you can do your work out-of-doors as long as you do work. How would you help yourself keep at your work?
>
> A new boy comes into your class and you find out that he is interested in science just like you are. It's his first day in class. You want to meet him and get to know him. How do you go about it?

These situations were discussed in the group in terms of how they could best be handled, and in some cases various solutions were role played by the members.

In order to encourage independent functioning after the group terminated, the leaders provided increasing opportunities for leadership within the group. In session 10, for example, two members acted as discussion leaders during the assignment review. A cue card with leadership tips was initially provided to the discussion leader and one of the adult leaders coached him if he needed some help (see Figure 6-3). After a while, the cue card was faded. The members also

---

CUE CARD LEADER ASSIGNMENT REVIEW

Ask the following questions.
  What was your assignment?
  What parts did you do this week?
      (Remember to praise)
  What was difficult to do? Why?
  Did you contact your buddy? (If not, why not?)
  What happened? Was it helpful?

FIGURE 6-3   Cue Card for Leader

took complete responsibility for organizing the picnic. The leaders arranged for each member to have a specific area to cover, for which he acted as leader. For instance, one person led a discussion on food, another on games, etc. When a member led the discussion, he chose volunteers, tried to keep others on-task, tried to draw each member into the discussion, offered suggestions, and praised the achievements of others.

During the last six meetings, in order to increase the attractiveness of relationships outside the group, the members were encouraged to bring guests to the final picnic meeting. At this meeting the members were encouraged to tell their friends what they did in the group and what they achieved.

In order to increase extra group incentives, parents and teachers were constantly informed of the procedures being used in the group, especially the use of positive reinforcement. The procedures were vividly demonstrated to the parents and teachers when they had the opportunity to review the videotape of a typical meeting which the members had developed for that purpose. In a discussion with the parents, the leaders encouraged the parents to try out some of the reinforcement procedures used in the group.

RESULTS

Skip's two target behaviors were to increase his friendly behavior, defined as positive interaction, and to decrease his inappropriate attention-getting behavior. The results indicated an increase in positive interactions of both the weekly teacher reports and systematic classroom observation. No data were available for attention-getting behavior.

Darryl's two target behaviors were the same as Skip's. The data indicated an increase in positive interactions; however, the teacher's weekly reports did not substantiate this. On the weekly reports a decrease in cooperative peer group interaction appeared.

Ike was working on class participation. On the systematic classroom observations, there was only a slight increase contrasted with the teacher's weekly reports. The teacher indicated great improvement and cited Ike's increase in class participation as the "most improvement" of all the group members.

Cal's target behaviors were attending to his written work and keeping his cool (keeping calm when pressed by his peers). The systematic observations and the weekly teacher observations indicated an increase in attending to his written work and a decrease in physical acting out.

Stan also was aiming to keep his cool and attend to his written work. Stan's physical acting act decreased; however, his verbal disruptions increased. Overall, his attending to his tasks increased.

The results of the Walker for each of the boys for both home and classroom behavior and before and after treatment is shown below in Table 6-1.

	ACTING OUT		WITH-DRAWAL		DIS-TRACTION		DISTURBED PEER RELATIONS		IM-MATURITY	
	pre	post	pre	post	pre	post	pre	post	pre	post
Ike										
Class	0	1	5	8	7	2	0	0	2	0
Home	7	0	1	0	4	0	0	0	0	0
Darryl										
Class	9	12	3	2	7	8	0	2	0	0
Home	10	7	6	6	6	2	5	0	3	0
Skip										
Class	14	17	0	0	7	4	1	3	0	0
Home	6	9	0	0	0	0	3	0	3	0
Stan										
Class	19	12	0	0	9	7	1	0	2	0
Home	—	0	—	0	—	1	—	0	—	5
Cal										
Class	20	18	0	0	9	9	3	3	4	3
Home	12	18	0	0	9	9	4	0	5	0

DISCUSSION

Ike seemed to progress rapidly and may not need a further group. Cal and Stan were better able to remain calm under stress, yet still demonstrated an occasional flare-up. They might both benefit from some additional relaxation and cognitive training, in response to feeling angry and tense. A token economy for Carl's completion of written assignments should be continued in his classroom. The results on Darryl and Skip indicate that a continued social skills group is probably necessary for them. Heavier reinforcement must be made contingent on acquiring some "friendly" skills, and thus decrease their inappropriate attention-getting behaviors.

The group was a small, structured situation which met only twice a week for a 10-week period. The structure and size were conducive to helping the members learn, practice, and acquire more adaptive behaviors since they each had difficulty in the normal size public school classroom. However, a detailed program of simulating the discriminative stimuli in their environments would probably still be necessary for generalization of learning to occur.

Follow-up data would also be useful and would most likely indicate the need for a booster program which could consist of infrequent meetings with the group members and group leaders to discuss their successes and difficulties. Continuing buddy contacts and establishing some means of meeting together every few weeks would also improve maintenance for the members.

More parent and teacher contact during the group is necessary since these people are significant in the members' natural environments. This contact could be perpetuated through an initial home visit, frequent newsletters, and regularly scheduled meetings.

In summary, the treatment package presented was successful in effecting a change in more adaptive social skills in four out of the five fifth-grade boys. A follow-up and booster session are suggested as added impetus to the maintenance and generalization of learning.

REFERENCES

Barrish, H., M. Saunders, and M. Wolf. Good behavior game: Effects of individual contingencies for group consequences of disruptive behavior in the classroom. *Journal of Applied Behavior Analysis*, 1969, *2*, 119-24.

Meichenbaum, D. *Cognitive-Behavior Modification*. New York: Plenum Press, 1977.

O'Leary, K. D., W. C. Becker, M. B. Evans, and R. A. Saudargas. A token reinforcement program in a public school: A replication and systematic analysis. *Journal of Applied Behavior Analysis*, 1969, *2*, 3-13.

Rose, S. D. *Treating children in groups*. San Francisco: Jossey Bass, 1972.

————. Children's Observation System, School of Social Work, University of Wisconsin, 1977.

Walker, A. M. *Walker problem behavior identification checklist manual*. Western Psychological Services, Los Angeles, 1970.

Wodarski, J. S., G. M. Rubeiz, and R. A. Feldman. Program planning for antisocial boys. *Social Work*, 1974, *19*, 705.

7

a transitional
activity group
for involving deaf clients
in community activities

INTRODUCTION

Transition groups are designed to help clients make a comfortable shift from the institutional setting to the community. Most of the emphasis during transition of the deaf has been concerned with helping the adult client to find work. If an individual has a job and is functioning well and returns to an apartment or other living situation without difficulty, the client is considered to be "doing well." Unfortunately, leisure time is ignored. It is during the nonstructured "free time" that so many individuals with behavior problems or social skill deficits have difficulty. They need not only knowledge of available recreation skills, but also the approach and social skills to become involved in activities in the community.

This chapter describes a transitional group consisting of five deaf individuals. The purpose of the group was to increase each member's knowledge of recreational activities in the city in which he/she lived and to teach him/her the approach responses and social skills necessary for getting involved in these activities. The specific goal was that each person would eventually be able to get involved on his or her own initiative in at least one ongoing community activity. Another less explicit purpose was to increase the small group interactional skills of each client.

ORGANIZATION OF THE GROUP

The transitional activity group was organized for deaf clients at the Deaf Treatment Center of a state mental health institute. These clients were preparing for a return to a community or family living situation. Data taken from the patient charts indicated that no clients sought involvement in a community activity even though they expressed interest in such activities as dancing, macrame, and basketball at various agencies in town (YMCA, school-community recreation department, and the area technical college). Although the group was formed on a voluntary basis, clients were encouraged to join, as it would help them further in making it on their own. There was a great deal of status attached to the group by all the clients in the center since it included only those preparing to leave the center. All members of the group knew each other well and had no difficulties getting along with one another prior to joining the group. Since the leader had already worked with all of them in developing recreation skills, she knew them well, was able to communicate with each one, and felt trusted by them.

A "sneak preview" meeting was held with the clients to explain the purpose of the group and what would be done. The leader was working with all the clients in recreation therapy so this type of group blended well with other things they were doing. All the clients described their plans for leaving the Center and their interest in the group. Refreshments were served and a role play was presented by several staff depicting some attractive activities. The group was to meet once a week for one hour, for a total of 11 weeks.

Treatment consisted primarily of information giving, contingency contracting of behavior assignments, and the use of behavior rehearsal, coaching, role played modeling, and group discussion to prepare them to carry out those assignments. The group was unique not only in terms of the deafness of all the group members and the communication patterns this established, but the fact that transfer of change from the sheltered environment was into a hearing world.

ASSESSMENT AND GROUP MEASUREMENT

Data taken from the Center charts on "Participation in Activities" indicated there was very little interaction in community activities other than those planned by the unit. Over a two-week period, only one member, who was the only outpatient, had been involved in a constructive activity in town. A questionnaire was given to each group member to check his/her knowledge of activities in town and procedures for getting into the activities.

Transitional Activity Group: Questionnaire

1. Do you know how to use the bus to get anywhere in town? (Describe.)
2. Do you know how to read a map of the town? (Show me!)

3. Do you know where you can go to find out about activities in town? (Give two examples.)
4. Do you know where the recreation department is? (Describe.)
5. Do you know where all the YMCAs and YWCAs are in town? (Describe.)
6. Do you know what W.A.D. and M.A.D. stand for? (What?)
7. Do you know where the state university is? (Tell me where!)
8. Do you know what the university union is? (What?)
9. Do you know what activities happen at the union? (What kind?)
10. Is there a deaf club in town? (Where?)
11. Do you know when the club (if any) meets? (When?)
12. Is there a church for the deaf in town? (Where?)
13. Are there activities for only deaf people in town? (What kinds?)
14. Do you know where the area technical college is and if it has activities? (What kinds?)
15. Do you know the name or location of one bowling lane in Madison? (Where?)
16. Do you know a place where you can play pool in town? (Where?)
17. Is there an indoor ice skating rink in town? (Where?)
18. Is there a roller skating rink in town? (Where?)
19. Do you know where the county coliseum is and what activities happen there? (What kind?)
20. Are there sports events you can watch in town? (Name three.)

(Two group members did not understand the question format. The leader signed all questions for them so they could understand and respond. For example, question 18 would be signed as "Roller skate place, here, Madison? Yes? No? Where?")

The questionnaire was designed to determine their knowledge of activities in the immediate community. If clients answered yes, they would have to describe what they would do. Testing results indicated a fairly even distribution of "yes" and "no" answers. Answers to the questionnaire gave information as to what group members knew about community services and aided in setting up behavior assignments.

Members reported on their achievements each week. These data were recorded on a group graph which clearly indicated what had been completed and by whom. This large graph was posted on the unit to show the group's achievements to other unit members. As various levels were achieved, the group earned various activities in the community, such as a game of bowling or a movie. An observer in the group kept data on one individual's eye contact and leader-member interaction. Two observers counting the above at the same meeting provided a reliability check on the accuracy of the observer. An audiovisual tape provided another means of reliability check. There was very little discrepancy between observers. Information was also available from unit charts of those residing at the Deaf Treatment Center. Each member in the group had a fellow "buddy," who provided feedback on task completion.

All members of the group filled out a reinforcement survey—money and food were the most popular. The reinforcement survey was nothing more than: "What do you like? Food? Pop? A talk with a friend?" The leader assisted each member in listing items. Any other format would have been too difficult for members to understand. Reinforcements were then included in the contracts, with aversive contingencies (such as payment by the group members to the leader) for noncompletion of assignments.

INDIVIDUAL ASSESSMENTS

Dave, a 38-year-old deaf male, was working at Goodwill and living at the YMCA. He became an outpatient of the Deaf Treatment Center because of a drinking problem. He stated he was bored and drank because he had nothing else to do. He had a low frequency of involvement in community activities and had been observed drinking on a number of different occasions. He enjoys sports and in the past had been involved in the deaf basketball team and recreation activities offered through work. Dave stated his goal in the group was to get involved in sports so that he wouldn't drink all the time.

John was a 28-year-old deaf male who was referred to the Deaf Treatment Center because of aggressive behavior and drinking. He worked at Goodwill and was in the process of changing jobs. Although now living at the center, he had lived on his own in the community, but became anxious and disorganized when faced with any problems. He shied away from large groups and preferred to be with a small deaf group. When living in the community, he had been withdrawn and had to be encouraged to do anything. He stated he wanted to get involved in a hobby group. John would soon be moving back into the community and needed to know how to get involved in activities on his own initiative. The goal for John was to increase his awareness of activities in town and to learn procedures for getting into the activities, and finally to attend and participate in an ongoing hobby group.

In the first group meeting, it was observed that John's eye contact with the speaker was limited. Because the speaker used sign language, it was apparent John was missing much of what was being said by not looking. An observer then kept data on this for the following three sessions and eye contact increased to the point where it was unnecessary to treat. It increased following a move by the group to a small room with few distractions.

Steve, a 33-year-old deaf male, was referred to the DTC for criminal observation. He stated he liked most activities and had been very involved in them in the past in a southern state. Since he would continue living in Madison while on probation, he wanted to know how to go about getting involved in a place that was unfamiliar to him. The goal for Steve was then the same as for John.

Sue, a 33-year-old deaf woman, was referred to the DTC because of extreme depression. She had been married and divorced and had two children living in a foster home. For the past seven years she had lived with her parents who had protected and sheltered her to the point that she felt there was little she could do on her own. After getting a job, she would be living in town, and wanted to know how to get involved in things to "keep her busy."

Joyce was a 15-year-old girl who was referred to DTC because of problems with school and her family. Although she heard well with a hearing aid, she had shifted to various special deaf education classes 12 different times. She stated she has always had to babysit for her brothers and sister, so has never gone to any school activities except for one football game. She was attending a local high school, but stated she had no desire to get involved in school activities and wanted to join something in town. This was appropriate, since Joyce would be returning to her own school in a nearby state. Joyce was primarily in the group as a model for the others, as she communicated well with everyone, participated in activities, and was conscientious about doing assignments. She was unaware that she was a group model and had as her goal the same areas as Sue.

INTERVENTION

In order to counsel a group of deaf individuals with diversified communication skills in something as broad as involvement in community activities, treatment had to consist of highly visual techniques. Some basic behavior assignments were developed and treatment consisted of contingency contracting, behavioral rehearsal, and role play. All these areas had to be simplified enough to be used (and understood) with the deaf clients.

Originally, the group stated two goals. The first was knowledge of and participation in community recreational activites. The second was that everyone in the group would get involved in at least one educational situation in Madison in order to improve his/her academic knowledge in some area that the individual felt needed improvement. An educational situation could be defined as a group or one-to-one learning experience in any area in which an individual needs academic improvement. Of particular importance to the members was better communication skills (writing, sign language, and speech therapy). After two weeks, the members complained that it would be too difficult for them to have assignments on anything but the recreational activities. Everyone was working or attending school full-time, so were limited in times they could work on assignments. The group decided to drop goal two and concentrate only on goal one.

Although assignments were given for two weeks, it was not until the third week that contingency contracting was instituted. An example of a typical contract is below.

Contract: Assignments 3 and 4   October 26, 19___

I, _____, agree to:

1. Find out where all the YMCAs and YWCAs are located in town, and bring in a map to the group with all Ys marked on it.
2. Go to the Y that is nearest to where you live now, or will live. Bring in an activity list from there.

If I do both of the above, I will help the group graph go up. I will also get 10 cents from Mary Smith (group leader) for each one (1 and 2) that I do. If I don't do all the assignments listed above, I must pay Mary 30 cents for each assignment I don't do. Bring assignments to the next group to meet on Tuesday, October 30, at 5:30. Further, if I arrive to this meeting on time, I will get refreshments at break time.

Also to be completed on Tuesday, October 30, is assignment 4, as follows:

1. Find out when the local Association for the Deaf (MAD) meets, where, and at what time. Write this on a piece of paper and bring to group.
2. Find out about one sports activity the deaf sponsor in Madison and write down when, where, time, and cost of this.

If I do both of the above, I will help the group graph go up. I will also get a group trip to the Circle Thing (expenses paid). I agree to bring assignments to the next group meeting on October 30.

Signed _____

_____

The main goal of the group (getting involved in at least one ongoing activity in Madison) was broken down into various behaviors that would increase the likelihood of involvement taking place. These behaviors were in the form of assignments that came under the headings of: *knowledge* of activities available in Madison, *procedures* for getting into the activity each individual chooses, and *attendance* at and *involvement* in the activity chosen.

Group Behavior Assignments

I. *Knowledge* of activities available in Madison.
   A. Clip out any article in the newspaper that shows some type of activity that is going on in Madison.
   B. Find out if there is a recreation department in Madison. If so:
      1. Bring in a slip of paper with the address on it.
      2. Bring in (to the group) any schedules of activities or literature that they may have.

      C. Find out where all the YMCAs and YWCAs are located in Madison and bring in a map of Madison with locations marked on it. Bring in a schedule of activities from the Y that is closest to where you live or will be living in Madison.

      D. Find out when the Madison Association for the Deaf Club meets, where, and at what time. Find out about one sports activity the deaf sponsor in Madison (when, where, time, and cost).

      E. Find out where Madison Area Technical College (MATC) is. Visit there and obtain a listing of activities available.

      F. Visit the University of Wisconsin Union (the old one and the new Union South). Bring back information on two activities they have that you could participate in (or attend as a spectator).

II.   *Procedures* for getting into the activity each individual chooses.

      A. From all the information you have on activities in Madison, choose two that you may be interested in and want to learn more about. For these two activities, find out all the details you will need to know before you can attend (dates, place, cost, if the group is limited in number, registration, can you get there by bus or walking, where do you sign up for the course, do you need special equipment to join, e.g., your own ski gear for a ski group).

      B. Contact the person in charge of the activity you want to join to find out if they are willing to have a deaf person in their group.

      C. Obtain an application blank from the agency sponsoring the activity. Fill it out and turn it in. If you have difficulty with the application, bring it to the transition group for help in filling it out prior to turning it in.

III. *Attendance* at activity chosen.

      A. Arrange for your transportation to the activity and make a "trial run" (meaning you practice walking, taking a bus, riding a bike, etc., to the place where the activity will be held several days before the actual acvitity) to be sure you know how long it takes to get there; where to leave from, etc.

      B. Attend the first session of the activity you applied for, and arrive there at least five minutes before the activity begins.

IV. *"Being involved"* in the activity.

      A. Attend the second session of the activity you have joined. Be prepared to bring the name of the leader and at least two other member's names to transition group.

      B. After attending the activity five times, be prepared to discuss what you are doing in the group. (Possibly the leader from the activity or a fellow group member could come discuss this with you.)

New contingency contracts were given to the group each week. In order to test the efficacy of the contracts, at the end of the fifth session contracts were discontinued for two sessions. They were reinstated in the seventh session. This is an example of a withdrawl design as it applies to a group context.

General Summary of Meetings

The questionnaire aided in setting up behavior assignments that would be contracted. On September 16 and again on September 23 the group was asked to do the first assignment (to clip out any article in the newspaper that showed some type of activity that was going on in Madison). There were no completions. On October 1, contingency contracts for behavior assignment 1 were filled out with each group member. The leader drew up the first contract and each one stated basically the same contingencies. Group members were to bring to the next meeting on October 7 an article they clipped from the newspaper telling about any sports activity going on in Madison. If this was done, the group graph would indicate progress, and each person would receive his/her choice of an item worth 20 cents (most specified pop). If this was not done, a payment of 25 cents was to be made to the leader (by previous agreement with the members).

Modeling and behavior rehearsal were used at every meeting in preparation for the new assignment. This will be discussed below in detail. Each group member was assigned a "buddy" from the group to remind and assist him/her in completing arrangements.

The second contract was broken down into more detail with reinforcements for each part. The contract stated that members should bring to the group the recreation department activity schedule showing they found the address and went to the Madison Public Schools' recreation department. The contract stated:

1. Find out where the recreation department is located in Madison and write this on a piece of paper.
2. Visit the recreation department this week (by Friday, October 11).
3. Get a schedule of their activities (orange folded sheet).
4. Bring this schedule to group next week on Tuesday, October 15, at 5:30.

Payment was then made for each part completed.

If an assignment was not completed, the client recontracted to do it the following week. If parts of an assignment were not completed, it was up to the individual if he/she wanted to contract only for those parts or add them on a contract with a new behavior assignment. Beginning with assignment 3, individuals drew up their own contracts. Contingencies became gradually higher as assignments became more difficult (i.e., receiving a 95-cent record for completing all of assignment 6 and if not, paying the leader $1.50). Every contract specified a 10-cent bonus for arrival to meetings on time, except for the last two (assignments 5 and 6).

Role playing was a vital part of the group meetings in preparation for behavior assignments to be carried out in the community. The second assignment involved going to the recreation department and asking for a schedule of activities. An observer and the leader modeled the procedure, then each member of the group went through it with the observer. There was some confusion at first when group members tried to use sign language and got no response. One young man insisted the observer knew signing so should answer him. It was apparent that several had some difficulty remembering what roles others were playing. Much of the role play had to be done in writing, as all but two of the group members had poor speech. Since assignments involved contacts with hearing people, practice in writing something that could be understood was just as important as rehearsing a speech.

In the fourth group meeting, role play was used for both the new assignment and evaluating the session. Members of the group paired up to do the planning. Several had difficulty understanding what to do so the leader drew up a list of choices. Cardboard signs were worn around the neck during role play to remind everyone of his/her part (for example, a sign stating "hearing person" or "deaf buddy"). The assignment involved finding out where all the YMCAs and YWCAs were located in Madison and marking the locations on a map. Members were also to get a schedule of activities from the Y nearest to where they lived. Choices for role play included:

1. Going up to the desk at the Y and asking for a schedule of activities.
2. Asking for a map of town at a gas station and directions to the nearest Y.
3. Getting help from a friend in learning how to read a map and locate where (in general) you are right now on the map.
4. Your buddy has not done his or her assignment and it is due tomorrow. How would you go about getting that person to do it?

This time, the leader and observer did not participate. The group had to role play all roles involved in their assignments.

Written evaluations were not effective with the group, so at the end of each meeting, the leader reviewed the agenda items and asked for their comments. In order to give the group ideas about responses (especially to encourage speaking out when they disliked something), a group member and the leader role played an evaluation session (member acting as leader) using the agenda.

Role playing was beneficial to the group and seemed to result in everyone understanding the assignments better and feeling more comfortable about actually doing the assignment. After use of role play for demonstrating response to an evaluation, all group members were able to give at least one response. Prior to this, only one group member responded during evaluation. The group also stated they enjoyed the meetings best when role play was used.

In summary, each session involved some discussion (as specified in each contract) of the week's assignment and individual reinforcement for all completions. This was paired with enthusiastic praise. Afterwards the leader filled in the group graph for all members to see. If assignments were not completed, the group members had to comply with the contingencies in their contracts. The group, and specifically the buddy, were then asked to help the member complete his/her contract the next week. It also involved writing and signing new contracts. Role playing all aspects of the behavior assignments in the new contract was also a necessary part of every meeting and finally every meeting was evaluated. Of course no meeting was complete without refreshments.

The group met in a comfortable lounge away from the unit. The lounge was small and well lighted, which is very important for a group that relies on sign language for communication. Attendance presented no problems and the group consistently stated during evaluation that they liked the group. The use of the buddy system, they also commented, aided in peer pressure for getting assignments completed.

Group Problems

Communication patterns with this particular group of deaf individuals presented unique problems. Only two members had any understandable speech, so sign language had to be used for all communication. Joyce (a model for the group) had good hearing with her aid on and good speech. Both young men had poor language skills and had difficulty understanding what was said. It was typical of group members to nod their head yes and say they understood when in reality they did not understand at all. Several explanations and receiving feedback helped alleviate this. Examples of typical responses (as with the evaluation) clearly show the problems in interpreting what is actually being said:

Leader: What do you think about this group?

Member 1: I don't know try like better learn any fast things.

Member 2: We would like done to work.

Intelligence was not a problem, but communication was. The question, "What do you think about this group?" was restated as: "Group here—good, bad, what?" (with a questioning look and shrug of the shoulders) and brought a response more in line with the question. Contracting and role play weren't understood until we stumbled through the actual process of contracting and role playing.

Distribution of participation was definitely affected by the communication problems. Repetition and reinterpretation for the leader by one group member of another member's signs made certain communication patterns unavoidable. Data was collected by an observer on leader-member interaction for a one-hour period of time, and some steps were taken to improve member participation. One method was to have everyone write down answers to a question. Responses often indicated they did not understand the question, and with difficulty we would try again.

Another effective method was to give tokens for both participation in role play and verbal responses to it. Regardless of the quality of a response, it was rewarded with tokens which could be turned in later for treats. It took all the treatment sessions to build up to this level of understanding. Increased member participation in leadership was the next goal.

All group members had difficulty giving any response (positive or negative) on the evaluations. On September 9 and 16, a one-question written evaluation was given and received only two responses. On September 23 and October 1, an agenda was used to encourage verbal responses with still very little response. On October 7 they role played making responses to the agenda (group member acting as leader). After this, every member made at least one response during evaluation at all remaining meetings.

On one occasion, John fell behind in assignments for two weeks in a row and was keeping the rest of the group from earning a free rollar skating trip. He was anxious about problems at work and wanted to leave the group. The group discussed this with him, explaining they wanted him to stay, as he had been doing well and maybe they could help. Two members worked with him over the next week in catching up on all assignments. This group assistance seemed to work, and the group earned its reward.

Although all members attended meetings, several (different ones at different times) arrived late (more than five minutes past the stated time of starting) to various meetings. On October 1, a bonus of 10 cents for arriving to the meeting on time was written into everyone's contract. This was done four times and all arrived on time, receiving 10 cents and a lot of praise. In subsequent meetings only praise was used, and all continued to arrive on time.

Transfer and Maintenance

One crucial problem that was dealt with for this group was transfer of change, which began as early as the very first meeting. At this time the leader explained to the group that most of the behavior assignments would be carried out in the community. The major purpose of the group was to prepare individuals for a transition from activities in the hospital to the community setting.

Several changes within the group meetings also helped facilitate transfer of change. The buddy system was not used by group members in completing their last two behavior assignments so they could practice doing it on their own. Praise replaced payment for coming to group on time, and poster signs were no longer used during role plays to cue members as to what they would say.

A posttreatment plan was developed. In January the group was to meet again to complete the goal of actual involvement in a community activity. When everyone was participating on an ongoing basis (attending their activity at least five times), then the group was to meet only once a month to discuss any difficulties. This follow-up would last until the end of May, when new schedules for summer programming would begin. The leader was to have carried out a follow-up interview with each individual through the summer to see if they were able to maintain involvement in a community activity on their own.

Prior to planning community involvement for clients away from the institutionalized setting, groundwork had to be laid with the community. Since the instructor at a YMCA program had never met a deaf individual, he may have found it difficult to include that person in a class—and thus the client would have been set up for failure. It was essential for the leader to work directly with a wide range of community people as well as the clients in selecting activities for them. This facilitated understanding, communication, and selection of the best possible situations for clients.

Individual Treatment Results

Sue—In two of the meetings (on September 23 and October 1), Sue did not complete the assignment that had been verbally given to the group. On October 1, contracting and role play began with pop, money, or tea bags as her reinforcement. Sue had 100 percent completion of all assignments until October 30, when she dropped to 25 percent. Two assignments over a two-week period had been contracted for that date (all other assignments were due after one week) and Sue stated it was too much to do at one time for her. No contracts were drawn up on October 30 (withdrawal) and assignments were given verbally and written down. On November 16, Sue had 0 percent completion. Contracts were once again used and Sue had 100 percent completion on November 12 and November 18. Sue tried to join a ceramics group at the local technical college, but had to wait for a new group to start in January.

Steve—Steve had 100 percent completion on all behavior assignments that were contracted and role played with the exception of October 30, when he dropped to 50 percent and during the no contract period on November 6, when he dropped to 0 percent. Pop or money were his main reinforcement. During this time, Steve was living at the YMCA and became active in their sports program.

Joyce—As stated previously, Joyce was the model for the group because of her communication skills and likelihood that she would encourage others to do their assignments. She was also helpful with some interpretation. She did state as a goal that she wanted to get involved in a ceramics group in town as opposed to something at school, since she would return to her old school in January. As stated earlier, Joyce had little involvement in school activities in the past. She had 100 percent completion of behavior assignments that were contracted and role played with the exception of October 30, when she dropped to 75 percent and during the no contract period on November 6, when she dropped to 66 percent. Pop, hot chocolate, or a 45-record were her main reinforcers. She was unable to join a ceramics group in town since they all were ending and did not start again until January. She did visit a group, however.

Dave—Dave attended all meetings in the beginning and had 100 percent completion on two different assignments contracted for. He then decided the meetings conflicted with other things so he dropped the group on October 16. One of the problems may have been that he lived in town and did not have the benefit of seeing his buddy daily.

John—John had 100 percent completion of all assignments contracted, with the exception of October 30, when he dropped to 0 percent and during withdrawal on November 6, when he dropped to 0 percent. Pop, cigarettes, and money were his main reinforcers. As explained under group problems, he did get discouraged when behind in assignment completions and wanted to drop the group. As stated in his contract, he had to pay money into the group treasury for noncompletion of task and was very upset about that. He did pay, but by November 6, when he saw he would have to pay again, he considered dropping out. The leader explained that it would be left up to the group to decide what to do. They felt he should not pay (it would be the "last straw" for him since he was having problems at work), and that he should draw up a new contract and they would help him complete it. That seemed to encourage him to remain.

In the beginning meetings, John had problems with eye contact and did not follow what was being said by others. Since everyone used sign language, by not looking at the speaker John was lost most of the time. Baseline data on September 9, 16, and 23 indicated he did not look at the speaker and missed what was said a total of 15 times in a one-hour period on September 9; 12 times on September 16; and 14 times in a one-hour period on September 23. This annoyed the group, as they always had to repeat things for him. At the September 23 meeting, the group confronted John with this and discussed ways to help. John complained that the room was too big. The group decided to change to a very small room with few distractions where everyone could easily see when someone was signing. After making this change, John's eye contact improved to the point where he failed to look at the speaker only once or twice in a meeting.

Group Results

On November 14, the group was given the same questionnaire as when the group first began to test their awareness of activities and facilities in Madison.

The test was set up for yes/no responses, but a yes was only counted if they were able to give the correct answer. For example: Do you know where the recreation department is in Madison and what hours it is open? If the answer was yes, then the person had to state where it was and the hours of operation. Yes (along with the correct answer) was the appropriate response to all questions. Originally, there were five individuals responding to the 20 questions, with an average correct response rate of 39 percent. Following treatment (with only four group members taking the questionnaire), an average of 90 percent correct response rate was obtained.

Results for the group indicated 0 percent completion of assignments prior to contracting and role play. When contracting began, there was a 100 percent completion rate on October 7 and October 15; a 37 percent completion rate on October 30; and a 14.2 percent completion rate during the no contract period. On November 12 and on November 18, when contracts were started again, there was a 100 percent completion rate of assignments by group members.

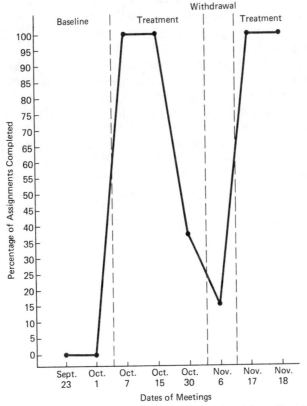

FIGURE 7-1 Percentage of Assignments Completed in a Transitional Activity Group for Four Deaf Clients

DISCUSSION AND RECOMMENDATIONS

The first meeting of the transition group required 40 minutes to explain and reach an understanding for four words: contract, assignment, agenda, and evaluation. The leader wondered then if the group would ever make it beyond this conceptual training. There was very little experience in or knowledge about group process. And yet, the program in part succeeded.

The project designed to increase community involvement was unique in leisure counseling. The clients had expressed a desire to be doing something in the community. This was especially critical to four of the group members who would probably experience employment difficulties throughout life. The leisure counseling entailed instruction in group decision making, social skills, and community resources. The ways of finding leisure pursuits were broken down into teachable components just like a recreation skill. The leader emphasized the activity aspects of leisure rather than the intrinsic values—the enjoyment, the state of mind commonly taught in leisure counseling. Individuals who required two hours of role play to *begin* to understand the difference between anger and being frustrated (or even that there is a difference) were not easily going to understand the state-of-mind aspect of leisure.

Members learned to role play, to communicate effectively with each other, to carry out assignments, to give each other feedback and to learn about the community. Actual participation in community activities was limited by the fact that most activities at the time clients were prepared to join (January) were filled or closed to new members.

In conclusion, group counseling with deaf clients involves time and patience. It involves a focus on specific behaviors taught in a step-by-step fashion rather than general concepts. It also requires community preparation if transfer of change is to be successful. Under these conditions, a group counseling program for the deaf may be an important approach in helping them to develop relevant social skills and find a place in the social and recreational pursuits of the hearing world.

AUDREY SISTLER and RAYMOND M. BERGER

8

the use of behavioral and group intervention in a nursing home discussion group for older men

INTRODUCTION

Although behavior modification procedures with a large variety of client populations have been reported in the literature for the past 25 years, until very recently
there have been few reports on the application of these procedures with the
elderly. The present authors found only three such reports prior to 1968 and
only eighteen reports between 1968 and 1976. These dealt almost exclusively
with the modification of simple operant behaviors such as unspecified verbalizations (Mueller and Atlas, 1972; Hoyer, Kafer, Simpson, and Hoyer, 1974), eating
(Geiger and Johnson, 1974; Baltes and Zerbe, 1976), and walking (MacDonald
and Butler, 1974). With a few exceptions these programs treated individuals
rather than groups.

    Mueller and Atlas (1972) successfully used cigarettes, candy, and token
reinforcement to increase appropriate interactions among members of a group
of five elderly men in a nursing home. Hoyer et al. (1974) increased appropriate
verbalizations among elderly male patients in two separate groups conducted
in an old-age ward of a state mental hospital. Linsk, Howe, and Pinkston (1975)
modified member behaviors in three ongoing group activities in a nursing home
for the elderly. They utilized stimulus prompting (i.e., leader question-asking

behavior) to increase a number of group social behaviors such as appropriate verbal behavior and attention to the group.

These reports represent a departure from traditional views of aging. Until recently it was assumed that social withdrawal behaviors of the elderly (e.g., reduced verbalizations, fewer interactions with others) were due to an irreversible biological process associated with aging. Lindsley (1964) first suggested the use of environmental manipulation to overcome behavioral deficits among the elderly. In recent years, social withdrawal behaviors of the elderly have been viewed as the result of environmental conditions rather than biological deterioration. For instance, a reduction in verbal interactions may be reinforced by nursing home staff because "quiet" patients are most easily managed. The implication of this view is that behavioral deficits which were once considered irreversible may readily be overcome by rearranging environmental contingencies. For example, staff may be taught to reinforce independent rather than dependent resident behaviors (Baltes and Zerbe, 1976). The purpose of the present report is to describe a behavioral group treatment program consistent with an environmental view of elderly behavior.

PURPOSE OF GROUP

Traditional social group work with the elderly has employed global and poorly defined treatment goals. (Klein, LeShan, and Furman, 1965; Euster, 1971; Mayadas and Hink, 1974). For instance, Saul and Saul (1974) define group goals as (1) motivation to live, (2) improvement of memory, (3) improvement of communication skills, (4) improvement of self-awareness, (5) improvement of social skills and social identity, (6) improvement of self-control, (7) development of a sense of comradery, and (8) development of a role and identify in the nursing home setting.

The goals of the present group were stated in such a way that they were amenable to verification by data collected during and after the group meetings. In addition they were meaningful indicators of social skills. They were formulated jointly by the coleaders and nursing home staff.

It should be noted that the first goal is a prerequisite for the second which in turn prepares the members to achieve the third goal. The goals were:

1. to increase the frequency of member-member interaction and decrease the frequency of leader-member interaction during group sessions;
2. to gradually increase the responsibility of group members in determining plans for the group;
3. to increase participation of group members in other nursing home activities.

ORGANIZATION OF GROUP

The coleaders contacted the activity director and the director of nurses at a large county nursing home located near Madison, Wisconsin. The coleaders indicated an interest in forming a behavioral treatment group directed to improving the social skills of residents. The staff directors indicated that a primary problem in the home was the social isolation and inactivity of residents. This problem was particularly acute on the second-floor wing of the home which housed approximately 20 elderly men who were isolated from nursing home recreational activities which all took place on the first floor. (The first floor was composed of six wings which all led to a common hallway area). Although daily recreational activities were open to second-floor residents, few attended. The nursing home staff were concerned about the social isolation of residents but had been unable to solve this problem because of lack of time. For second-floor residents the problem was exacerbated by the fact that no staff were permanently stationed on the second-floor wing. Therefore, it had not been possible for staff to encourage interaction among these residents. It was decided that a group program would be initiated in the day lounge of the second floor, as an activity directed at the particular needs of the second-floor residents.

A total of six men ranging in age from 63 to 91 years were selected by the activity director and the director of nurses on the basis of three criteria. The resident (1) seldom interacted with others, (2) rarely attended regularly scheduled nursing home activities, and (3) spent most of the time in his own room. However, the staff had not worked with social workers prior to this program and were not familiar with the process of identifying those residents who might need social skills training. Thus, in retrospect it appeared they may have omitted some residents who might have benefited from the group and instead chose some who already had adequate social skills.

Each of these residents was interviewed by one leader who requested his participation and provided him with a description of the purpose and procedures of the group (see Figure 8-1). The residents were told that the meetings would be enjoyable, that they would be attended by other residents who had interests similar to theirs, and that refreshments would be served. (These procedures were suggested by Goldstein, Heller, and Sechrest, 1966, pp. 73-145.) In addition, individual interests of group members and potential reinforcers were elicited in these interviews for use in the group.

Nurses' assessments were also used to acquire information on individual residents that would be used in the group. An inventory of resident behavior adapted from Williams (1973) was administered to several nurses in order to assess residents' mental alertness, agreeableness, level of social interaction, and general mood. The inventory also requested nurses to list activities and objects which might be employed as reinforcers in group treatment (see Figure 8-2).

FIGURE 8-1   Pretreatment Resident Interview Schedule

PURPOSE OF THE INTERVIEW

1. To learn as much as possible about the resident: activities, events, and objects which are reinforcing for him; his most frequent activities.
2. To increase the probability of his attending the group meetings.
3. To let him ask questions about the group: the reason for the group, why he was invited to join the group, etc.
4. To let him ask questions about the leader: what the leader enjoys doing, why the leader is conducting this group.

SOME QUESTIONS TO GUIDE THE DISCUSSION

1. What do you like to do?
2. How do you spend your time here?
3. If you did not live here, what would you do?
4. What do you dislike about living here? (Empathize)

ALSO, INCLUDE THE FOLLOWING INFORMATION

1. He will enjoy the group: a chance to talk to others.
2. Other members have similar interests.
3. Refreshments will be served.
4. You need him: the group is necessary in order for the leaders to satisfy a course requirement.
5. If he is reluctant, ask him to try the first meeting, and then decide whether to join.

FIGURE 8-2   Nurses' Inventory of Resident Behaviors*

I would like to know more about _____.

Please answer this questionnaire, giving me your opinion. Thank you!

MENTAL ALERTNESS

	Below Average	Average	Above Average
1. responsive to greetings and requests			
2. attends to things around him			
3. knows person, place, and date			
4. interested in current events			

5. Popularity with other patients
   ___ A. tends to be ignored or rejected by others
   ___ B. neither among the first or last to be chosen by others
   ___ C. is likeable or popular

6. Agreeableness
   ___ A. opposes ward routine
   ___ B. goes along with suggestions some of the time
   ___ C. is usually agreeable to suggestions

7. Relationships to others
   ___ A. is often in disagreement with others
   ___ B. occasionally disagrees with others
   ___ C. always gets along well with others

DEGREE OF SECURITY AND CALM

8. Anxiety level
   ___ A. is always very calm
   ___ B. has a moderate level of anxiety
   ___ C. continually nervous

INVOLVEMENT IN GROUP ACTIVITY

9. Activity participation
   ___ A. does not participate in activities
   ___ B. goes to activities sometimes
   ___ C. always attends activities

10. Social interaction
    ___ A. rarely talks to others
    ___ B. talks to others sometimes
    ___ C. very talkative

11. What are his major daily activities? (Talking, reading, TV, etc.)
    A.

    B.

12. What things does he like? (candy, books, magazines, records)
    A.

    B.

    C.

13. What is his general mood?
    ___ A. happy, content
    ___ B. sometimes happy, sometimes sad
    ___ C. grouchy
    ___ D. depressed, sad

14. Are there any physical difficulties?
    A.

    B.

*Adapted from Williams (1973).

All six residents agreed to join the group. One resident was unable to follow through on his agreement because of illness. The other five continued with the group until termination.

GROUP COMPOSITION

Group members ranged in age from 63 to 91 years. Their length of residence at the home ranged from two months to over five years. Three members were single, one widowed, and one divorced. Their occupations were farmer, accountant, salesman, and gardener. The men chosen for the group were rather varied in age, interests, and level of participation in recreational activities at the home.

GROUP MEASUREMENT PROCEDURES

Each group session was recorded on audio tape. At the first session the presence of the tape recorder was explained and members were told that the tapes would be used to inform the group about the nature and frequency of interactions. In addition, it was explained that the tapes would be kept strictly confidential, i.e., only the coleaders would listen to them. The members quickly adjusted to the presence of the tape recorder.

Following each session both coleaders listened independently to three 10-minute segments chosen at random. Each leader recorded the number of times each member spoke (an instance of speaking was terminated when another group member or leader spoke) and whether the interaction was directed at member(s) or leader(s). This task was relatively simple, since members almost always spoke one at a time.

Four variables were derived from these data:

1. The total frequency of leader-member interactions (i.e., the number of times a leader spoke to a member or vice versa).
2. The total frequency of member-member interactions (i.e., the number of times a member spoke to another member).
3. The rate of interaction for each member was computed by dividing the number of times a member spoke by the number of minutes observed.
4. The average range of interaction for the group was computed by dividing for each member the number of members spoken to at least once by the number of members present, and averaging across members.

In addition, the following outcome measures were computed

5. Promptness, an indirect measure of group attractiveness, was computed by recording the number of minutes early each member arrived

at the meeting room by the number of members present at each session.

6. Group attractiveness was computed by averaging for each session the members' responses to the following question on session evaluations: "How did you enjoy the meeting?" (1 = not at all to 5 = very much.)

7. Proportion of assignments completed was computed by dividing the number of members who had completed the assignment by the number of members in the group. Member self-report was used to determine assignment completion and partially completed assignments were not considered completed.

8. The number of recreational activities each member attended per month was recorded by the activity director. (The activity director regularly kept a record of all residents' attendance at recreational activities.)

9. Group responsibility was measured by the number of agenda items suggested entirely by the members.

INTERVENTION

A broad range of treatment procedures was employed to increase the frequency and quality of social interactions among group members and between members and other residents during the eight one-hour group sessions. The coleaders provided direct instruction for the members to address each other more often and to address the leaders less often. Each session was tape-recorded and data on frequency of member-member and member-leader interactions were obtained (see Figure 8-3). These data were fed back to the group at following sessions in order for members to evaluate their progress on this variable.

Direct instruction was augmented by the use of praise which was contingent on member-member interactions. Initially, each such interaction was followed by praise from one of the coleaders. After the level of member-member interaction increased, praise was provided intermittently.

The coleaders also rearranged stimulus conditions to facilitate interaction among group members. For part of each meeting the coleaders shuffled papers in the corner of the room away from the members or left the room entirely for 5 to 10 minutes. During this time the tape recorder continued to run, providing a continuous record of frequency of interactions.

After the initial three meetings a task-leader procedure was implemented. At each meeting one member was assigned to present a topic of interest to the group and then to serve as a discussion leader to the topic for about 20 minutes. Topics ranged from interpreting the stock market to cultivating roses. When necessary, leader modeling and member rehearsal were used to train the member in presentation and discussion behaviors.

A modified reversal design was employed to assess the effect of these interventions on the level of interaction in the group. The first three sessions served as baseline—i.e., leader praise was not contingent on member-member interaction, the leaders did not shuffle papers, and there were no task-leader exercises. At session four these interventions were instituted. They were withdrawn for session five and reinstituted for sessions six through eight (see Figure 8-3).

Modeling and behavioral rehearsal were used in other aspects of the program as well. At the first two meetings these procedures were used to train each member how to introduce himself to the group and how to direct statements to the group. Both coleaders and group members served as models for these behaviors.

Modeling and behavioral rehearsal were also employed between group sessions. Assignments involved approaching and interviewing another resident (not a group member) about that resident's hobbies and interests, inviting another resident to attend one group meeting, and passing a book among group members. It was hoped that these assignments would facilitate increased social interaction among group members and between members and other residents in the home. An additional assignment required members to record the frequency of interactions with other members between group sessions.

Shaping procedures were employed to get members to assume greater responsibility for planning group sessions. The first two meetings were planned entirely by the coleaders. At the third and fourth meeting the coleaders pro-

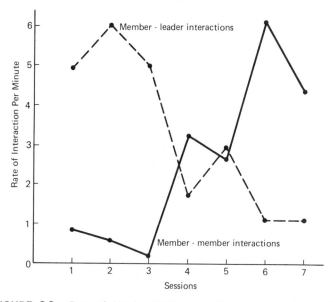

FIGURE 8-3   Rate of Member-Member and Member-Leader Interaction During Group Sessions (For All Members)

vided agenda items from which members selected those items to be included at the following meeting. The last four sessions were planned almost entirely by the group members themselves. Throughout the program members were encouraged to participate in decision making regarding the group. Members decided which presentation and discussion topics were chosen, and they negotiated assignments with the coleaders.

At the end of each session members completed a written evaluation of that session. These evaluations asked members to rate on a five-point scale how much they enjoyed the session and to make suggestions for improving the meetings. The results of the previous meeting's evaluation were summarized at the beginning of each session.

Summary of Group Meetings

Fifteen minutes before the first meeting, the leaders went to each member to remind him of the time. The men arrived very curious about the leaders and about the content of the group. They asked the leaders several questions and interacted very little among themselves.

When they were asked to learn about the person next to them and to introduce him to the group, they responded that everyone knew each other and that it was a silly idea. However, when the leaders questioned them further, they did not know names, only faces. The leaders modeled the introduction between each other, which consisted of two steps: (1) ask the other person what he likes to do; (2) report this to the group. The group was still reluctant, so they finally just asked each other's names, and introduced each other by name only. The rest of the session was spent discussing what topics could be talked about in the future meetings. Members were asked to attend every meeting if at all possible.

Members arrived early to the second meeting with no reminder from leaders, and chatted with the leaders. Since the leaders were not staff members, they agreed to keep topics of discussion confidential if the members requested. The members were pleased with this arrangement, and talked freely with the leaders.

An interesting discussion followed regarding their loneliness and isolation. Their reason for not interacting with other residents and staff was that they were afraid of offending someone. This would cause tension, which might be intolerable in the highly confined environment of the home. They postulated that living with several others 24 hours daily, one had to try to keep things running smoothly. They did not want a resident or staff member complaining about them.

One of the leaders was from Hong Kong, and at the third meeting she showed her slides of that area. The members had requested the slides, so they came very early, and commented afterwards that they would like to see more slide shows. During the meeting, all the members eagerly asked the leader several questions about the slides and about Hong Kong. Since they knew very little about the subject, they could not discuss it among themselves, so that most of the interaction that session was between the leader and members, not among members. As an assignment for the next session the members agreed to approach and carry on a conversation with another resident of the home who was not a group member.

The fourth meeting marked the beginning of the task-leader procedure. Mr. J., the oldest member, and a former gardener, talked about roses and how to care for them. He described the different varieties and the pros and cons of each. The other members were interested and asked questions quickly and smiled often during the discussion. Only two of the members had completed the assignment for this session. As a result, no assignment was given at the fourth session.

At the fifth meeting, the leaders explained that the assignments were given to encourage the members to talk to each other and other residents during the week. The members said they understood this, but that they did not want to be told what to do. After a short discussion, both the leaders and members agreed to negotiate assignments with the members. The assignment negotiated for the next session was to talk to someone outside of the group. At this meeting, the members talked about Madison and its landmarks. As old-timers, they enjoyed telling the leaders (who were new in Madison) what to see and do.

At the sixth meeting, Mr. K. led the discussion on a book he had read, and then the problems of living in a nursing home were discussed. The members stated that it was hard to keep hobbies of interest when they seldom visited outside the home. Since experiences at the home were rather limited, the members were not stimulated to think about hobbies or other interests. The leaders praised any hobbies that members were involved in. In addition the leaders suggested as their assignment that group members invite other residents to the next group meeting. It was hoped that this would encourage interaction between group members and other residents.

At the seventh meeting, Mr. W. completed his assignment successfully and brought Mr. L., another second-floor resident, to the meeting. Mr. L. led the discussion at this meeting. Patients' rights were also discussed, since at that time this topic was getting a lot of publicity in the news. Two of the members expressed a cynicism for continual rules and rights "put on" them by others, without any of their input, but the other members seemed hesitant to complain. The leaders encouraged them to speak up at the residents' council, a monthly meeting of resident representatives from each ward.

The eighth meeting consisted of the last task-leader discussions. Mr. B. talked about farming and how methods and machinery had improved, and Mr. H. discussed a book about wild animals. Then the group planned the slide show about China to be shown the following week for other residents. Each member agreed to invite at least one resident who was not a group member to the program. Finally, the leaders thanked the members for the enjoyable and worthwhile meetings, and presented the data from the sessions. The members expressed an interest for the group to continue, and all stated they had liked the sessions.

Group Problems

Two difficulties became apparent over the course of the group meetings. The first concerned the between-session assignments. Initially there was a great deal of member reluctance to perform the assignments. At the third session members were first asked to count the number of interactions with other group members during the week. At the fourth session two members had not completed this assignment and the other members forgot to bring their data to the meeting. For the eighth session, they were again asked to count the number of interactions with other group members. This time all members completed the assignment and brought their data to the meeting.

After the fourth session all assignments were negotiated with the group members. Allowing members to determine the nature of their assignments appeared to make the members more responsive to this task. After the fifth meeting assignment completion was 80 percent, 80 percent, and 100 percent (see Figure 8-4).

The second difficulty that developed in the group became apparent when two members stated after the first and third group sessions that they disliked

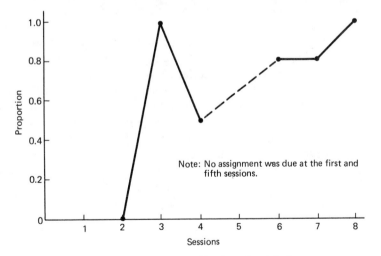

FIGURE 8-4   Proportion of Members Who Completed Assignments

Mr. H's "ramblings." Mr. H. did indeed have a very high level of verbal responses in the group. However, other members avoided interactions with Mr. H. and would often frown when he spoke. Prior to the fourth session coleaders spoke to Mr. H. outside of the group about this problem and at subsequent meetings he spoke less frequently. As a result the other members began to interact with him during the sessions and reported no further negative comments about him.

RESULTS OF INDIVIDUALS

Mr. B., and 80-year-old man, had lived in the home for two months, and was the newest resident among the group members. Although he talked little to the other members, he always came 10 to 15 minutes early to the meetings to talk to the leaders. He gradually began to interact with Mr. H. and mentioned to the leaders that he enjoyed talking to Mr. H. They often left the meetings together.

Mr. B. had been a farmer and appeared to lack the social skills which the other members had. He told the leaders he did not know what to say in his presentation to the group, so the leaders visited him in his room and modeled a way to give a talk, which he then rehearsed. In the group situation he gave his talk about farming the way he had rehearsed it, and all the members paid attention to him and asked questions. During this presentation, his rate of interaction jumped from .15 per minute to 1.8 per minute. If he had given his presentation at an earlier meeting, perhaps his subsequent rate of interaction would have been higher. It appears the modeling and behavioral rehearsal did aid in increasing his interaction and in lessening his self-reported anxiety. Mr. B's attendance at other nursing home activities increased from 4 in January to 15 in April.

Mr. J., the other less verbal member of the group, was a 91-year-old man who had lived in the home for a year and a half. He was a pleasant man, often smiling, but very hard of hearing. Consequently, he did not interact often because he could not hear the discussion. Members would have to ask him a question at least twice before he understood, which was not very reinforcing to them. Although the leaders discussed this problem with the group, most of the members did not think the extra effort was worth it, since Mr. J. forgot easily. Mr. J. interacted the most (.8 per minute) during his presentation on how to grow roses which the other members enjoyed.

His memory was very poor, and he could never remember the meeting from one week to the next. In fact, he never did learn to recognize the leaders, but would ask each week for their names. Because of his advanced age and poor memory, he did not really have much in common with the other members. He needed a more structured environment to aid his memory. The leaders did attempt to set up a schedule for him for each day, but he did not remember to look at it. Perhaps later the group members could have provided the needed structure for him, but in order to promote cohesiveness, common interests were stressed. Mr. J. was the only member who did not increase his attendance at other nursing home activities, probably because his poor memory hindered any generalization effects.

Just the opposite from Mr. J., Mr. K. was an outspoken, 64-year-old former alcoholic, who had lived at the home two-and-a-half years. He had a master's degree in accounting from the University of Wisconsin. He modeled several leadership behaviors which the leaders praised in front of the rest of the group, such as asking questions, giving suggestions, and praising others. He was quite alert and articulate and seemed capable of living in a less supervised environment.

The leaders praised any assertive interaction he mentioned having with the staff (asking for better living arrangements), and other independent activities (going to Madison alone). He became a member of a committee on patients' rights and a month after the last meeting he moved to an apartment in Madison. His plans were discussed periodically in the group, and the other members, especially Mr. W., reinforced his efforts. The group appeared to be an important factor in his decision to leave the home. He and Mr. W. did appear to become close friends throughout the meetings, talking more and more to each other. The leaders saw them together in their rooms prior to the last two meetings. Mr. K. increased his attendance at other nursing home activities from two in January to seven in April.

Mr. W., like Mr. K., was a former alcoholic, 62 years old, and a five-and-a-half-year resident of the home. Although he was quite articulate and intelligent, he did not have the social skills Mr. K. had. He interacted primarily with Mr. K. and did not pay much attention to other members. His presentation on the stock market was directed totally toward Mr. K. and was long and uninteresting to other members. He was the most persistent about not wanting assignments outside of the meetings, saying he did not like being told what to do. However, after the leaders negotiated a few assignments with the members, and allowed one week with no assignments, Mr. W. consented to doing them. In fact, he was the first member to invite another resident (Mr. L.) to the meeting. Furthermore, he spoke adamantly against other nursing home activities at the first meetings, but in April he attended nine activities as compared with none in February.

Mr. H., the 69-year-old roommate of Mr. J., had lived at the home for two years. He was very talkative during the first three meetings, interrupting the leaders, and often telling long stories, off-task. For instance, during his introduction at the first meeting he talked about a fire in a residence hall 10 years ago. After other members complained verbally and in the evaluations, the leaders talked to Mr. H. alone, and set up a contract that both he and the leaders talk less. He did not attend the next meeting, because he had a visitor, but at the following meeting he did not talk as much, which the leaders praised. Furthermore, his conversations were on-task. He did not rate the meetings as highly after the leaders requested that he talk less. He was late to one meeting but came early to the others and stayed late. He completed all of the assignments, but often would forget the time of the meeting. After he was reminded, he would come with his roommate, Mr. J. His monthly participation in other nursing home activities increased from 14 events in the month prior to the group to 21 in the month after termination.

DISCUSSION

Despite the brief duration of treatment (eight one-hour group sessions), members increased their level of interaction with other group members, their attendance at recreational activities outside of the group (see Figure 8-5), and their responsibility for planning group sessions. Both the group members and staff responded positively to the program. Elderly nursing home residents are often seen as suffering from irreversible biological deterioration which precludes positive behavior change. Planned activities for these residents are frequently confined to simple and repetitive tasks such as basket weaving or floral arrangement. The present program illustrates the feasibility of inducing complex behavioral changes in elderly patients through group treatment.

A number of procedural changes may be helpful in future applications of behavioral group training for the elderly. During the course of treatment,

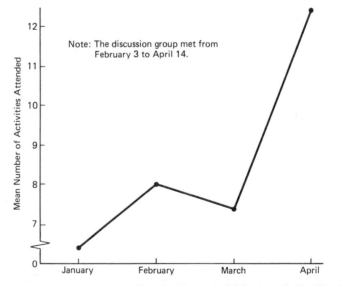

FIGURE 8-5   Mean Number of Nursing Home Activities Attended by Members

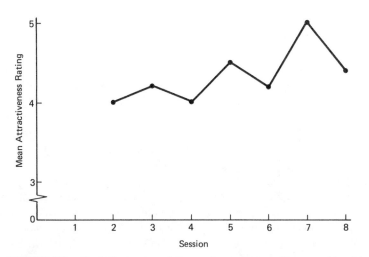

FIGURE 8-6 Mean Evaluation of Group Attractiveness. (Computed by Averaging for Each Session Members' Responses to the Following Question: "How Did You Enjoy The Meeting? 1 = Not At All to 5 = Very Much.")

it became apparent to the leaders that the group itself could serve as a potent resource (see Figure 8-6) as evidenced by the increase in satisfaction of group members over the course of the meetings. For example, in several instances the group helped an individual member to resolve a problematic situation. One of the functions of group treatment in the nursing home may be to encourage interaction among residents so that they may begin to draw upon the accumulated experience of their peers to solve individual problems. This may be best accomplished when group commitment and cohesiveness are high. Cohesiveness may be enhanced by planning common group tasks such as taking a short trip, planning and directing a nursing home activity, or engaging in cooperative activities. Commitment to the group may be enhanced by soliciting input from members in the planning of the group. This may include selection of members, selection of time and place of meetings, selection of agenda items, and treatment techniques.

Examination of the results of the present program suggests some ways in which program effectiveness could be increased. Although the frequency of interaction during sessions increased during the program, this was due largely to an increase in the frequency of statements addressed to one or two other members. Each member tended to become friendly with only one other member and directed most of his statements to that member. More attention needs to be paid to increasing the range as well as the frequency of interaction.

Despite the emphasis on role playing by both the leaders and members, the members reported discomfort in role playing, even during later sessions. Role playing (or rehearsal) has been shown to be an important therapeutic

215

component. Especially in the group context it provides a highly realistic "test run" and practice opportunity for new behaviors. However, in order for the use of role plays to be successful, associated anxiety must be diminished. Group members can only be expected to role play if it is reinforcing to them. In the present program more attention could have been paid to the gradual shaping and reinforcement of role play behavior itself. With repeated practice in a positive context, anxiety associated with role playing is likely to be desensitized.

Reinforcement is another crucial treatment component. In order to shape and maintain behavioral change, the group leaders must assist the residents in finding and programming reinforcement. Although group members were very responsive to verbal praise, it was felt that the use of additional reinforcers would be helpful in developing and maintaining new behaviors. In soliciting potential reinforcers from staff and members themselves, it became apparent that there was a very limited range of events and objects that were both reinforcing to these residents and readily available. As one member expressed it, "It's hard to get interested in anything because there is so little stimulation around here. Things are always the same." Since there are so few naturally occurring reinforcers it is incumbent on the group leader to provide new sources of reinforcement. These may take the form of refreshments, or specially planned events or activities. The leader must be careful, however, to ascertain the actual reinforcing value of potential reinforcing events. For instance in the present group, tokens (poker chips) were briefly introduced as reinforcers for increased group interaction. Although tokens have proved useful with other populations, the members in the present group objected to the use of the tokens, which were withdrawn.

Another important consideration in program effectiveness is transfer and maintenance of learning. This is related in part to patterns of reinforcement, since new behaviors learned in the group will not transfer to the resident's natural environment unless these behaviors are also reinforced in other settings. Staff can be very important in this regard. Ideally the leaders should share with staff the details of the behavior change programs of individual group members. For instance if a group member's goal is to decrease negative and increase positive self-statements, staff members may help in achieving this goal by ignoring the former and praising the latter types of statements. Consultation with staff may also help to avoid developing resident behaviors in the group which are likely to be punished between sessions. For instance if a member's goal is to become more "assertive," consultation with staff will help the leaders to determine which types of assertive statements will receive a positive response from staff and which ones will not. It may also be helpful to involve staff in other aspects of the program as well. Staff persons may be good resources for information that will help in the selection of group members, identification of problematic behaviors of group members, and identification of potential reinforcers. Staff should be consulted in the drafting of session agendas. Treatment techniques should be explained to staff and group progress and final results should be shared with them. All of these steps will ensure staff cooperation with the program. It should be kept in mind that staff time is generally very limited and it may be difficult to engage staff in substantial participation with the program. However, it is both feasible and perhaps essential to the success of a program that at very least, staff be informed of the program's progress on a regular basis.

Another technique which will enhance transfer of learning is to vary the setting of group meetings (Goldstein, Heller, and Sechrest, 1966, pp. 212-258). These settings should approximate "real life" settings (i.e., sessions could be conducted in the auditorium, day room, or individual members' rooms).

Behavioral group treatment with the elderly is an area in which systematic research is sorely needed. As a first step it is important to develop an empirical base for the content of treatment programs. In other words it is important to study this population systematically to determine what types of problematic situations occur frequently, what kinds of behaviors should be included in a training program to enable residents to resolve these situations, and what criteria should be used to judge the effectiveness or appropriateness of resident behaviors (Goldfried and D'Zurilla, 1969). In addition, assessment procedures are needed that are more inclusive and empirically based than the procedures employed in the present program. These may take the form of "real life" observations or simulated behavioral role play tests around situations determined to be problematic by the systematic study of this population.

REFERENCES

Baltes, M. M. and M. Zerbe. Independence training in nursing home residents. *The Gerontologist*, 1976, *16*(5), 428-32.

Euster, G. L. A system of groups in institutions for the aged. *Social Casework*, 1971, *52*(8), 523-29.

Geiger, O. G. and L. A. Johnson. Positive education for elderly persons. *The Gerontologist*, 1974, *14*(5), 432-36.

Goldfried, M. R. and T. J. D'Zurilla. A behavioral-analytic model for assessing competence. In C. D. Spielberger (ed.), *Current topics in clinical and community psychology*, vol. 1. New York: Academic Press, 1969.

Goldstein, A. P., K. Heller, and L. B. Sechrest. *Psychotherapy and the psychology of behavior change.* New York: John Wiley, 1966.

Hoyer, W. J., R. A. Kafer, S. C. Simpson, and F. W. Hoyer. Reinstatement of verbal behavior in elderly mental patients using operant procedures. *The Gerontologist*, 1974, *14*(2), 149-52.

Klein, W. H., E. J. LeShan, and S. S. Furman. *Promoting mental health of older people through group methods: A practical guide.* New York: The Manhattan Society for Mental Health, Inc., 1965.

Lindsley, O. R. Geriatric behavioral prosthetics. In R. Kastenbaum (ed.), *New thoughts on old age.* New York: Springer, 1964.

Linsk, N., M. W. Howe, and E. M. Pinkston. Behavioral group work in a home for the aged. *Social Work*, 1975, *20*(6), 454-63.

MacDonald, M. L. and A. K. Butler. Reversal of helplessness: Producing walking behavior in nursing home wheelchair residents using behavior modification procedures. *Journal of Gerontology*, 1974, *29*(1), 97-101.

Mayadas, N. S. and D. Hink. Group work with the aging. *The Gerontologist*, 1974, *14*(5), 440-45.

Mueller, D. J. and L. Atlas. Resocialization of regressed elderly residents: A behavioral management approach. *Journal of Gerontology*, 1972, *27*(3), 390-92.

Saul, S. R. and S. Saul. Group psychotherapy in a proprietary nursing home. *The Gerontologist*, 1974, *14*(5), 446-50.

Williams, J. R. Preliminary studies aimed at increasing the reliability of a behavior rating scale for use with geriatric and infirm patients. *Journal of Gerontology*, 1973, *28*(4), 510-15.

STANLEY L. WITKIN and JAY J. CAYNER

9

communication and problem solving skills training for couples: a case study

This chapter describes the communication skills workshop (CSW), a group train-ing program for couples wishing to improve their communication and problem-solving skills. Development of the CSW began in 1974 at the University of Wisconsin-Madison, as part of the Interpersonal Skills Training and Research Project, and has been conducted with approximately 75 couples. Since concep-tual and empirical information on the workshop has been reported elsewhere (Witkin, 1976, 1977; Witkin and Rose, 1976, 1977), the present focus is on the operational aspects of the program. Specifically, our objective is to describe the training procedures used in the CSW and provide actual workshop examples to illustrate their application.

OVERVIEW OF SKILLS TAUGHT

Communication skills are related to three interrelated concepts: accuracy, open-ness, and quality. Skills related to accuracy are those which improve consistency between the intent of a person attempting to express a message and the interpretation of the person perceiving that message. Probably the most important skills in this area are specificity skills, such as learning to express messages in observable and operational terms.

Communication openness reflects the notion that messages can have multiple interpretations. Feedback is the principal skill that expresses this concept. As used in the CSW, feedback consists of messages which explicitly express a person's interpretation of another's message, the effects of another's message upon the interpreter, or an evaluation of a message. For example, the statement, "I felt embarrassed when you joked about my accident" would be a feedback message. The extent to which feedback is used to improve mutual understanding and facilitate productive change is the measure of a couple's communication openness.

The cognitive, behavioral, and affective effects of message exchanges illustrate communication quality. Quality is influenced by two sets of skills: those which increase positive messages and those which decrease negative messages. In this context, positive and negative messages refer to the interpretation of messages as putdowns, attacks, and the like, versus pleasing, constructive or, at least, neutral interpretations. Thus, quality can be determined on a continuum on which spouses evaluate messages from pleasing to displeasing.

As we mentioned earlier, the skills necessary to achieve accuracy, openness, and quality of communication are interrelated. For instance, feedback will be most effective if it is expressed in specific terms and in a positive manner, and, thus, does not evoke the perception of attack in the interpreter. Similarly, communication quality can only be improved if partners provide each other with feedback on their interpretations and the effects of each other's messages.

These groups of skills provide the backbone of the communication skills taught in the first half of the CSW. Their application to relationship problems is the focus of the second half of the workshop.

METHOD OF INSTRUCTION

Groups of three to five couples meet weekly for six two-hour sessions. Currently, participation is open to couples seeking an educational or enhancement type of experience. The program is not oriented toward those couples experiencing severe relationship distress or seeking marital therapy. Since groups are conducted with an educational orientation, they do not emphasize the disclosure or resolution of highly personal or distressing problems. Rather, the atmosphere of the group tends to resemble a small, highly cohesive seminar in which couples attempt to gain useful knowledge and skills.

Each group is led by female and male coinstructors. Basically, the instructors facilitate group process, provide didactic information, model group procedures and various applications of skills, and provide corrective and positive feedback to the participants. The instructors also perform important administrative functions such as monitoring completion of homework assignments and returning of deposits.

Following instruction and modeling, group members practice implementing the skills. Group exercises are provided to facilitate learning by emphasizing specific skills. The content of the exercises is varied to permit couples to gain practice using these skills with both standardized workshop material and experiences from their own relationships. Feedback from other group members is frequently elicited. As members increase their knowledge and ability to use communication skills, additional comments are proportionately encouraged.

A crucial aspect of the CSW is the homework assignments given at the end of each session. These assignments provide review exercises of recently learned material. More important, however, they encourage the couple to utilize their new skills in their actual day-to-day interactions. These assignments help make the workshop material more meaningful to the couple and increase the likelihood of transfer and maintenance of learning.

To increase assignment completions, three procedures are implemented. First, the last five minutes of each session are devoted to a review of all assignments. This includes short demonstrations by the couples as well as the leaders. Second, each couple is contacted by telephone within two days following a session. This contact has proven extremely important as it allows for early reclarification of misunderstood assignments, encourages at-home practice while the material is relatively "fresh," and reinforces (through instructor and peer praise) couples who have begun their assignments. Couples who have not started their assignments are called again in two days. The third procedure used to increase assignment completions is the monitoring of completed assignments at the subsequent group session. This is accomplished in two ways: through recording sheets provided to the couples at the previous session, and by ingroup demonstrations of the assignments by the couples. These demonstrations also provide opportunity for feedback from the instructors and other members. Each session begins with these demonstrations and thus serves as a review prior to the learning of new skills. The remainder of this chapter is concerned with the elaboration of these various aspects of the CSW and an illustrative case example.

CSW SUMMARY

The first workshop session serves as a general introduction to the CSW and an introduction to the concept of effective communication as applied to couples. Skill training focuses on prerequisite behaviors for effective communication beginning with attending procedures. Session two continues with preliminary concepts focusing on increasing message clarity and accurate interpretations. The latter half of the session is devoted to methods for developing and increasing positive communication. Session three continues with the theme of increasing positive messages and methods of decreasing negative messages are introduced and practiced. Also, in this session, couples are familiarized with the importance of nonverbal communication. Session four marks the beginning of the application of skills and concepts learned in the first three sessions to areas of decision making and conflict. To this end, negotiation and problem solving training are introduced to the group. Session five continues with the negotiation process with additional training in contracting procedures. Session six provides couples with additional practice of their skills in more difficult situations. Intrapersonal communication is emphasized and procedures for improvement practiced. Selected topics such as communication avoidance of certain subjects are discussed and dealt with. Finally, procedures for maintaining skills over time are taught and practiced. To enhance understanding of the workshop, a detailed case example will be presented.[1] This example will emphasize the concepts and procedures presented to the couples as well as problems which arose during group meetings. For clarity, the program will be described session by session. Prior to this description, however, background information on the five couples who participated in the workshop will be presented.

Group Composition

Group members were recruited by means of newspaper advertisements, posters distributed throughout the city, and letters sent to randomly selected married couples. (See Edleson, Witkin, and Rose, 1979, for a more detailed description of recruitment procedures.) Table 9-1 summarizes member characteristics.

As shown in this table, the group members were heterogeneous with respect to age (range 21 to 68), number of children (range 0 to 4), length of marriage (range .5 to 40 years), and occupation. Educationally, all members had at least three years of college and three had graduate school experience.

All persons who indicated interest in the workshop were invited to attend a pretraining assessment session. At this meeting each couple participated in a structured interview during which the program was described and questions answered. If, following this interview, the couple still wished to participate, they were asked to separately complete a short marital adjustment questionnaire (Locke and Wallace, 1959). Couples with mean scores of 80 or above on the Marital Adjustment Questionnaire (MAQ) were allowed to participate. This liberal criterion (100 is the traditional cut-off score between distressed and non-distressed couples on the MAQ) allowed all but severely distressed couples to participate in the program. Once participants were selected on the above criteria

---

[1] This example is drawn from a larger study previously reported (Witkin, 1977).

TABLE 9-1 Demographic Data of Five Couples

COUPLE	AGE	SEX	YEARS MARRIED	PREVIOUS MARRIAGE	NO. OF CHILDREN	EDUCATION	OCCUPATION	PREVIOUS THERAPY
Sandy	25	F	2.5	—	1	16	housewife	no
Richie	32	M		1		16	sales	yes
Patty	40	F	14	—	4	15	nurse	no
Jack	42	M		—		15	sales	no
Mary	22	F	.5	—	0	16	med. tech.	no
Frank	21	M		—		16	student	no
Robin	65	F	40	—	3	19	housewife	no
Tom	68	M		—		18	lawyer	no
Ann	27	F	7	—	1	15	sales	no
Bob	27	M		—		22	student	no
Mean	36.9		12.8		1.8	16.8		

the workshop began. The following is a session-by-session description of the training workshop.

Session One

Couples were introduced to the concepts of accuracy, openness, and quality that constitute effective couple communication. With these in mind, attending skills were introduced as prerequisite to effective communication. Procedures were taught to elicit and maintain attention ranging from common everyday types of behavior, e.g., eye contact, to a more highly structured technique requiring prior planning. The main procedures were as follows:

Asking for a response.   By requiring a response from the intended message recipient, the probability of his/her attention is increased (Hartman, 1963). Phrasing messages in a manner requiring responses (e.g., using questions) was discussed and practiced by the couples.

The following demonstration by the leaders illustrates the use of the technique.

Model I (no response required)

Leader A:	There was another bank robbery on the east side today.
Leader B:	(reading the newspaper, raises eyebrows and grunts)
Leader A:	It seems like there have been a lot of bank robberies lately.
Leader B:	(silence)
Leader A:	Maybe we should withdraw our account and leave our savings in the mattress.
Leader B:	What!?

Model II (response required)

Leader A:	Sue, did you hear about that bank robbery on the east side today?
Leader B:	Yeah.
Leader A:	It seems like there have been a lot of robberies recently. What do you think is the cause?
Leader B:	I'm not sure, maybe it's because the one last month appeared successful.
Leader A:	That's interesting. Perhaps we should withdraw our money and keep our savings in our mattress. What do you think?
Leader B:	Not unless the mattress begins paying interest. Actually I'm not worried.

Paraphrasing.   Restating a message in one's own words is a useful attending behavior, especially for important topics. Couples were each given a few minutes to relate experiences which occurred to them during the day. Their partner then practiced paraphrasing after the speaker indicated the expression of a complete thought. Feedback by the original speaker completed this exercise. Partners then switched roles so each obtained practice in this skill.

Paraphrasing in important topics is illustrated by this example:

Tom:	Robin, I have something important I want to discuss with you. Today, I was reviewing our money situation for the month. I think we have been careless about the way we've been budgeting. I'm not sure how we will make the car payments this month.
Robin:	You feel like we were lax this month in our budgeting practices. You're quite concerned that we will not be able to make car payments this time and you want to talk about this.
Tom:	That's right.

Message exchange.[2]   This was presented as a method of structuring a "communication only" time period. This procedure involves a prearranged time interval (e.g., 7:00 to 7:30) which is devoted to discussion of a particular topic without outside distractions. Emotionally charged issues, conflicts, and topics requiring lengthy discussion are particularly well-suited for this procedure. The message exchange is used in the session assignments as a way of devoting a specified amount of time to skill practice.

The following description and example demonstrate the use of the message exchange:

Ann:	We used the message exchange three times last week. Two times, we discussed general issues, the day, children, work, etc. The other time, we discussed some of the techniques of communication skills we learned here. For this one, we set it up formally. Almost like a date. We had an agenda with three items on it. We specified a time, the length of discussion, turned off the TV and sat at a table facing each other.
Bob:	It was very successful, efficient. We got a lot accomplished.
Leader A:	Can you show us a part by role playing your talk time?
Ann:	Sure. I really enjoyed the group. I think it will be interesting. Everybody seemed as uneasy at first as I did. There are completely different people in the group. This will make things interesting.

---

[2] This procedure is similar to Stuart's (1974) "talk times," and to "administrative time" used by Weiss, Hops, and Patterson (1973).

Bob:	How do you mean different?
Ann:	Different ages, different backgrounds. Some people have been married a long time, some only a couple of months, some have kids. Tom and Robin have been married 40 years, they're so full of life.
Bob:	Well, I agree, but what do you think about the group itself, the program. It made sense to me that for the first part of the workshop we will practice skills and in the last part learn to apply the skills to everyday situations.
Ann:	I also like the idea of learning and trying new things.

Session Two

Discussion of ambiguous messages and their role in misunderstandings occurred in this session. Methods of rendering vague messages more specific were modeled and couples were given practice in changing general statements to specific ones ("Stop being so lazy" becomes "I'd like you to mow the lawn"). Paraphrasing and questioning were then reintroduced and briefly practiced from the perspective of clarifying messages.

The following dialogue from the group illustrates this process:

Leader A:	I think our relationship would be a lot better if you'd appreciate me more.
Leader B:	How can you say that? I do appreciate you!
Leader A:	No you don't!
Leader B:	Yes I do!
Tom:	(laughing) I've heard that before. (group laughing)
Leader B:	Well (pause), what did you notice about this interaction?
Robin:	It sounded like the start of an argument.
Leader B:	Yes, anything else?
Jack:	I don't think the couple realized what they were arguing about.
Leader B:	Good, what could this couple have done differently?
Sandy:	I found this frustrating, I was getting mad, I wanted to ask the couple what it was that they meant by "being appreciated." To me it could have meant helping with dinner when the baby is crying. To Richie it could mean commenting on how helpful he is, or how well he fixed something.
Leader B:	These are very good observations. The point of this demonstration was to illustrate just that. To show how lack of specificity and ambiguity can contribute to unpleasant interactions and even arguments. What are some ways that we show appreciation? Sandy has already given some good examples.

Richie: Holding hands, taking time to talk, smiles, thank yous.

Robin: Doing favors, doing things together, like walks or rides.

Jack: Surprising your wife, flowers, you know, out to dinner.

Leader B: These are excellent examples. Okay, so what might be a better way of phrasing that first statement (Leader A's first statement)?

Sandy: I really like it when you help with the dinner, or it's nice when you do the dishes on days that I cook the meals.

Robin: (laughing) After a rough day, talking and rubbing my back helps me to relax, unwind.

Leader A: Very good. In your revisions of the statement you hit on an important aspect of being more specific. All of your examples and improvements describe *observable* behaviors.

There is a strong relationship between talking about behaviors and specificity. Actually, I think it would be difficult to describe an observable behavior and not have it be specific.

Up to this point we have been focusing on what the sender of a message can do to make a communication more specific. Now let's look at what the interpreter can do to help.

Paraphrasing and questioning are just two examples of what the receiver or interpreter of a message can do to make it more specific or to clarify. We would like to give you a little example:

Leader A: We never seem to do anything special anymore.

Leader B: What were some of the special things we used to do?

Leader A: Oh, you know, like a drive out in the country, time to talk, just you and me.

Leader B: Like things we did when we first met?

Leader A: Right, that was really a lot of fun. I've been thinking about how pretty the countryside is, especially since it will soon be too cold to go out much.

Leader B: We should take advantage of the good weather and spend some time together in the country like we used to.

Leader A: I think it would be fun.

Leader B: Me too. How about if we go this weekend?

Leader A: (to group) How did Leader B help clarify my messages?

Robin: She wouldn't let you be vague, she asked *what* the "special things" were.

Richie: She paraphrased, I think, your entire thought, what you liked, the good weather, the country, time together.

Patty: Even specified a time, this coming weekend. Maybe it could be better if she suggested Saturday afternoon at 2 o'clock!

Leader A: Excellent, you seem to understand the notion of specificity. In addition to paraphrasing and questioning, you can help your partner become more specific by asking for examples, illustrations, or analogies. Now we are going to give each of you a chance to practice using some of these specificity skills. (Index cards with one unspecified message printed on each card were passed to each group member.)

Leader B: On each card is an expression or message which can be further specified. We'll give you about 15 seconds to convert the statement into a specific one and then we'll see if your partner and the rest of the group can understand it. Let's go around the room clockwise. (On the left, Couple 1, Sandy and Richie; Couple 2, Jack and Patty; Couple 3, Frank and Mary; Couple 4, Tom and Robin; Couple 5, Ann and Bob.)

Richie: (*Doing things together is fun.*) I enjoy going with you for walks, out to dinner, to a movie or play, or just knocking around the house, just the two of us.

Sandy: You enjoy my company?

Richie: Yes, especially when the two of us are alone.

Patty: (*I need help around the house.*) I would like it if every other day you would take out the garbage and on the weekend help with shopping or cleaning the kitchen or watching the children so I can run errands.

Jack: Sounds like my work schedule at home for the next week; you'd like me to do those things to help out around the house.

Patty: Yes.

Frank: (*I like it when you compliment me.*) It makes me feel good, close to you, and appreciated when you note some of the things I do, like fixing the car, or working on a paper; like when you thank me for taking out the newspapers or starting a fire (in the fireplace).

Mary: You like to be appreciated and having compliments.

Frank: That's it.

Ann: (*You make me feel good.*) I like it when you smile, hold my hand, suggest doing things together, when you joke, when you do things for me, these all make me feel close to you.

Bob: I'm not sure, you like things that I do for you?

Ann: Yes, you make me feel good with these things.

Leader B: Good, Bob.

Leader B: Okay, you all did very well with this exercise. Without exception you described specific desires or events in observable terms. In addition, after receiving the specified message, you all chose to check out the message by paraphrasing your partner's statement. By making statements which are observable, using examples, most of you sort of cataloged your examples; by paraphrasing and questioning for further clarification, you can eliminate a great deal of misunderstanding and potential conflict.

Following the above exercise, couples were taught a special case of specificity called operationalizing (see Weiss, Hops, and Patterson, 1973). Operationalizing is used to specify an expectation. For example, "I'd like you to change your attitude" is put into operation as "I would like you to smile more often when playing with the children." The aim of this procedure was to describe exactly *how* an expectation can be met. Specificity, in contrast, often is confined to *what* is intended in a message, not necessarily how something is to be done. Once the message was operationalized, the initial message sender evaluated his/her partner's response.

A role reversal procedure was taught as a message clarification technique, especially with emotionally tinged, unclear messages. The basic sequence followed was: (1) an individual described some situation and attendant emotions; (2) message recipient took the first person's role and "replayed" original message as he/she perceived it; (3) original message source provided feedback on the interpretation. Couples were encouraged to actually try to "be" the other person when switching roles. Accordingly, they were instructed to speak in the first person and utilize perceived nonverbal cues.

This technique is illustrated as follows:

Jack: (upon returning home from a party) You seem upset about something. Didn't you enjoy the party?

Patty: (loudly) I'm sick of parties! That Bill S. really turns me off. He has an opinion on everything, especially at parties. His wife is such a nice person, I can't see what she sees in him.

Jack: Wow, I hear a lot of messages and strong feelings in what you're saying. How about if we do a role reversal to see if I am understanding what you're saying? I'll play you and relate to you what I heard.

Patty: Okay.

Jack: Parties could be a lot of fun if some people wouldn't act so dumb. Bill really made me feel angry with the things he was saying to me. I feel especially bad because I like his wife and was hoping to get to know her better.

Patty: That was close. In addition, I was really looking forward to the party and was quite surprised with Bill's behavior. It was a let-down.

The focus of the workshop shifted slightly at this point toward analyzing negative communication patterns, decreasing their occurrence, and increasing positive interactions. A "coercive" interaction (Patterson and Hops, 1972) was modeled by the leaders and its various features (demand for immediate change, mutual reinforcement of aversive behaviors) and consequences (likelihood of negative change efforts being repeated, original issue unresolved) were pointed out. A second interaction, based on positive message exchanges, was again modeled and the procedures followed above repeated.

The group leaders modeled a coercive interaction (taken from Patterson and Hops, 1972):

Leader B: You still haven't fixed the screen door.

Leader A: (no observable response)

Leader B: (raises voice) A lot of thanks I get for all I do. You said three weeks ago . . .

Leader A: Damn it, stop nagging me. As soon as I walk in here and try to read the paper, I get yelling and bitching.

Leader B: (shouting) You're so damn lazy, that's all I can do to get things done.

Leader A: All right, all right, I'll fix it later. Now leave me alone.

The same message was then modeled using positive messages.

Leader B: Honey, I know you have been busy, but I was wondering if you will be able to fix the screen door.

Leader A: Oh, yeah, I've been awful busy. I'll get to it soon. I'd like to just sit down and relax a little.

Leader B: Sounds good. How about after supper?

Leader A: Okay.

Leader B: Thanks, you are very helpful.

As a method of closing this session and increasing participants' repertoire and use of positive messages, members were asked to list on cards all those ways in which their partner communicates that makes them feel good, loved, etc. Categories of positive messages (appreciation, understanding, compliments, positive feelings) were given to assist couples in formulating these "pleasure lists." In order to increase use of these messages, it was requested that these lists be placed in a prominent place in the home (e.g., refrigerator) and added to periodically.

Session Three

This session began with a role reversal exercise aimed at modifying aversive communication patterns. In this exercise, group members identified communication patterns which they found unpleasant. The focus was on *how* particular types of messages are expressed, rather than the "legitimacy" of the message.

For example, the "condescending" manner in which one spouse told the other to leave him/her alone might have been an appropriate topic for this exercise. The *right* to spend time alone was assumed to be an issue the couple agreed on. If not, they would attempt to resolve their differences using problem-solving procedures. Following message identification, the couples used role reversal to illustrate this pattern to their partner. After some feedback, the role was replayed. This time, however, the offended partner demonstrated how he/she would have *liked* his/her partner to communicate in the same type of situation. If the partner positively evaluated this new method of communicating, he/she then rehearsed it with the partner.

This method of decreasing unpleasant message exchanges between partners is illustrated by the following:

Leader A: On the cards we've just passed around we would like you to write as specifically as you can how your partner communicates either verbally or nonverbally that makes you feel unloved or not good. It could be a particular phrase or a non-verbal expression. It could be very situational. Write it in enough detail to remind you of how your partner acts. Any questions? Okay, good. We'd like to use this information to do a role reversal exercise. Using the situation that you have described on your card, we'd like you to follow the steps written on the board.

On chalk board:

1. role play partner's aversive message (demonstrate to partner the message you have identified).
2. give opportunity for partner feedback.
3. role play more desirable way of expressing same message (demonstrate desired method to partner).
4. allow partner to respond, ask for feedback.
5. have partner practice modified message.
6. provide feedback for partner's performance of modified message.

Leader A: (after a short discussion regarding above points) Before asking you to try this technique, we will give a brief demonstration of how the role reversal might work. Suppose that my coleader has a way of correcting my mistakes that makes me feel pretty lousy. I might say: Listen, Sue, I realize that when you correct my mistakes your intention is to help me improve as a group leader; however, the way it comes across leaves me feeling kind of bad and more nervous. I'd like to show you how I'm seeing it so we can work it out in a more positive way, then I won't be so nervous, and will probably make fewer mistakes.

Leader B: Okay.

Leader A: (role playing coleader) You really screwed up that last exercise (sounding critical with disapproving facial expression).

Leader B: Do I really come across that critical to you?

Leader A: Yes, and it makes me pretty nervous the next time I have to speak. How about if you expressed your message like this: "You appeared to be struggling with that last exercise;" or alternatively, "Did that last exercise cause you some difficulty?"

Leader B: That's the idea I wanted to communicate. Would that be better for you?

Leader A: Yes, how about trying it out?

Leader B: All right. Leader A, there was one spot in that last exercise that seemed difficult for you; would you like to practice it?

Leader A: Great! That was a lot less threatening.

At this point, questions were answered by the leaders and the couples were encouraged to practice the procedure.

Leader A: Okay, who would like to try this role reversal?

Jack: This frequently occurs when Patty is riding with me while I'm driving, especially in traffic. (Jack, role playing Patty:) Jack!! (on the verge of screaming) Don't drive like that, when you get so close, my heart almost stops! Slow down.

Patty: I sound like that?

Jack: Yes. It scares me, sometimes I almost slam on the brakes.

Patty: But I'm concerned, it bothers me when you get too close.

Jack: I know, tailgating is dangerous, usually I don't know that I'm doing it. I'm just moving with traffic. You know when you say something I always back off. For me it would be better if you would say it but calmer, something like: (in calmer voice) "Hey, Jack, you're getting a little too close," or, "Back off a little, honey."

Patty: Okay, I could try it that way. How about, Jack, you're a bit too close. Could you back off a little?

Jack: That's great, just call it to my attention.

Patty: I'll do it but I'm not sure it will work.

Jack: Sure it will, I don't drive closely to scare you on purpose, it happens as we are moving in traffic, I don't do it on purpose! If you just remind me, it will work better for both of us.

Even with all the previous emphasis on positive messages, couples will still occasionally use negative messages in their interactions. The following procedures were designed to teach responses to negative messages which would decrease the probability of a reciprocal negative exchange sequence.

What, how, why.   Couples were then taught to view requests or demands for change from a "what" (specificity) and "how" (operationalizing) perspective, rather than from a "why" point of view. Various problems leading from an insistence on knowing why a behavior occurred were explained and illustrated. Problems associated with why type questions were illustrated by this leader-modeled role play:

Leader A:	Answers, the right answers to "why" questions are often unknowable. For example, Leader B, why do you feel so bad?
Leader B:	My parents moved frequently and I didn't get to meet people. It could also be that I have been insecure for a long time.
Leader A:	Why do you feel like that?
Leader B:	Because my father was a plumber.
Leader A:	Why so resentful?
Leader B:	I was weaned too early.
Leader A:	In this example, the why questions received answers that were untestable, as a result unknowable. One answer could fit all questions. All answers were equally plausible. Another problem with why questions is that they imply guilt. Notice that when I asked Sue why she felt resentful, I implied that I actually knew she felt resentful. Our point is that when the answer to why is untestable or unknowable, it will probably be more beneficial to ask what and how.

What and how questions were then role played by group leaders:

Leader A:	Why do you feel so bad?
Leader B:	What am I doing that gives you the impression that I am feeling bad?
Leader A:	You're not talking as much as you usually do.
Leader B:	I guess I'm still preoccupied by the day's events.
Leader A:	How can I get your mind on other things?
Leader B:	Let's try a little walk together.

Responding to content.   In some instances, aversive interchanges can be avoided by responding only to the content of a message. For example, when negative feelings are ambiguously expressed, responding to the message content might avoid lighting the match to a potentially explosive situation. Another situation often appropriate for this procedure is when a spouse's negative feelings are a consequence of a nonrelationship-related incident, e.g., stubbing one's toe. Once again, responding to unpleasant expletives (e.g., "Where are my damn shoes!") by focusing on the content ("Here they are.") may provide the time necessary for these short-lived feelings to pass. Role playing exercises such as the following are given for couples to practice this procedure. A successful example of responding to content is illustrated by this interaction:

> *Mary:*   (sternly, loudly) Are you going to spend the entire damn evening working?
>
> *Frank:*   No, I'll be done in a half-hour or less.

Selective communication.   Stuart (1974) suggests partners ask themselves three questions before disclosing potentially unpleasant information to their partners: Is it true? Is it timely? Is it constructive? These three criteria are further broken down into specific message problems associated with each question. For example, descriptions which use always and never classifications or labels are rarely true. Couples were given practice in recognizing these communication problems by observing each other's interactions. Supervised discussions provided opportunities for communication without these pitfalls, and subsequent reinforcement from the leaders and group.

Being an optimist and using constructive feedback.   The objective of these procedures was to improve communication quality by having couples adopt a more optimistic orientation. This position was operationalized by increased expression of desired activities, changes, etc. and by utilizing feedback which suggested positive alternatives to an undesirable situation. Frequently, communication problems arise when couples consistently phrase their change requests in terms of what a spouse should not do, e.g., "Don't mess up the house with your dirty clothes!" Although "cease and desist" messages may be necessary at various times, they can often be developed into positive interactions. For example, the above statement when rephrased illustrates these techniques: "You help a lot when you pick up around the house," or "It works much better for me when you put your clothes in the hamper, thanks." As with other techniques, both ingroup rehearsal and at home practice was utilized.

Nonverbal messages.   Couples were introduced to the concept of nonverbal messages and the role they play in message interpretation. A "freeze technique" (having couples "freeze" in the middle of a conversation) was utilized to increase awareness of the relationship of nonverbal factors (e.g., body posture, facial expression, distance) to the spoken messages. This theme was elaborated by having couples continue their conversations with instructions to deliberately attempt to use nonverbal modes of expression. Finally, following discussion and feedback, group members were encouraged to add nonverbal messages to their "pleasure lists" of session two.

Beginning with this session, couples were taught to apply the skills learned in the first half of the workshop to areas of decision making and conflict. Identification of actual or potential trouble spots in the relationship was aided through the use of a small chart (the "tune-up checklist") which each partner completed.

The tune-up checklist was designed to help couples identify potential conflict areas and articulate their concerns in these areas. An example of the checklist is presented in Figure 9-1.

FIGURE 9-1   Tune-Up Checklist

Finances (how much to save, paying bills, etc.)
    Specify a.
             b.

1. Decision based on
   a. mutual discussion/negotiation
   b. tradition
   c. withdrawal
   d. skill/ability
   e. control of resources
   f. coercion
   g. other (specify)

2. Would like decision to be based on
   a. mutual discussion/negotiation
   b. tradition
   c. withdrawal
   d. skill/ability
   e. control of resources
   f. coercion
   g. other

3. Negotiation/discussion necessary?   Yes   No
   a. Date
      Topic
      Outcome
      Satisfaction—Very High 1 2 3 4 5 6 7 Very low
      Next exchange

In this example the general area of finances was the focus (there are similar checklists for a number of problematic areas, i.e., sex, personal habits, leisure activities, household responsibilities, etc.). Completing their checklists independently, each spouse first attempted to specify the relevant issue or issues within this general area. Then, utilizing guidelines 1 and 2, spouses further pinpointed the source of discord. More specifically, spouses determined how they believed decisions were made in this area and further, how they would have liked them to be made. Written definitions of the six methods of decision making were given to the couples and discussed. Brief definitions are given in Figure 9-2.

FIGURE 9-2   Brief Definitions of Decision Methods Used by Couples

1. Mutual discussion/negotiation: decision based upon joint discussion of various issues involved, alternatives considered, resolution agreed upon.
2. Tradition: decision based on beliefs about who *should* perform certain activities, e.g., men should handle finances.
3. Withdrawal: decision by default, that is, one spouse withdraws or refuses to participate in decision-making process.
4. Skill/ability: decisions based on belief that one spouse has greater skills than the other in the particular area, and that this skill is important for decision making. For example, arithmetic skill might determine who makes financial decisions.
5. Control of resources: occurs when decisions are determined by the ownership or control of a perceived crucial resource, e.g., control of the checking account.
6. Coercion: decisions based upon aversive methods, e.g., screaming, threats.

Following completion of this part of the checklist, spouses compared checklists for possible "weak spots" in their relationship. Brief discussion of differences led to the decision of whether further, more focused discussion was necessary (question 3). If it was, couples were encouraged to make an appointment for a message exchange time and to rate their satisfaction with their communication.

Negotiation.   Once problematic areas had been defined, guidelines for negotiation of problems were taught and rehearsed. A structured negotiation procedure was presented over the next two sessions. As in all the problem-solving procedures covered, a heavy emphasis was placed upon the integration of previously learned communication skills with the problem-solving framework.

Information gathering.   The first part of the negotiation process involved the gathering of sufficient information about the problem. The following five points were intended to serve as guidelines in this information gathering process: (1) recognition of the problem; (2) description of the nature of the problem; (3) reasons for labeling the situation a problem; (4) past effects upon the relationship; (5) future implications of nonresolution for the relationship.

For brevity of presentation, one couple will be followed through these five steps.

Leader B: Before we can effectively deal with a problem, that is, resolve it satisfactorily for both partners, we must first recognize it as a problem. Gathering information is the first step. Gathering information helps define the problem, define the boundaries, establish the seriousness, etc. Five points are usually dealt with in the process of gathering information: First, *recognition of the problem*, one or both individuals must perceive the existence of the problem; the "tune-up checklist" can be helpful here. Second, the *nature* of the problem needs to be described. Here the type and boundaries of the problem are identified. For example, visits from in-laws during holidays. Specificity is very important in this step. Third, *reasons for labeling* the situation as a problem should be ascertained, for example, when X happens, then I feel bad. Fourth, *past effects* on the relationship should be identified. As an example, when they left we both were short with each other; we seemed to argue a lot. Here it is important to stick with observable behavior. Fifth, the *future implications* for the relationship need to be discussed. As in the example above, if our in-laws continue to come, chances are that we will continue to argue and not enjoy our holidays.

Following questions, a couple was picked to try out this procedure. It is usually important at this point to remind couples not to try to solve the problem, but just gather information.

Tom: The problem that we have selected to work on is where to live. We have been renting for about nine years and we are considering building or buying soon, in about a year. We disagree on where to live. I want to live in the country, Robin wants to live in the city. We both have good arguments, but we can't decide.

Robin: We both agree that it is a problem, we both selected it on the "tune-up checklist." In terms of the type and boundaries of the problem, it's about where to live. We agree on the type of house, everything but where. The difficulty now is between us. Our child is too young to care.

Tom: The difference is a problem for a couple of reasons. At this point, we are slowing down in our progress, we are not looking for land or at open houses, we don't talk about it as much. We used to be excited, now it's getting to be a bother to talk about it. If we don't get this resolved we may not ever get settled. We will never develop equity, our income taxes will continue to go up. There are all sorts of reasons that it is a problem.

Robin: I agree, it's a real sore spot. As far as past effects on our relationship, it hasn't been too much of a problem. Either we couldn't afford to buy, or we weren't staying in one place long enough for it to pay off. Just recently it has become a problem. Before, we used to daydream about owning a house. I think Tom has already described the future implications for us very well. It's a hardship on us. It has reduced our enthusiasm for owning a home. It will begin to cause us loss of money in terms of taxes and equity. At this rate we will have to keep renting.

Generation of alternatives.   This step, extrapolated from the problem-solving literature (for example, see D'Zurilla and Goldfried, 1973), is based on the idea that quantity (of alternatives) breeds quality. Couples were encouraged to be creative and suspend all judgment while formulating a written list of possible solutions.

An example of generating alternatives is illustrated by the following:

Leader A: The next step in problem-solving is generating alternatives; you try to identify as many alternative solutions as possible. At this point do not try to select a solution or one alternative. Come up with as many alternatives as possible. When doing this, it is helpful to follow two rules: One, suspend judgment, don't reject an alternative because it seems impractical or weird. Two, remember quantity breeds quality. The more alternatives that you are able to come up with, the greater your chances of finding workable solutions. Some strange or unusual alternatives can often be combined to form a reasonable solution.

Leaders modeled examples of alternatives to problems they are working on. Couples were given five minutes to work with partners and develop their own list of alternatives.

Tom: This is the list Mary and I have come up with. You know it's very hard not to cancel out impractical solutions—I mean alternatives. Well, here they are:

Live in the city.
Live in the country.
Live at the edge of town.
Live on quiet cul-de-sac or dead-end street with large yard.
Rent house in the country to see if Robin likes it.
Continue to rent.
Move to a smaller city.
Live apart, one in the city, one in the country.
Rent house in town to see if Tom likes it.

Robin: Even the possible good solutions have problems. We are hard to please.

Leader A: Any other suggestions?

Bob: Take turns, live in the country for two or five years or whatever, then move into town, or vice versa.

Leader A: Good. Any others?

Sounds like you have a good list. You can enlarge the list by combining some of the alternatives. As you review your list, see if you can't add more.

Session Five

In this session, couples continued to learn how to negotiate solutions to problematic situations. Topics covered included evaluation of alternatives, development of plans, evaluation of the plans, and contracting.

Evaluation of alternatives.   After an adequate list of alternatives was generated, couples were asked to decide which "solutions" were most likely to resolve the conflict relative to costs incurred. To assist couples in this task, "consequence cards" have been developed. The following dialogue illustrates how these cards were used in the group.

Leader B:	Once you have developed a fairly complete list of alternatives, the next step is to evaluate them. This is the third step of negotiation/problem solving. To assist you in selecting the best alternative, we have developed some guidelines for sifting out the alternatives that are less likely to lead to satisfactory outcomes.
	Obviously, a quick "once over" of the list will probably eliminate some alternatives right away. In some cases, an alternative will be out of the question because of high cost or because it is unethical and/or illegal. Go through your list and together decide which alternatives you can eliminate. Now that you have eliminated some of the more obviously inadequate alternatives, you are faced with the dilemma of selecting from those remaining. One approach that can be useful is to look at the consequences of each of the remaining alternatives for ourselves, our partners, and for others. The "consequence cards" we are now passing out are designed to help you with this task.

FIGURE 9-3   Example of Consequence Card

Solution	for self	for partner	for others
1			
2			
3			

These cards provide a framework for each of you to evaluate or rate the consequences of your remaining proposed alternatives. To use the cards, independently rate each proposed solution on a scale from −3 (least satisfactory) to 0 (neutral) to +3 (most satisfactory). Two advantages of this approach to solution selection are that it encourages you to consider the points of view of all persons involved in the situation, and it aids in the process of compromise.

After rating the alternatives, the decision to use one solution over another equally plausible solution can be reached by how you and your partner scored the alternatives. Generally, we will look for level of agreement and how positively (mutually satisfying) each solution is viewed. The solution in which there is the greatest and the largest amount of mutual satisfaction will be our first choice.

The following four solutions were rated by Tom and Robin. Their respective ratings:

FIGURE 9-4

Tom

Solution	for self	for partner	for others
1. Rent on cul-de-sac	−1	0	0
2. Rent in country	+2	0	+1
3. Buy in country	+3	−1	+1
4. Buy in city	−2	+3	0

Robin

Solution	for self	for partner	for others
1. Rent on cul-de-sac	+1	−1	0
2. Rent in country	0	+2	0
3. Buy in country	−3	+3	−2
4. Buy in city	+2	−3	+2

Robin: According to the guidelines, solution number two (rent a home in the country) is the best immediate solution.

Tom:	Yeah, it is still renting; we haven't solved that problem. The plan would call for renting a certain number of months, then making a decision. I agree it's the best solution. It would give us a chance to weigh the pros and cons of making a more permanent decision.
Leader B:	In this case, this is probably the best solution, neither partner rates it as negative, they generally seem to agree on the consequences for themselves, each other, and others.
Robin:	This would have to be an intermediate plan, it doesn't solve the renting problem.
Tom:	Absolutely, it's a good test, a first step in making the decision. I might see some big problems with living in the country, or you might fall in love with it.
Leader A:	Both of you have done well. More important, you've noticed the importance of having a more specific plan, and the need to evaluate your plan. We will discuss these topics next.

Planning.   The evaluation stage terminates when the couple decides upon an appropriate solution. In the planning stage the focus shifts from *what* is a viable alternative in the present situation to *how* we can get there. In other words, couples move from goal formation (specificity) to operationalization, how to reach the goal. As in the previous step, couples again began by generating alternative plans and then evaluating these plans (via consequence cards).

This stage is often overlooked by couples, especially when the solution seems to be a relatively straightforward task, e.g., our example of renting a house in the country. However, even these seemingly simple solutions can become problematic if the means to accomplish them are not specified. Continuing with our example, Tom's task was to check the "for rent" listings of a variety of papers each day, while Robin was to register with the local rental service. In addition, they agreed to spend Saturday mornings exploring different locales which met their definition of "country."

In summary, although the consequence cards should not be used in a rigid manner (i.e., where there is obviously no need), they are often useful in developing a plan of action to reach the agreed upon solution. Once a plan is determined, the steps involved in its implementation must be specified for optimum benefit.

Follow-up evaluation of plan and solution.   Couples were encouraged to hold periodic evaluation sessions to assess how well their plans were working and/or how satisfied they were with their solutions. Message exchange sessions (discussed earlier) are ideal times for reviewing progress on various problems. If the plan and solution appeared to be working as intended, couples were reminded to use the time as an opportunity to give each other positive feedback on their ability to work together to solve their relationship problems.

Contracting.   Formalization of the final plan in terms of a contract (initially written) was presented. Various forms of contracts were presented and advantages and disadvantages discussed. Basically, contracts increased the likelihood of implementation of the plan by helping couples specify the reward/cost ratio for their individual efforts in the plan and thus allowing for appropriate compensation.

For example, a plan for handling finances might include one partner paying all the monthly bills. Performance of this task may "earn" a backrub from his/her partner. As can be seen from the example below, couples were encouraged to exchange *positive* behaviors for completing their agreed upon tasks.

I, Frank, agree to spend two hours every other Tuesday evening for paying bills and taking care of financial concerns. In return I will be excused from drying dishes the following evening and will receive a 20-minute backrub from Mary.

Two types of contracts were discussed with the group: those in which the problem centered around behaviors in each other, e.g., lack of affection and more time together, and those which were viewed as a mutual problem by the couple, e.g., finances, relatives. Finally, negotiation and evaluation clauses were presented as essential to every contract. The contract developed by Tom and Robin illustrates these concepts:

Contract Example

Tom and Robin
Selecting a Site of Residence

This will be the first in a series of mutually negotiated contracts; the goal of this and following contracts is to move toward an equitable decision regarding the site of our residence.

I, Robin, agree to a six-month trial of living in a rented home in the country. During this time I will develop and maintain a daily diary of pros and cons (subjective) regarding country life.

I, Tom, agree to a six-month trial of renting a home in the country. Further, I agree to develop a daily diary of pros and cons (subjective) regarding country living.

Completion of diary of pros and cons will earn one dinner out every other week (choice of place on a rotating basis).

Completion of the above will earn Robin a new outfit of her choice.

Completion of the above will earn Tom a two-day fishing weekend in June at a resort.

If I do not complete my specific task, then I, Robin, will wash the car once every two weeks for three months.

If I do not complete my task, then I, Tom, will do weekly shopping every Saturday for two months.

This contract will be evaluated in two weeks at a message exchange to review the progress made in renting a country home. Thereafter, the contract will be evaluated at one-month intervals from the date of signing.

The contract will be modified at the end of six months. Also, it can be renegotiated at any time if one or both parties deem this necessary.

Signed: _____

Date _____   _____

Prior to formulating their own contracts, couples were presented with a hypothetical situation and requested to develop a contract together to help implement the agreement. This procedure often clarifies the principal difficulties couples have in writing contracts, e.g., lack of specificity, overuse of negative sanctions, etc. In addition, this exercise gave the group leaders another opportunity to stress the importance of integrating communication skills with problem-solving procedures.

Session Six

The last session elaborated upon some of the topics taught previously and continued to teach couples how to apply their communication skills to problematic areas of their relationships. Particular emphasis was given to methods and practices which facilitated the maintenance and transfer of skills learned.

Mixed messages. Nonverbal communication was reintroduced in session six with a discussion of "mixed messages," i.e., messages with incongruous verbal and nonverbal content. Two types of mixed messages were modeled by the groups leaders:

1. messages which express ambivalent feelings:
    H: "Do you want to go to the party tonight?"
    W: "Yeah . . . sure."
2. negative messages expressed with neutral or positive words:
    W: "How do you like that painting I hung over the fireplace?"
    H: (sarcastic tone, sour facial expression) "It's a real beauty, all right."

Following discussion of the difficulties involved in interpreting such messages, couples were encouraged to suggest constructive responses. A useful procedure for most couples has been to *check out* and *clarify* their message interpretation. Paraphrasing and requesting further information about the ambiguous aspects of the message were two skills used to check out and clarify.

In order to practice these skills, couples took turns expressing a mixed message written on cards passed out by the group leaders. Group feedback and, when necessary, prompting, were also utilized.

This interpretation demonstrates mixed messages and how they can be checked out and clarified:

Ann: How do you feel about my mother staying the weekend?

Bob: (sigh, frown, shrugged shoulders) It's okay with me.

Ann: Your facial expression and sigh seem to contradict your verbal message. It is not clear to me what you really want. What is your preference?

Bob: I was actually hoping to spend the weekend with you. I wanted to go cross country skiing and sleep in late. Although I like your mother's visits; this weekend I would rather have to ourselves.

Ann: How about if she comes next weekend?

Bob: Sounds good! (smiling)

Another example using role reversal to clarify mixed messages:

Sandy: How do you like my new outfit?

Richie: (studying Sandy modeling new outfit) It looks good on you.

Sandy: I'm not sure what you mean. Let me show how your response hit me. It looks okay, but the price detracts from its appearance.

Richie: (laughing) You said it. I was actually saying that we are tight on money this month, and while the outfit is nice, really quite flattering, I wished you would have waited a couple of weeks.

Intrapersonal communication.   Since message interpretation is essentially a cognitive process, it is important to devote some attention to the *intrapersonal* aspects of communication. In the CSW, the group leaders illustrate the influence of intrapersonal communication on relationship interaction by role playing a couple trying to deal with a "taboo topic." A taboo topic is a subject which evokes high anxiety in one or both spouses. Furthermore, taboo topics are often characterized by implicit couple contracts *not* to discuss a particular subject. As a result of not being made explicit or discussed, these topics remain sources of ambiguous messages and conflicts.

Taboo topics are usually associated with poor intrapersonal communication. For example, if sex is a taboo topic for a couple, they will tend to engage in a great deal of intrapersonal communication around this subject. These self-generated messages might deal with the anticipated negative consequences of disclosing a certain sexual fantasy to one's partner. Such thoughts—although unexpressed and unvalidated—may in turn evoke severe self-critical messages. To the extent that similar message exchanges occur within both spouses, interpersonal communication about sex becomes very difficult.

Couples were taught to deal with intrapersonal messages from a similar conceptual framework used to clarify interpersonal communication. Briefly, the criteria of accuracy, openness, and quality were modified in the following manner. *Accuracy* now refered to the degree of correspondence between one's interpretation and "reality." For example, when lying in bed, a spouse might interpret the attempt of his/her partner to get more comfortable as an indication of sexual rejection.

Openness in intrapersonal communication was operationalized as the extent to which a person "checks out" his/her messages with other sources of information. A simple example of openness would be whether a spouse asks for feedback from his/her partner concerning his/her intrapersonal message ("Are you trying to move away from me?"). Intrapersonal message *quality* reflected the relative proportion of self-generated messages that were interpreted as positive or negative. That is, a spouse who engaged in a high proportion of self-critical messages related to his/her sexual behavior would be characterized as having poor intrapersonal communication in this area.

Utilizing this framework, couples were taught to improve their intrapersonal message exchanges. Space does not permit a detailed account of training in this area, but procedures taught included discriminating thoughts and feelings; assessing their logical adequacy; checking-out in relation to partner's behavior; generating alternative messages based on the accuracy, openness, quality categories; and providing oneself with positive feedback for using communication skills.

In addition to the above, couples discussed previous high anxiety topics, how they dealt with them intrapersonally, and the effects of their self-generated messages on their interpersonal behavior. Finally, alternative methods of dealing with these topics were demonstrated and practiced.

Dealing with new conflicts. In order to encourage transfer of skills learned in the workshop to future conflicts which might arise, couples were presented with a series of conflictual situations. This exercise attempted to simulate potential conflicts by presenting each partner with a written description of an interpersonal situation slanted to lead them to different conclusions about what should be done.[3] Couples role played these situations utilizing

---

[3] Some of these situations were drawn from the Inventory of Marital Conflicts (Olson and Ryder, 1973).

whatever skills they deemed necessary to resolve the issue. Once again, feedback was provided by other group members. An important aspect of this procedure was the practice it provided couples in dealing with the conflict at the issue-specific level.

Session six and the CSW program were ended with a review of the skills presented and practiced. Emphasis was directed at reinforcing continued use of skills acquired during the program. Further, participants were encouraged to use specificity skills in discussing relationship issues and to avoid "global" problem solving.

DISCUSSION

The CSW is not a therapeutic program for highly distressed couples. Early experience revealed that couples experiencing serious discord (as evidenced by Locke-Wallace scores of below 80) had difficulty with many of the exercises. This in turn detracts from the learning of other group members.

Couples of limited educational backgrounds might have difficulty with some of the concepts and terminology of the CSW. In these situations the instructors must simplify the language used and spend additional time on key concepts such as specificity. Such modifications might require the addition of an extra session or longer sessions. (More recent experience with these groups suggests that lower socio-economic groups can indeed participate in these programs.)

Another difficulty occasionally encountered involved hesitancy on the part of one couple to engage in role plays. The methods used to overcome the reticence were to re-emphasize the importance of role plays for learning, additional modeling by the leaders, modeling by a couple who are not hesitant to role play and praise by the leaders. Alleviation of another couple's anxiety over role playing was also achieved by initially having a leader play the part of one partner or having the couple role play privately.

CONCLUSION

The training program described in this chapter represents a growing interest in the use of groups as a form of treatment for couples (for example, see Liberman, Wheeler, and Sanders, 1976). While the efficacy of a group approach to couple therapy has some empirical support (c.f., Cookerly, 1976; Witkin, 1976), many potential benefits remain unexplored. For example, our understanding of how group variables (e.g., interaction patterns) can be utilized to facilitate change has only begun to be systematically investigated (see Rose, 1977, Chapter 10).

The above situation suggests the general need for increased research in at least three areas: identification of group variables associated with positive treatment outcome; the most effective means of manipulating those variables; and the evaluation of treatment approaches which integrate specific intervention strategies (e.g., behavioral techniques) with principles of group dynamics. Progress in these areas seem prerequisite to significant advances in a group approach to marital treatment.

REFERENCES

Bienvenu, M. J., Sr. Measurement of Marital Communication, *Family Coordination*, 1970, *1*, 26-33.

Cookerly, J. R. Evaluating different approaches to marriage counseling. In Olson, D. H. (ed.), *Treating Relationships*. Lake Mills, Iowa: Graphic, 1976.

D'Zurilla, T. R. and M. R. Goldfried. Problem solving and behavior modification. In Cyril M. Franks and Terence Wilson (eds.), *Annual review of behavior therapy, theory and practice*. New York: Brunner-Mazel, 1973.

Edleson, J. L., S. L. Witkin and S. D. Rose. Recruitment process: An initial investigation, *Journal of Social Service Research*, Spring, 1979.

Hartman, R. R. A behavioristic approach to communication: A selective review of learning theory and a derivation of postulates. *Audio Visual Communication Review*, 1963, *11*, 155-90.

Hops, H., T. A. Wills, G. R. Patterson and R. L. Weiss. Marital interaction coding system. In *Training and reference manual for coders*. Marital Studies Center, University of Oregon, 1975.

Liberman, R. P., E. Wheeler and N. Sanders. Behavioral therapy for marital disharmony: An educational approach. *Journal of Marriage and Family Counseling*, 1976, *2*, 383-95.

Locke, H. J. *Predicting Adjustment in Marriage*. New York: Holt, Rinehart, and Winston, 1951.

Locke, H. J. and K. M. Wallace. Short marital adjustment and prediction tests: Their reliability and validity. *Marriage and Family Living*, 1959, *21*, 251-55.

Olson, D. H. and R. G. Ryder. Inventory of marital conflict (IMC): An experimental interaction procedure. *Journal of Marriage and the Family*, 1973, *32*, 443-48.

Patterson, G. R. and H. Hops. Coercion, a game for two: Intervention techniques for marital conflict. In R. E. Ulrich and P. Mountjoy (eds.), *The experimental analysis of social behavior*. New York: Appleton-Century-Crofts, 1972.

Patterson, G. R. and J. B. Reid. Reciprocity and coercion: Two facets of social systems. In C. Neuringer and J. Michael (eds.), *Behavior modification in clinical psychology*. New York: Appleton-Century-Crofts, 1970.

Rose, S. D. *Treating children in groups.* San Francisco: Jossey-Bass, 1972.

―――. *Group therapy: A behavioral approach.* Englewood Cliffs, N.J.: Prentice-Hall, 1976.

Stuart, R. B. Behavioral remedies for marital ills: A guide to the use of operant interpersonal techniques. In A. S. Gurman and D. G. Rice (eds.), *Couples in conflict: New directions in marital therapy.* New York: Aronson, 1974.

Weiss, R. L., H. Hops and G. R. Patterson. A framework for conceptualizing marital conflict: A technology for altering it, some data for evaluating it. In L. A. Hamerlynck, L. C. Handy, and E. J. Mash (eds.), *Behavior change.* Illinois: Research Press, 1973.

Witkin, S. L. *Development and evaluation of a group training program in communication skills for couples.* Dissertation Abstracts, University of Wisconsin, Madison, 1976.

―――. *Communication skills training for couples: A comparative study.* Paper presented at the 11th Annual Convention of the Association for the Advancement of Behavior Therapy, Atlanta, 1977.

――― and S. D. Rose. *Communication skills workshop.* Paper presented at 15th Annual Meeting of the Council on Social Work Education, Philadelphia, 1976.

―――. Communication skills workshop. In S. D. Rose (ed.), *Group therapy: A behavioral approach.* Englewood Cliffs, N.J.: Prentice-Hall, 1977.

―――. Group training in communication skills for couples: A preliminary report. *International Journal of Family Counseling*, 6, 1978, 45-56.

STEVEN P. SCHINKE and STEPHEN E. WONG

10

group in-service training
for paraprofessionals
in group homes

This chapter describes the organization, implementation, and evaluation of a behavioral in-service training program for paraprofessional staff in two group homes for mentally retarded adults.[1] To provide a context for the program, we first review the background and need for empirically tested paraprofessional staff training models. Following a conceptual overview of the interventive model, we detail our in-service training program and evaluative procedures, closing with a discussion of the program's major strengths and limitations.

BACKGROUND

Recent state and federal mandates for deinstitutionalization of mentally retarded persons have identified the group home as one residence alternative (see, for example, President's Committee on Mental Retardation, 1976). Group homes

[1] Preparation of this chapter was supported in part by National Institute of Child Health and Human Development Grant No. HD-02274, Maternal and Child Health Project No. 913, Social and Rehabilitation Service Grant No. 84P-00170/0-02, and the Washington State Association of Group Homes. The authors express appreciation to Courtenay Bell and Ellen Ryerson of the Washington State Association of Group Homes, to Lewayne Gilchrist who served as a group leader, and to the student assistants who served as observers.

249

give retarded persons an opportunity to develop and maintain close ties with family and friends, to work or attend school in the community, and to test out independent living skills in a protected environment. A recent review by Whittaker and Small (1977) details the myriad therapeutic advantages of a group setting. Kugel and Shearer (1976), in a Presidential Committee report on residential services for mentally retarded persons, suggest that group homes offer great potential for all but the most profoundly handicapped of the six million retarded persons in the United States. Unfortunately, development of group home in-service training programs and techniques has not paralleled current deinstitutionalization trends.

Paraprofessional group home staff are often ill-prepared to meet the needs of their resident population in this demanding job. High staff turnover, low job satisfaction, and staff frustration are frequently attributed to lack of proper in-service training. A survey of the 43 certified group homes for mentally retarded persons in Washington State (Bell, 1976) revealed staff training and education as the second highest priority for improvement (a better salary scale was first). As a result of these data and other anecdotal information, a federation of Washington State group homes for mentally retarded persons asked the Child Development and Mental Retardation Center at the University of Washington to develop and implement an in-service training program for group home staff.

A number of studies propose and validate a technology for paraprofessional staff working with institutionalized retarded persons. Spradlin and Girardeau (1966) and Warren and Mondy (1971) recommend operant techniques for the care and treatment of retarded children and adults. A study by Baker and Ward (1971) showed staff trained in reinforcement procedures, when compared to untrained staff, significantly reduced retarded children's self-destructive behavior in a state school. Roos and Oliver (1969) compared attendants taught in a behavioral workshop, teachers using traditional special education techniques, and a control condition of no unusual staff attention in developing retarded children's self-help skills. Independent ratings on the Vineland Social Maturity Scale showed children assigned to attendants from the behavioral workshop realized significantly greater gains than children in either of the other two conditions. Grabowski and Thompson (1972) demonstrated that behaviorally trained technicians in a hospital for retarded persons can train residents in adaptive self-care behaviors, and positively affect a wide range of problematic responses. The operant model, therefore, seems well suited for staff working with institutionalized retarded children and adults.

The behavioral approach appears equally appropriate for paraprofessional staff in group homes for retarded persons. Group homes encountered in the present study, however, required an in-service training model substantially different from those used in institutions. Most Washington State group homes for mentally retarded persons are converted private residences or small motels, and have fewer than 20 residents and three to four staff. Floor plans and organizational structures of the homes usually resemble a familial setting with common resident and staff living quarters. Staff and residents frequently interact in diverse situations, often developing close personal attachments. In many homes, residents and staff are regarded, and referred to, as "children" and "parents." Because of the physical structure and interactional patterns of this setting, the present investigators selected a staff-resident interventive model originally developed for family interactional work by Patterson and his colleagues (Patterson, 1974, 1976; Patterson, Cobb, and Ray, 1973; Patterson, Reid, Jones, and Conger, 1975). Patterson's model assumes a reciprocity of behavior between parents and children. Simply stated, parents and children learn how to maximize their own rewards and respond contingently to the behavior of others. For the present program, Patterson's family interaction model was directly translated to the group home milieu.

This family-based model was introduced to group home staff through a variety of behavioral training techniques. Specific techniques, empirically validated by previous research, included positive reinforcement (Bricker, Morgan, and Grabowski, 1972; Clark, Macrae, Ida, and Smith, 1975; Montegar, Reid, Madsen, and Ewell, 1977), role playing (Gardner, 1972), modeling (Gladstone and Spencer, 1977), behavior rehearsal (Carpenter and Baer, 1976; Gladstone and Sherman, 1975), feedback (Kirigin, Ayala, Braukmann, Brown, Minkin, Phillips, Fixsen, and Wolf, 1975; Panyan, Boozer, and Morris, 1970; Panyan and Patterson, 1974; Quilitch, 1975), cueing (Fielding, Errickson, and Bettin, 1971; Iwata, Bailey, Brown, Foshee, and Alpern, 1976), and contingency contracting (Schinke and Rose, 1976). The resulting in-service training program (cf. Schinke, in press; Schinke and Wong, 1978) was delivered on-site, in the home normally occupied by each staff, with small groups serving as the training context. Both in-service groups followed identical training agenda and protocols. Ongoing measures of group process, and a multivariate assessment battery, administered at pre- and posttraining, evaluated the in-service training program's impact.

METHOD

Group Homes and Staff

Training was conducted in two Washington State certified group homes for mentally retarded persons, located in the Seattle area. Participation in the program was based on staff requests for in-service training in job-related skills. The two homes differed in physical layout, staff to resident ratio, and staffing pattern. Home 1 was staffed by a live-in married couple, employed five days a week in the care of eight residents. This home was a two-story house indistinguishable from other single family residences on the block. Home 2, staffed by one male and two females, had 20 mentally retarded residents. Home 2 had a motel floor plan, with living quarters in separate units of an elongated building. The only common facility was a central dining room. The staff in Home 1 worked a five-day week, with a relief staff covering the other two days. Home 2 had a different staffing pattern, with one staff member living on the premises, one frequently staying overnight, a third person working in the home only during the day shift, and no additional relief staff.

The two Home 1 staff were 27 and 28 years of age. The woman had three years of college and was not employed outside the group home; the man had a high school degree and was currently employed at a state institution for retarded persons. The Home 2 staff were 19, 24, and 31 years old. The two women had high school educations, the man had a BA in psychology. All five full-time staff, in both homes, participated in training groups.

Training Procedure

Staff in both homes received eight 90-minute group sessions in applications of behavior modification with retarded persons. Two master's level social work students provided group leadership and training for all sessions in both homes. Each leader had taken a minimum of two courses in behavior modification; neither had previously led such an in-service training group. Group leaders attempted to achieve a balance between presenting information and maintaining staff interest. Therefore, one became the primary leader, with responsibilities of organizing and presenting a major portion of didactic material. The second was designated coleader, with tasks of observing staff members for attentiveness, eliciting questions and answers, and reinforcing staff participation. The coleader regulated instructional rate, and to a lesser degree, assisted in disseminating information.

Group leaders' sensitivity to a workable ratio of information exchange and staff involvement was further enhanced when the senior author provided feedback after an observational visit, midway through the program. This observer/evaluator took data on leader actions that appeared to hinder or advance the instructional process. Group process and content were evaluated for adherence to prepared agenda and optimal interactive patterns. Leaders were monitored for frequency of positive comments, attention to staff, interruptions, relative rates of speaking, and potentially distracting idiosyncratic behaviors. Immediately following the training session, the observer gave specific and constructive feedback to leaders on their ingroup behavior. For example, the leader was alerted to his habit of referring to the retarded adults in the home as the "little residents." In another instance, the coleader was shown her high frequency of speaking relative to the leader and other group members. This pattern appeared to prevent her from increasing staff participation, an important part of her coleader role. Such performance feedback helped improve the quality of subsequent training sessions.

Training rationale and organization. The in-service group training program was forced to deal with unique constraints of the group home setting, including on-duty status, limited time, and diverse educational backgrounds of staff. Organization of training, therefore, tried to meet these needs by conducting the groups in the home, keeping sessions brief, and beginning instruction at a nonabstract level. In addition, all training focused on principles and techniques with immediate relevancy for problems routinely encountered in the group home. Training proceeded on a logical progression of topics and specific assignments designed to gradually increase staff skills, and eventually foster independence from leader direction.

The eight 90-minute sessions reflect this progression and can be grouped into subsections covering four central concepts. In the first subsection, session one, the leaders gave a brief overview of the in-service program, including an explanation of the social learning theory approach to human behavior. In addition, leaders asked staff for a tour of the group home, and spent approximately half the session discussing day-to-day routines and problems of group home living. These activities seemed to foster a warm and trusting relationship with the staff, especially important since a successful group process appeared more likely if the leaders respected the staff members and understood the demands of their job. Session one also delineated the formal training contract. This contract outlined staff responsibilities of attending all meetings and staying current with readings and other assignments, and trainer responsibilities of consulting, furnishing instructional materials, and making midweek monitoring telephone calls to the group home. The second subsection, comprised of sessions two through five, covered basic behavioral concepts and techniques, most applied to a resident behavior-change project. The third subsection, session six, gave additional methods and initiated a second resident behavior-change project, planned largely by staff members with limited group leader consultation. The fourth subsection, sessions seven and eight, focused on transfer of change principles and maintenance of modified resident behaviors. Exercises in this last subsection encouraged staff self-sufficiency in planning, implementing, and evaluating behavioral programs.

General session format. Regardless of subsection or session number, all weekly meetings shared common structural components. A standard format permitted continuity throughout the program and gave each group meeting a task-oriented framework. Written weekly agenda enhanced the mutual understanding of group leaders and members about session topics and the order in which these topics were discussed. These detailed outlines of the meetings also served as technical notes and reminders for staff future reference. The common process components across all meetings and incorporated in all agenda were:

Review of previous week. A brief review of activities, assignments, and problems related to the training program was the first item on every agenda, except for the initial meeting. The review component gave group leaders an opportunity to praise staff for assignments and tasks completed, and to identify and deal with specific concerns and problems encountered during the week or given on the previous meeting's evaluations. For example, session two began with a review of session one's reading assignment, including clarification of unclear concepts and terms. Next, the group discussed other homework assignments from session one, with leaders giving social reinforcement for attempts to apply session content. Leaders then advanced to content relevant to session two. Thus, the review period often provided a natural transition from "old" business to the current session's "new" business.

Presentation of new concepts, principles, and techniques.   New material was introduced by readings, didactic presentation, case examples, role plays, and behavior rehearsals. All readings were drawn from copies of *Families* (Patterson, 1975), given to the staff. Short reading assignments involved 10 to 15 pages each week. As previously noted, one group leader took primary responsibility for preparation and delivery of a didactic overview of new concepts. This presentation was brief, usually no more than ten minutes, minimizing abstract theoretical material in favor of principles and techniques germane to the group home setting and population. Case examples, drawn from clinical cases seen at the Child Development and Mental Retardation Center or the professional literature, described practical applications of new techniques. Next, group leaders role played a hypothetical situation demonstrating a technique or principle. Finally, staff were encouraged to "try out" the techniques in a behavior rehearsal. Group leaders provided coaching and social reinforcement throughout this process. Presentation and suggested uses of new material set the foundation for *in vivo* application in the group homes.

Resident behavior-change project.   The planning, implementation, and evaluation of a resident behavior-change project applied the behavioral principles and techniques covered in the group training program. Each week, group leaders helped staff use their learning to assess or change the behavior of selected residents. Staff members were advised to choose residents with problems of a relatively uncomplex nature to increase the probability of early success with the social learning approach. The behavior-change project progressed in small steps over the eight-week training program to allow staff familiarity with each phase of a "model" interventive regimen. These steps included behavior specificity, assessment, baseline data collection, intervention planning, intervention implementation, and data-based evaluation of project effectiveness. All steps of the behavior-change project were operationalized, negotiated, and developed into weekly assignments carried out between group meetings.

Group process surrounding one resident behavior-change project is illustrated by recounting the second training session in Home 1. Ingroup tasks were to specify a target behavior and to develop a monitoring plan for a group home resident. In this instance, staff selected asking-for-approval responses of Judy (whose complete behavior-project is detailed later). Staff first verbally described Judy's annoying behavior. To gain a better understanding of Judy's behavior, group leaders asked one staff member to act out Judy's approval-asking behavior while the other staff member role played herself responding to Judy. From this demonstration, leaders and staff specified the verbal and nonverbal components of Judy's requests, subsequently developing a viable monitoring plan.

Weekly contract.   Each program-related activity planned for the crucial interval between meetings was written into a weekly contract. Typical weekly staff assignments included readings in *Families* and implementation of an assessment or interventive phase of the resident behavior-change project. An important feature of the weekly contract was the arrangement of a between-meeting telephone call from one of the group leaders. This call provided leaders an opportunity to monitor assignment completion, and give appropriate reinforcement and consultation. Staff completed each contract in duplicate so group leaders had a copy to refer to for the telephone call and to review for the next session.

A case example of the contracting process is again provided by Home 1's behavior-change project with Judy. Figure 10-1, showing the form and content of a weekly contract for session two, outlines the major responsibilities for staff member Karen. After negotiating with the other staff member and group leaders, Karen notes that she is responsible for observing and counting instances of Judy's asking for approval when completing routine tasks during lunch preparation. This behavior-in-a-situation was first role played in group so all involved parties understood clearly the target behavior. Karen's weekly contract also shows her intention to read two chapters in *Families*. Finally, Karen indicates that she has arranged with group leader Lewayne to report on her contracted activities during a midweek telephone call.

Session evaluation.   Each weekly meeting ended with a brief written evaluation of the process and content of that session. The evaluation form asked group members for specific feedback on group training techniques, behavioral principles, readings, and other topics covered in the session. This information enabled group leaders to alter subsequent sessions to more closely approximate group needs. Summarized evaluation results were given to the group during the review component of the next week's agenda.

A frequent use of weekly evaluation results was clarifying ambiguous behavioral principles or jargon. In one set of weekly evaluations, for example, Home 2's staff reported not understanding the meaning or relevance of the Premack Principle. Apparently, leaders had assumed too quickly that staff comprehended fully this concept after a brief description and case example.

WEEKLY CONTRACT

Staff Member's Name _Karen D._____ Date _March 7, 1977_____

Group Meeting Number __2_____

1. This week I will observe ___Judy_____ and will count the following:

_____
            behavior   under these conditions   at this time

Asking for approval   When she has finished   Lunch making
_____ _a small job in the_____
_____ _kitchen (buttering bread_____
_____ _or cutting carrots)_____

2. This week I will work with _____ and will use the following procedures when the
    following behaviors occur:

_____
        work with these   under these   with these
        behaviors   conditions   procedures

_____

_____

_____

_____

3. This week I will read the following materials:

_Chapters 4 and 5 in Families (pp. 33-57)_____

_____

4. I am expecting ___Lew____ to call on __Thursday___ at __7:30 P.M.___
    I will report any project problems or changes at that time.

___Karen D._____   ___Luwayne D. Gilchrist___
Staff Member   Group Leader

FIGURE 10-1   Sample Weekly Contract for Group Home 1

Justifying subsequent clarification with the previous week's evaluation addressed the need for further explanation of the principle and validated group members' feedback.

WEEKLY SESSION CONTENT

Session content followed the progressive stages of a behavioral interventive program. Each session was organized around a central theme, and reiterated that theme throughout the agenda by techniques previously described. The following outline represents an overview of major thema, topics, assignments, group process, and problems identified in each of the eight weekly group sessions.

Session One

Thema: Overview and introduction to the in-service training program.

Topics: Program mechanics; distribute books, complete forms and set time for subsequent meetings. Introduction to assessing behavior in an environmental context; defining antecedents, behaviors, and consequent events.

Assignments: Choose a resident and select three behaviors as targets to increase and three to decrease.

Group Process: Because much introductory material had to be covered, session one was dominated by leader didactics. In addition to introducing the behavioral content, leaders also needed to preview the format of in-service training, including readings, behavior-change projects, weekly contracts, and session evaluations.

Problems: Leaders' verbal dominance, and perhaps the novelty of in-service training, resulted in low levels of staff participation in both group homes during session one. Following suggestions by Rose (1972, 1977), leaders dealt with this problem in subsequent meetings by reinforcing staff verbalizations and incorporating frequent staff role plays into each agenda. For example, staff were asked to role play themselves and group home residents in routine interactions. After these techniques were implemented, group leaders noted marked increases in staff participation and general interest in both homes.

Session Two

Thema: Behavioral specificity and base rates.

Topics: Importance of preinterventive data collection. Counting procedures, rate computation. Monitoring plan for selected resident and behavior.

Assignment: Monitor one behavior of target resident for the coming week.

Group Process: Session two yielded premonitoring reports on potential behavior-change projects, and thus involved lively discussions of group home residents. In fact, leaders expended considerable energy keeping these discussions on-task and directed toward establishing monitoring plans. As leaders learned more about group home life and pressures on staff, and as staff gained a better understanding of the training model, less time was devoted to issues peripheral to in-service goals.

Problems: In Home 1, leaders quickly realized that one staff member had not read the *Families* assignment. It seemed that reading was usually attempted during prime-time television, and this stimulus almost always won the greater share of attention. Through an extemporaneous negotiation process, the staff member agreed to begin reading 30 minutes before the television was turned on, resulting in contingently reinforcing the less preferred reading behavior.

Session Three

Thema: Graphing, reinforcement, and fundamental interventive techniques.

Topics: Graphing principles and applications; frequency, cumulative, and rate graphs. Reinforcement and extinction.

Assignments: Complete reinforcement survey hand-out for selected resident and continue base rate monitoring.

Group Process: Detailed reviews of the week's monitoring experiences occupied most of this session in both homes. Fortunately, such discussions gave way to respecifying targeted behaviors, and to preliminary interventive planning. Although staff were eager to begin intervention, leaders emphasized the need for an additional week of baseline data collection.

Problems: The midweek call to Home 2 revealed that the behavior slated for monitoring had spontaneously remitted. Staff and leader therefore identified an alternate target response and monitoring plan so a full week's data were not lost. This action proved wise since the original targeted behavior was not manifested again throughout the in-service program.

Session Four

Thema: Contingency contracting.

Topics: Review of reinforcement survey. Contingency contracting exercise, practice, and application to resident behavior-change project.

Assignments: Implement contingency contract with resident; continue monitoring.

Group Process: Staff in both homes were very active in contingency contracting and interventive planning exercises comprising the bulk of session four. Leaders were pleased to note that staff already showed good theoretical and working grasps of most behavioral principles covered. Staff in Home 1 especially enjoyed developing a point system and contingency contract for their first behavior-change project.

Problems: Enthusiasm for creating elaborate interventive programs occasionally obscured the exercise's original intent. For example, Home 2's staff planned a series of complete contingency contracts that appeared far beyond the understanding of the targeted severely retarded resident. Despite staff protests, leaders advanced a much simpler plan. This active leadership role tapped a crucial decision: Should interventive plan creativity override the pragmatics of implementation? Or, should a dull but feasible plan be foisted on staff? Compromising between these extremes resulted in extensive negotiations, but yielded a plan satisfactory to both staff and leaders.

Session Five

Thema: Additional interventive techniques.

Topics: Shaping, modeling, and cueing.

Assignments: Continue intervention plan, revising if necessary. Continue data collection.

Group Process: Session five witnessed preliminary reports on intervention programs and subsequent program modifications. For example, staff in both homes lowered their intermediate goals for resident behavior change, thus extending their estimates of the total time necessary to achieve terminal goals. Additional interventive techniques covered in this session readily offered a number of opportunities for staff role plays and behavior rehearsals.

Problems: The only notable group problem in either home during session five was considerable off-task talk in Home 2. But, since group leaders were disinclined to lower the overall frequency of staff participation, they did not intervene.

Session Six

Thema: Restatement of behavioral methodology; second resident behavior-change project.

Topics: Ground rules for effective behavior-change programs including problem definition, specificity, counting procedures, recording, contracting, and evaluation. Application of behavioral paradigm to a second resident.

Assignments: Continue first resident project and data collection. Specify new target behavior and monitoring plan; begin monitoring.

Group Process: Reviewing the major components of the behavioral approach and negotiating a second resident behavior-change project interdigitated well in session six. As the group covered each step in developing behavioral programs, they were able to immediately apply most steps to the new behavior-change project. This process also evidenced staffs' increased expertise since group leaders provided limited substantive consultation on the second behavior-change project.

Problems: Off-task talk continued in Home 2, apparently sanctioned by leaders' tacit approval of this behavior during the previous session. Leaders dealt with the problem in the present session by telling staff that although most off-task content was interesting, important agenda items were being jeopardized. Leaders then suggested that off-task issues be tabled until after the agenda was covered, thereby making these reinforcing discussions contingent upon on-task behavior. Once again, the Premack Principle demonstrated its clinical utility.

Session Seven

Thema: Advanced interventive techniques, transfer of change, and maintenance procedures. Intervention plan for second resident project.

Topics: Overcorrection and response cost. Development of interventive plan for second resident. Overview of principles, and application of transfer and maintenance of change to first resident project.

Assignments: Begin interventive plan and continue monitoring with second project. Continue monitoring and begin transfer of change program with first resident behavior-change project.

Group Process: Session seven's agenda, with considerable new material, required leaders to devote over half the session to didactics. The remaining time was taken up with discussion and negotiation around resident behavior-change projects. Staff in both homes initially developed rather complex contingency contracts for the second project, possibly due to a desire to experiment with additional behavioral principles. Leaders again cautioned against becoming seduced by the elegance of an interventive plan, stressing the need for simple, straightforward plans, especially in the early stages of intervention.

Problems: Low frequency of staff participation, similar to session one's process, represented a major problem in session seven. Leaders addressed this problem by eliminating three agenda items, favoring more opportunities for staff involvement. The strategy seemed effective, as the latter half of the session showed increased staff participation.

Session Eight

Thema: Summary of program and transfer of change with staff.

Topics: Review of resident behavior-change projects, with emphasis on generalizing principles to other behaviors and residents. Discussion of how potential future problems will be handled; application of "soft" (no data) behavioral programs. Utility of social learning theory in day-to-day routine. Plans for telephone follow-up, and future home visits for "refresher" course.

Assignments: Continue with all projects. Send in copies of collected data in two weeks.

Group Process: This session focused on preparing staff for a nontraining environment supportive of continued resident behavior-change projects. Working toward this end, leaders proposed that the behavioral approach be viewed not as a set of immutable laws applied in a lock-step sequence, but rather as a common sense approach to everyday interactions. To validate such a conceptualization, leaders and staff examined their interactions with coworkers, friends, and family. Indeed, the husband-wife staff team in Home 1 even developed a reciprocal contract specifying how they could spend more time together! In both homes, Session 8 ended with light refreshments, convivialities, and well-deserved off-task talk.

Problems: Perhaps because of a shared motivation to end the training program on a pleasant note, no problems were encountered in either group home.

Measures

Efficacy of the eight-session group training program was evaluated on two levels. Group process data gave ongoing and summative evidence of the viability and success of training sessions. Outcome data, collected at pre- and posttraining, provided self-report and objective parameters of change in staff and resident behavior. Since these evaluation sources represent important components of a behavioral approach to in-service group training, they will be described in detail.

Process measures.   Leaders' subjective evaluation of weekly group interaction was one measure of session quality. Additional quantitative process indices were: meeting attendance, staff responses on weekly end-of-session evaluations, and rate of assignment completion. Finally, staff progress and success with resident behavior-change projects were viewed as an integral part of process evaluation.

Outcome measures.   The second level of evaluative measures examined staff and resident behavior before and after the in-service training program. All pretraining measures were taken two to three weeks before the first group session; all posttraining testing was completed within two weeks of the last training session. Outcome measures included:

1.   A 25-item objective knowledge questionnaire, covering basic social learning theory principles, behavioral techniques, and terminology.

This questionnaire, developed from similar instruments reported by Becker (1971) and Patterson et al. (1975), was completed by all staff at pre- and posttraining.

2. A job satisfaction rating form, as developed by Brayfield and Rothe (1951). Each staff member completed one form at both assessment periods.

3. An attitude checklist (Becker, 1960) measuring each staff member's impressions of selected group home residents. At pretraining, staff were asked to complete checklists relative to three residents designated as potential behavior-change project candidates; at posttraining, staff were asked to address checklist responses to the same three residents.

4. Observational data on resident-staff interactions were also collected. An observational system described by Schinke and Wong (1977a) gave real-time indexing for frequency, duration, and latency of 29 resident and staff behaviors. Two trained observers collected four hours of observational data at each of two pre- and posttraining group home visits. All visits commenced shortly before the dinner hour to increase the likelihood of resident-staff interactions. During these two-hour periods, each observer recorded two 12-minute time samples of behavior for each of the three residents chosen by staff as potential behavior-change project candidates. Observers coded staff behaviors only when staff members interacted with the target resident.

RESULTS

Process Measures

Group interaction.   All staff in both homes attended all group meetings. This 100 percent attendance rate enhanced group interaction during the sessions and the quality of the entire training program. Group leaders' notes on group process, as itemized earlier under individual sessions, generally indicated a positive and smooth information exchange with staff members. Except for occasional problems of low staff participation and off-task talk, leaders saw the group process as a consistently effective in-service training vehicle.

Weekly evaluations.   Group members' satisfaction with session process and content was derived from weekly evaluations. Responses relative to session content, readings, and training techniques were rated on a three-point scale of positive, neutral, and negative. Summed ratings for the two staff of Home 1 across all evaluations were 83.3 percent positive, 16.7 percent neutral, and none rated negative. Responses on all evaluations for Home 2's staff were rated 82.4 percent positive, 11.8 percent neutral, and 5.8 percent negative. Additional staff feedback from both groups supported these data as representing a positive and satisfying experience with the training process.

Assignment completion. Behavioral clinicians working with groups have used percentage of assignments completed as a quantitative measure of successful delivery and use of session information (Rose, 1972, 1977; Schinke and Rose, 1977). Similarly, in this study, summed completed assignments were divided by the total number of tasks given in all weekly contracts. In Home 1, 23 of 25 assignments, or 92 percent, were completed; in Home 2, 28 of 38 assignments, or 73.7 percent, were completed as contracted. Assignment completion rates confirmed leaders' impressions of the two groups: Home 1 was well prepared and coordinated with the training schedule; Home 2 was less dependable with assignments, and seemed distracted by events external to the program. Leaders attempted, albeit unsuccessfully, to deal with Home 2's low rate of assignment completion by giving copious social reinforcement for completed portions of an assignment. The lack of tangible reinforcers for improving staff performance was often frustrating.

Resident behavior-change projects. Group Home 1. Home 1 staff selected Judy, a 31-year-old female resident, for the first behavior-change project. Judy assisted in many of the household duties in the home, but habitually asked for praise after finishing each task. She typically said, "I did it, I did it, dear," waited for approval from the staff, and repeated the phrase if not praised. Judy disturbed the home staff as she requested approval for completing routine chores clearly within her repertoire. After staff recorded baseline rates of the targeted behavior, group leaders and staff jointly designed an interventive plan. First, leaders asked staff to develop an interventive plan based upon their newly acquired knowledge of behavioral principles. When staff were unable to suggest a concrete plan, the leaders proposed one. Finally, staff modified the leaders' plan to fit Judy's preferences and capabilities, resulting in the following:

Behavior-Change Plan for Judy

1. When Judy completes the following simple tasks and asks for approval, we will ignore her. (Special procedures to be used when Judy insists on receiving approval are: restatement of the new conditions; leaving the room.)

2. When Judy completes the following simple tasks and does not ask for approval, we will compliment, praise, and reward her with a point placed on her record sheet.

SIMPLE EXPECTED TASKS

   a. Following basic instructions.
   b. Fixing the lunches.
   c. Getting food items in the kitchen.
   d. Making coffee or tea.
   e. Folding clothes.

The extinction and point reinforcement program (points exchangeable for the privilege of buying a desired item) was implemented for three weeks. The number of requests for approval following an expected task, recorded during baseline and treatment conditions, are shown in Figure 10-2. Staff were highly satisfied with the results of the project, which reduced the frequency of a behavior previously resistant to change. A telephone follow-up, conducted approximately five months after the beginning of the project, indicated a near zero rate for this behavior.

A second behavior-change project with another resident aborted during the second week of baseline when the resident was transferred out of the home. But staff were able to specify and monitor the chosen behavior of noncompliance, successfully demonstrating a working knowledge of the techniques and principles involved.

Group Home 2.   The first resident behavior-change project in Home 2 focused on grooming behaviors of Georgina, a 26-year-old female. Specifically, staff wanted Georgina to comb her hair more frequently. A monitoring plan identified four daily time periods for spot checks of Georgina's grooming. One week's baseline data are given in Figure 10-3, upper graph. Georgina's treatment plan designated that stars be awarded each time her hair was combed during a spot check. Three stars earned in any single day could be exchanged for an extra soft drink in the evening, or veto power over choice of evening television programs. Project results indicate an initial increase in frequency of hair combing, eventually returning to base rate level. Staff suggested that the program had lost its effectiveness because rewards in the treatment plan had lost their reinforcing

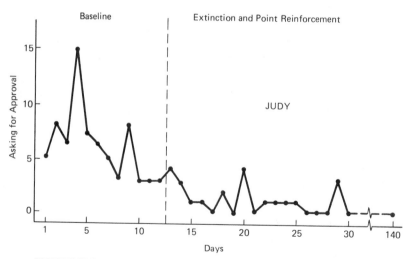

FIGURE 10-2   Resident Behavior-Change Project in Group Home 1

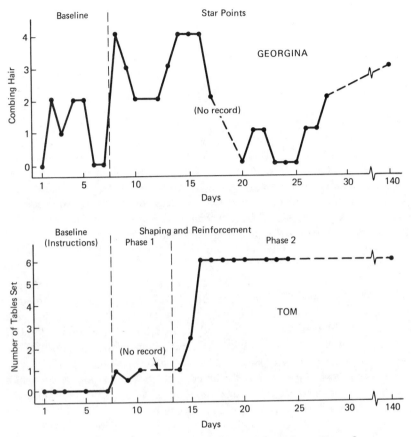

FIGURE 10-3   Resident Behavior-Change Projects in Group Home 2

value. The project was discontinued when a staff search for more powerful rewards proved unsuccessful.

A second project launched with Georgina was also abandoned. The presenting problem selected by the staff in this effort was Georgina's toileting hygiene. This behavior had high nuisance value to the staff and other group home residents. A series of unworkable monitoring plans led to the reluctant rejection of Georgina as an ideal behavior-change project resident.

The third behavior-change project in Home 2 focused on Tom, a 35-year-old male. Staff considered Tom the most severely retarded resident in the home, and wanted to involve him in productive activities. Tom was the only resident in the home not helping with any of the daily household chores, but staff questioned his ability to learn these tasks. Staff proposed training Tom to place napkins and silverware on the six dining room tables before each mealtime. One female staff member had tried to train Tom in this particular job, previous to the in-service program. She was asked to continue her old instructions for one week to determine the behavior's baseline rate. One week's baseline data, shown in the lower graph of Figure 10-3, revealed no recorded occurrences of the target behavior. To establish and strengthen this behavior, the group developed a program of successive approximations and cueing, using food and praise as reinforcers.

When a staff member attempted to work on the shaping procedure with Tom, however, the resident became highly excited, laughed repeatedly, and engaged in stereotypic handbiting. After the third day of intervention, staff stopped the program because of other priorities in the home and their feeling that "the program wasn't working." Despite this initial frustration, leaders urged staff to reinstitute Tom's program. Leaders suggested a bit more patience with the project, and posited that Tom was temporarily overstimulated by increased staff attention and the novelty of shaping procedures.

Reestablishment of intervention in Phase 2 is shown in the last interval of the lower graph of Figure 10-3. In this phase, staff routinely left drinking glasses as cues for the proper spots for place settings; and Tom would put napkins and silverware near those cues on all the tables. The data recorded in Phase 2, showing Tom setting all six tables every day, represented the first time staff had ever observed Tom helping with a household chore. Home 2's staff were most pleased with these results. At a follow-up telephone call, staff reported that Tom was correctly setting silverware and napkins on all dining room tables at every meal. During the follow-up contact, staff also reported Georgina's hair combing had stabilized to three times daily (when staff intermittently monitored), even though intervention was not consistently used.

Outcome Measures

Knowledge questionnaire. All knowledge questionnaires were blind scored by totaling the correct number of responses out of a possible 25. Total mean scores for all staff in both homes, at pre- and posttraining, are shown in the top graph of Figure 10-4. Although staff in both homes began training with similar mean scores, Home 1's staff scored over six points higher at posttraining than did staff in Home 2. The staff from Home 1 learned the behavioral principles and terminology so well, in fact, that their posttraining mean is 90 percent of a perfect score. Gains for Home 2 are not nearly as impressive since their posttraining mean is 64 percent of a perfect score.

Job satisfaction rating. All staff job satisfaction rating sheets were scored according to guidelines given by Brayfield and Rothe (1951). This procedure yielded one positive or negative two-digit score for each staff member at pre- and posttraining. Group home means, shown in the middle graph of

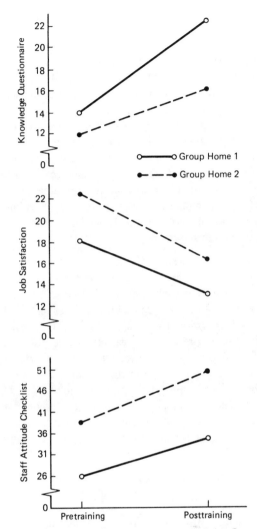

FIGURE 10-4 Group Home Mean Scores for Knowledge Questionnaire; Job Satisfaction Rating; and Staff Attitude Checklist at Pre- and Posttraining Assessment

Figure 10-4, indicate parallel decreases in job satisfaction over the eight-week training period.

Attitude checklist. A total of three staff attitude checklists relative to each targeted resident, at both pre- and posttraining assessments, were scored on the six subscales identified by Becker (1960). Composite mean scores across all targeted residents and all six subscales are given in the bottom graph of Figure 10-4. Staff in both homes show an upward trend, pre- to posttraining. Home 1's staff rated their residents consistently lower than Home 2's staff, at both assessment periods.

Behavioral observation data.   Interrater agreement.   Agreement between the two observers was checked for 12 of the 48 recorded 12-minute observation periods in both group homes. Two agreement coefficients were computed on observed resident-staff interactions. The first coefficient indicated agreement on the frequency of categorized resident-staff interactions. Observer agreement occurred when both observers concurrently coded a resident-staff interaction within the same category. A coefficient of 79 percent resulted from dividing agreements by agreements plus disagreements. The second coefficient designated agreement on the latency of staff responses in any interactive sequence with the targeted resident. Observer agreement, computed by dividing the smaller recorded latencies of one observer by the larger latencies of the other observer, averaged 73 percent across all sessions.

Resident-staff interactions.   All 29 resident and staff behaviors were divided into three categories identifying the responses as positive, negative, or neutral, similar to a format described by Wahl, Johnson, Johansson, and Martin (1974). The data were next transformed into staff-response indices with a procedure reported by Durward and Whatmore (1976). These investigators describe an observational study in a residential treatment center for retarded children, in which the nature and frequency of resident-staff interactions were viewed as measures of treatment quality. One such measure, the reinforcement index, identified the proportion of appropriate child behavior followed by staff contact.

The present study developed an analogous outcome measure of staff positive responses to substantively meaningful resident positive responses. This index, the ratio of contingent staff reinforcement, was computed by the formula:

$$\frac{\text{Total occurrences of positive resident behavior}}{\text{Total occurrences of positive resident behavior}}$$
$$\text{followed by positive staff responses}$$

A second index, made possible by the continuous real-time recording system, gave an additional measure of staff reinforcement by quantifying the immediacy of each staff response. This index, the mean latency of contingent staff reinforcement, was computed by the formula:

$$\frac{\text{Total latency of staff positive responses}}{\text{Total frequency of staff positive responses}}$$
$$\text{to resident positive behaviors}$$

Table 10-1 shows the ratio and the mean latency of contingent staff reinforcement for both group homes at pre- and posttraining observational periods. These data indicate that staff in both homes were more frequently positive to resident positive behaviors after in-service training than before training. Values given for reinforcement latency show Home 2's staff taking longer in delivering renforcement than Home 1's staff at both assessment periods. Pre- to posttraining change scores show Home 1 increasing their reinforcement latency and Home 2 decreasing on the same measure. This inconsistent movement is difficult to interpret, but does not negate the importance latency may represent in the evaluation of reinforcer effectiveness.

TABLE 10-1   Ratio and Mean Latency of Contingent Staff Reinforcement for Both Group Homes at Pre- and Posttraining Assessment

	HOME 1		HOME 2	
	Pretraining	*Posttraining*	*Pretraining*	*Posttraining*
Ratio of Reinforcement	.28[1]	.32	.15	.24
Mean Latency of Reinforcement[2]	10.30	14.11	29.87	27.00

[1] All values are based on 21 12-minute observation sessions.
[2] Latency is the number of elapsed seconds from the onset of resident behavior to the onset of staff behavior.

DISCUSSION

The purpose of this chapter was to describe the rationale, procedures, and effectiveness of an in-service program for training paraprofessional group home staff in the appropriate use of a variety of behavior management skills. The in-service training program was composed of eight 90-minute in-home, group sessions led by two social work graduate students. Process and outcome measures indicate that the training was favorably received by group home staff, correctly applied to group home residents, and resulted in positive changes in self-report and objective parameters of staff behavior.

Individual evaluative measures suggest that instruments directly related to the in-service training program were more sensitive to positive changes than those tangentially measuring staff perceptions or performance. For example, resident behavior-change projects indicated that interventive plans carried out by staff were effective. Staff behavioral knowledge, another measure of program impact, showed increases for both staffs. Attitude checklists, again directly related to the program since staff completed these relative to residents involved in behavior-change projects, also indicated positive movement for both homes, pre- to posttraining. Job satisfaction ratings, only vaguely related to in-service training, decreased for both homes over the two assessment periods. A study comparing responses of trained and untrained group home staff on this instrument, however, found job satisfaction tended to decrease over time for all staff members (Schinke and Wong, 1977b). The final assessment instrument, observed resident-staff interactions, measured generalized changes in group home behavior as a result of specific interventive projects with targeted residents. Pre- to posttraining increases on this instrument, in both homes, suggested an improved ratio of positive responses to adaptive resident behaviors after the training program.

Future in-service training programs for paraprofessional group home staff working with special populations should focus on important areas only touched upon by the present study. Results from this report suggest that staff who volunteer for in-service training may not require special contingencies motivating them to participate. Additional research, however, could compare the relative success of staff motivated in training by material incentives, compensatory time away from the job, and social rewards. Investigation of differences between staff trained in-home and those trained out-of-home represents another area of research potential. Finally, the efficacy of groups led by indigenous staff or previously trained paraprofessionals warrants further inquiry. The limited successes documented in the present report should furnish guidelines for clinicians and researchers working in this challenging area.

REFERENCES

Baker, B. L. and M. H. Ward. Reinforcement therapy for behavior problems in severely retarded children. *American Journal of Orthopsychiatry*, 1971, *41*, 124-35.

Becker, W. C. The relationship of factors in parental ratings of self and each other to the behavior of kindergarten children as rated by mothers, fathers, and teachers. *Journal of Consulting Psychology*, 1960, *24*, 507-27.

―――――. *Parents are teachers: A child management program.* Champaign, Ill.: Research Press, 1971.

Bell, C. W. *Working in group homes.* Unpublished manuscript, Washington State Association of Group Homes, Seattle, 1976.

Brayfield, A. H. and H. F. Rothe. An index of job satisfaction. *Journal of Applied Psychology*, 1951, *35*, 307-11.

Bricker, W. A., D. G. Morgan, and J. G. Grabowski. Development and maintenance of a behavior modification repertoire of cottage attendants through T.V. feedback. *American Journal of Mental Deficiency*, 1972, *77*, 128-36.

Carpenter, C. J. and D. M. Baer. Teaching the trainer―Descriptive feedback and corrective practice: An experimental analysis. Paper presented at the meeting of the Association for Advancement of Behavior Therapy, New York, December 1976.

Clark, H. B., J. W. Macrae, D. M. Ida, and N. R. Smith. The role of instructions, modeling, verbal feedback, and contingencies in the training of classroom teaching skills. In E. Ramp and G. Semb (eds.), *Behavior analysis: Areas of research and application.* Englewood Cliffs, N.J.: Prentice-Hall, 1975.

Durward, L and R. Whatmore. Testing measures of the quality of residential care: A pilot study. *Behaviour Research and Therapy,* 1976, *14,* 149-57.

Fielding, L. T., E. Errickson, and B. Bettin. Modification of staff behavior: A brief note. *Behavior Therapy,* 1971, *2,* 550-53.

Gardner, J. M. Teaching behavior modification to nonprofessionals. *Journal of Applied Behavior Analysis,* 1972, *5,* 517-21.

Gladstone, B. W. and J. A. Sherman. Developing generalized behavior modification skills in high school students working with retarded children. *Journal of Applied Behavior Analysis,* 1975, *8,* 169-80.

Gladstone, B. W. and C. J. Spencer. The effects of modeling on the contingent praise of mental retardation counselors. *Journal of Applied Behavior Analysis,* 1977, *10,* 75-84.

Grabowski, J. and T. Thompson. A behavior modification program for behaviorally retarded institutionalized males. In T. Thompson and J. Grabowski (eds.), *Behavior modification of the mentally retarded.* New York: Oxford University Press, 1972.

Iwata, B. A., J. S. Bailey, K. M. Brown, T. J. Foshee, and M. Alpern. A performance-based lottery to improve residential care and training by institutional staff. *Journal of Applied Behavior Analysis,* 1976, *9,* 417-31.

Kirigin, K. A., H. E. Ayala, C. J. Braukmann, W. G. Brown, N. Minkin, E. L. Phillips, D. L. Fixsen, and M. M. Wolf. Training teaching-parents: An evaluation of workshop training procedures. In E. Ramp and G. Semb (eds.), *Behavior analysis: Areas of research and application.* Englewood Cliffs, N.J.: Prentice-Hall, 1975.

Kugel, R. B. and A. Shearer (eds.). *Changing patterns in residential services for the mentally retarded* (rev. ed.). Washington, D.C.: U.S. Government Printing Office, 1976.

Montegar, C. A., D. H. Reid, C. H. Madsen, Jr., and M. D. Ewell. Increasing institutional staff to resident interactions through in-service training and supervisor approval. *Behavior Therapy,* 1977, *8,* 533-40.

Panyan, M., H. Boozer and N. Morris. Feedback to attendants as a reinforcer for applying operant techniques. *Journal of Applied Behavior Analysis,* 1970, *3,* 1-4.

Panyan, M. C. and E. T. Patterson. Teaching attendants the applied aspects of behavior modification. *Mental Retardation,* 1974, *12*(5), 30-32.

Patterson, G. R. Interventions for boys with conduct problems: Multiple settings, treatments, and criteria. *Journal of Clinical and Consulting Psychology,* 1974, *42,* 471-81.

————. *Families* (rev. ed.). Champaign, Ill.: Research Press, 1975.

————. The aggressive child: Victim and architect of a coercive system. In E. J. Mash, L. A. Hamerlynck, and L. C. Handy (eds.), *Behavior modification and families*. New York: Brunner-Mazel, 1976.

————, T. A. Cobb, and R. S. Ray. A social engineering technology for retraining the families of aggressive boys. In H. E. Adams and I. P. Unikel (eds.), *Issues and trends in behavior therapy*. Springield, Ill.: Charles C. Thomas, 1973.

————, J. B. Reid, R. R. Jones, and R. E. Conger. *A social learning approach to family intervention*, vol. 1. Eugene, Ore.: Castalia, 1975.

President's Committee on Mental Retardation. *Mental retardation: Century of decision*. Washington, D.C.: U.S. Government Printing Office, 1976.

Quilitch, H. R. A comparison of three staff-management procedures. *Journal of Applied Behavior Analysis*, 1975, *8*, 59-66.

Roos, P. and M. Oliver. Evaluation of operant conditioning with institutionalized retarded children. *American Journal of Mental Deficiency*, 1969, *74*, 325-30.

Rose, S. D. *Treating children in groups*. San Francisco: Jossey-Bass, 1972.

————. *Group therapy: A behavioral approach*. Englewood Cliffs, N.J.: Prentice-Hall, 1977.

Schinke, S. P. Staff training in group homes: A family approach. In L. A. Hamerlynck (ed.), *Behavioral systems for the developmentally disabled*, vol. 1. New York: Brunner-Mazel, in press.

———— and S. D. Rose. Interpersonal skill training in groups. *Journal of Counseling Psychology*, 1976, *23*, 442-48.

————. Assertive training in groups. In S. D. Rose, *Group therapy: A behavioral approach*. Englewood Cliffs, N.J.: Prentice-Hall, 1977.

———— and S. E. Wong. Coding group home behavior with a continuous real-time recording device. *Behavioral Engineering*, 1977, *4*, 5-9. (a)

————. Evaluation of staff training in group homes for retarded persons. *American Journal of Mental Deficiency*, 1977, *82*, 130-36. (b)

————. Teaching child care workers: A behavioral approach. *Child Care Quarterly*, 1978, *7*, 45-61.

Spradlin, J. E. and F. L. Girardeau. The behavior of moderately and severely retarded persons. In N. R. Ellis (ed.), *International review of research in mental retardation*, vol. 1. New York: Academic Press, 1966.

Wahl, G., S. M. Johnson, S. Johansson and S. Martin. An operant analysis of child-family interaction. *Behavior Therapy*, 1974, *5*, 64-78.

Warren, S. A. and L. W. Mondy. To what behaviors do attending adults respond? *American Journal of Mental Deficiency*, 1971, *75*, 449-55.

Whittaker, J. K. and R. W. Small. Differential approaches to group treatment of children and adolescents. *Child and Youth Services*, 1977, *1*, 1-13.

glossary

Aggressive behavior   behavioral responses to situations that degrade the other person(s) with whom one is interacting (Alberti and Edmons, 1975). Aggressive behavior may accomplish the client's goal in the situation, but will do so at the expense of the other(s) involved. It is sometimes confused with assertive behavior because of the fact that it often facilitates goal accomplishment. (Compare with **Assertive** and **Non-assertive behaviors.**)

Anger starvation   a defensive technique which is used to 'defuse' anger in someone who confronts a client aggressively (Booraem and Flowers, 1975). Client recognizes that the other is angry but suggests that they discuss the situation in a more pleasant setting (e.g., over coffee, in private office, etc.). It gives time for both parties to think over what is happening. See also **Time out.**

Antecedent conditions   the immediate environmental context of a given behavior or set of behaviors. It includes the interaction of such dimensions as time, place, material attributes of the situation, persons present, behavior and personal characteristics of those individuals, and relation of those individuals to the given client. For example, the antecedent condition for John's complaining in the group is any criticism, overt or implied, directed toward any member of the group.

Assertive behavior   a behavioral response to a situation that accomplishes goal of client without imposing unfairly on other(s) involved or putting them down (Alberti and Emmons, 1975). Assertive behavior is the honest but appropriate expression by the client of his or her own will or feelings that tries to take into account the risks involved (including the possible reaction of the other(s) involved).

Baseline   a condition in which data collected during a specified period reflect stability and/or predictability to a degree which allows differences between that data and other data to be discriminated (White, 1971, p. 11). For example, in groups baseline data are collected on average rate of member participation. If these turn out to be low, then intervention follows the baseline period. Baselines are often used in **Time series research designs.**

Behavior modification   the general application of principles of learning and related concepts to human functioning with a change in or maintenance of some aspect of behavior as a goal. Some authors (e.g., Bandura 1969) use the concept of behavior modification interchangeably with behavior therapy. Others suggest (e.g., Rimm and Masters, 1974) that behavior modification stresses operant change procedures while behavior therapy is broader based.

Behavior rehearsal   a procedure that involves a client in practicing a new set of responses in a role-played or simulated situation. The client in behavior rehearsal plays his or her own role and speaks his or her lines aloud as if in the actual situation. Behavior rehearsal usually follows a modeled role play demonstration and is followed by group feedback. (See also **Covert rehearsal** and **Role play.**)

Behavior specificity   the formulation of general complaints of clients in terms of specific behaviors that can be observed directly or indirectly. A general problem or complaint, thus, is translated into a set of problematic behaviors in a specific situation.

Behavior therapy   the process of changing behavior with a set of therapeutic methods based on experimentally established principles of learning. It is further defined as "the beneficial modification of behavior in accordance with experimentally validated principles based upon SR concepts of learning and the biophysical properties of the organism" (Franks, 1969, p. 2).

Behavioral role play test   a simulation test used to evaluate the response to specific situations not readily available for observation. The client is instructed to respond to a set of standardized situations as if he or she were in the situation. The response is recorded (audio-or-videotaped) and later rated by trained observers. The client usually rates his or her satisfaction with and anxiety about each of the responses immediately afterwards.

Booster sessions   a meeting or session set some time after the termination of the regular group sessions to monitor and reinforce the continued work toward long range treatment goals of the group members, as well as to develop new long range goals.

Brainstorming   a procedure in which group members attempt to develop a large number of solutions to a problem. In order to generate creative solutions, all criticism is ruled out and wild ideas are encouraged. These are later evaluated. Brainstorming is often a step in the systematic problem solving process.

Broken record   a technique which consists of repeating what you want in a calm voice until the other person agrees to your request or you work out a compromise. It is a technique that is used only when all other techniques fail (Booraem and Flowers, 1975) since it tends to be viewed as aggressive.

Buddy system   a commonly used extra group procedure in which members are paired off and encouraged to meet outside of the group for the purpose of helping each other complete behavioral assignments. Members may role play, discuss problem situations, encourage each other, or discuss readings. Contact may be by telephone or face-to-face.

Clipping   a technique used in situations in which one is under verbal attack or challenged and it is unclear if the person under attack is right or wrong. It is a method of letting the attacked person clarify an issue before responding; it is not a technique to be used in place of a response. When clipping one answers "yes" or "no" to a question or comment with a minimum of free information, waiting for the other person to clearly specify their issue (see Booraem and Flowers, 1975).

Coaching   a treatment procedure used to aid the client in responding to a problem situation. The trainer or therapist usually reminds the client of wording of selected response or suggests response to problem situation during the behavioral rehearsal. The trainer may sit beside client during role play. Members may also serve as coaches to other members (similar to **Prompting** and **Cueing**).

Cognitive correction   a procedure for providing clients with new information to correct previously held distorted beliefs. For example, in a group of adolescent boys, factual information on masturbation was provided to correct their impression that masturbation was linked with mental illness. This distortion had been causing them considerable anxiety (see also **Cognitive distortion**).

Cognitive distortions   the misperceptions by an individual of his or her environment in the form of thoughts and related images, including what one anticipates is going to happen, how one views past events and how one evaluates one's own behavior and that of others (Gambrill, 1976, p. 112). (See **Cognitive correction**.)

Cognitive restructuring   a technique designed to teach clients to relabel anxiety-eliciting thoughts in a more rational manner (Foreyt and Rathjens, 1978, p. 19).

Cohesiveness (cohesion). See **Group cohesiveness**.

Consequation   process of using a reinforcer that bears a definite arrangement to the emission or repeated emission of a specified response (White, 1971, p. 26), (see also **Reinforcement** and **Contingency**).

Contingency   the temporal or physical conditions under which a response is followed by a positive or negative reinforcing stimulus or the removal of either (White, 1971, p. 26). To dispense a reinforcer contingently is to dispense it following a desired behavior (one whose frequently is to be increased) and to take care that the reinforcer be dispensed only following desired behaviors. Contingency management consists of the contingent presentation and withdrawal of rewards and punishments (Rimm and Masters, 1974, pp. 165-166). A contingent relationship is best described as an if-then statement. *If* you do X, *then* Y will happen.

Contingency contract   an agreement usually written in contract format which includes a statement of what the client will do over a given time period and what the client will receive as a consequence of completing that sequence of behaviors. It may include how the consequence will be delivered and by whom. It may also include what will (not) occur if the behaviors are not performed.

Covert rehearsal   a procedure in which the client is asked to imagine exactly what he or she would do in response to a set of previously stressful stimuli. It is similar to behavior rehearsal except that the rehearsal is carried out in one's imagination (see also **Behavior rehearsal**).

Cue cards   cards with written key words or statements as reminders of important questions or principles one needs to keep in mind while participating in interactive situations.

Cueing   the process of presenting a stimulus to bring forth a desired response (also called prompting). In a role play, one member may cue another to use more eye contact by pointing to his or her eye.

Defensive techniques   procedures for dealing with others who are putting the client under excessive pressure. Such techniques as time out, broken record, negative assertion, and clipping are examples of defensive techniques. They are sometimes viewed by the antagonist as aggressive or manipulative and usually used sparingly.

Degree of discomfort   a client's response to the items on the Gambrill-Richey (1975) Assertion Inventory on a five-point Likert type scale in terms of the client's perceived internal discomfort in each of the situations described by the items.

Desensitization (systematic)   a procedure that focuses on the development of approach responses to feared situations. It often involved confronting the individual with successively more anxiety-producing situations (imagined or real) while in a state of relaxation (see Wolpe, 1969, for more detail).

Extinction   the process of reduction in frequency of a behavior as a function of occurences that are nonreinforced (Rimm and Masters, 1974, p. 312). For example, in the group when leader and members totally ignored Mr. X's sexist remarks, the remarks disappeared (see also **Ignoring, planned**).

Fading   the operation of gradually changing a stimulus, reinforcer, or contingency controlling a subject's performance to another stimulus, reinforcer, or contingency, usually with the intent of maintaining the performance without loss or alteration, but under new conditions (White, 1971, p. 63). In group therapy with children, an example of fading is the gradual elimination of concrete token reinforcement and replacing it with praise during group meetings (see also **Thinning**).

Feedback   a procedure in which an observer gives information to a client about the observer's impression, reaction to, or even description of the client's behavior or attitudes within or out of the treatment situation. **Group feedback** refers to feedback from group members according to prescribed criteria.

Food exchange system   a system of dieting in which the dieter is permitted a certain number of foods in several categories. The dieter may exchange certain categories for others.

Foreshadowing   a procedure in which a therapist or parent talks to an individual (most often a child) about a new situation or difficult event; for example, going to a dentist or seeing a new relative for the first time. It involves telling what the therapist or parent thinks might happen, helping the child to figure out what he or she might do or say, and practicing the responses.

Generalization   the process in which learning occurring in one situation is carried over into other situations. For a discussion of generalization principles as they apply in group therapy, see Rose (1972) and (1977).

Group cohesiveness   the degree to which the members, therapists, and group activities have reinforcing value for each other. It is often measured by rates of attendance and promptness, or by asking members how much they like the group.

Group contract   an agreement between client and trainer, outlining philosophy of training, fees and deposits, group rules, meeting times and places, role of group trainer, and expectations for clients. The group contract is usually in written form and copies are signed by and for client and trainer.

Group feedback   (see **feedback**).

Group productivity   (see **Productivity, group**).

Ignoring (planned)   a procedure in which inappropriate verbal behavior is not answered or reinforced or responded to by plan (see also **Extinction**).

Lesiure counseling   a helping process which facilitates interpretive, affective, or behavioral changes in others toward the attainment of their leisure well-being (McDowell, 1976).

Maintenance of change strategies   activities or strategies oriented toward maintaining the goal level of behavior achieved during the course of treatment for an indefinite period following treatment.

Modeling   the technique of demonstrating a response or chain of responses to a subject and then directing the subject to immediately imitate the performance (White, 1971, p. 98). This treatment procedure usually is included as a step in behavioral rehearsal. In modeling, one member (or leader) takes on the role of another member with a presenting problem and role plays one or more ways of responding to that situation. The member with the problem may then evaluate the response in terms of his or her own comfort, potential effectiveness, and personal style. Modeling may be role played or may occur planned or unplanned in the natural environment.

Monitoring   the process of observing and measuring, that is assigning numerical values to the frequency, intensity, duration, or appropriateness of a behavior. Monitoring may be carried out by the leader, observers, other members, parents, or the client's self. **Self-monitoring** involves monitoring one's own behavior or internal responses. Monitoring may occur in or out of the group.

Monologues   the way one talks to oneself about oneself. Negative monologues are usually self defeating statements or negative self descriptions. Positive monologues are usually self statements of praise or appreciation of one's strengths. Monologues are usually spoken subvocally (i.e. one thinks the statement). However, in the training process, the client may be urged to first say them aloud.

Negative assertion   a defensive technique employed when the client is being attacked and perceives himself or herself to be wrong. The client first admits the error and then follows with a positive self statement (Booraem and Flowers, 1975).

Negative reinforcement   the removal or termination of an aversive stimulus following the emission of the desired response (White, 1971, p. 137). In the group, the leader was negatively reinforced when the members, immediately following the leader's behavior of starting the film, ceased their raucous yelling and running about. The showing of the film was negatively reinforced by the termination of the noise. (See also **Punishment** and **Response cost**.)

Negotiation   a procedure where a person makes his or her interests clear and seeks to clarify those of others with whom he or she is negotiating. The person seeks to obtain the realization of his or her goals, preferably in such a way as to allow for or even to facilitate goal attainment by the other parties with whom he or she is involved.

Non-assertive behavior (also **unassertive behavior**)   a behavioral response to a situation that is ineffective and most often passive from the perspective of the client. The client lets others dominate a situation without expressing own opinion or feeling. He or she does not accomplish his or her own goal for the situation.

Observation code (Rose-Hall)   observational categories derived from Bales' Interaction Code and from clinical experience with assertiveness training groups. Includes variables for who is speaking, for what is said (a 17 category code), and for the receiver of what is said (a member or a leader or the group). Observers record who says what to whom every 10 seconds for five minute units. (Rose and Hall, 1979.)

Operant conditioning   conditioning procedure involving responses which operate in the environment to produce direct consequences. It usually involves a target behavior followed by an environmental response on a predetermined schedule. (See also **Positive reinforcement**, **Responsive cost**, **Punishment**, and **Extinction**.)

Paraprofessional   a staff person or volunteer, usually in the health services, who has limited training or experience, as compared to a fully trained professional, who assumes treatment responsibilities, usually under a professional's supervision.

Positive reinforcement   the occurrence of a positively reinforcing event following the emission of the desired response (White, 1971, p. 138). (See also **Social reinforcement**, **Token economy**, **Contingencies**, **Schedules of reinforcement**.)

Premack principle   the principle of establishing preferred events as contingencies for less-preferred events as a means of increasing future occurrence of the latter. For example, parents may place children's television viewing contingent on school homework completion.

Problem-solving   the process of dealing with a problem systematically. It is "a behavioral process, overt or cognitive in nature, which makes available a variety of potentially effective response alternatives for dealing with the problematic situation and increases the probability of selecting the most effective response from among these various alternatives" (D'Zurilla and Goldfried, 1969).

Productivity group   an index of how effective the group is from meeting to meeting. It is usually estimated by the weekly average of assignment completion by members of the group.

Prompting (see **Cueing**).

Punishment   the presentation of painful or aversive stimulation. In some usages, it also refers to the taking away of positive reinforcers (see **Response cost**).

Rational emotive therapy   a method in which the group members challenge or defend their self-perceptions and assumptions, using group discussion, roleplaying, or confrontation. (Ellis, 1970.)

Recreation therapy   an approach which utilizes recreation programming and activity for rehabilitative and habilitative purposes.

Relaxation training   a set of procedures designed to train a client to produce a state of muscle relaxation. It usually involves instructing the client in alternately tensing and relaxing various muscle groups throughout the body.

Respondent conditioning   a process occurring when a reinforcing stimulus reliably elicits a particular response, but not necessarily increasing the rate of a response which it follows (Whaley and Malott, 1971).

Response cost   the process of withdrawing reinforcers or tokens. For example, in some groups the clients are fined a certain number of tokens for the performance of previously agreed upon, undesirable group behaviors. (Compare with **Punishment**.)

Response latency   the length of time between the discriminative stimulus and the given behavioral response. For example, in groups, if the leader asks a question, the response latency is the time elapsing between the end of the question and a member's response.

Response probability   a five point Likert type scale used in the Gambrill-Richey (1975) Assertion Inventory in which clients rate the likelihood of their performing a given response.

Role play   the process of one person stimulating or acting out a set of behaviors in a situation with one or more other persons in other simulated roles. Role play in behavioral groups is used for assessment, for demonstration, for practice in new behavior, or gaining some perception for a given client of how a person in a given role (other than the client's own) might be feeling. Role play is a major tool in behavior-cognitive group therapy. (See also **Modeling, Behavior rehearsal, Role reversal**.)

Role play test (see **Behavioral role paly test**.)

Role reversal   a message clarification technique for use especially with emotionally tinged, ambiguous messages. The basic sequence followed is: 1) an individual describes some situation and attendent emotions; 2) message recipient takes first person's role and "replays" original message as he or she perceived it; and 3) original message source provides feedback on interpretation.

Schedule of reinforcement   the manner or pattern in which reinforcement is delivered or made contingent upon responding. In groups, the most commonly used schedules are continuous, fixed intervals, fixed ratios, and mixed. However, other schedules also exist (see Whaley and Mallott, 1971, for more detail).

Self-reinforcement   the process in which the client provides either verbal or tangible reinforcement to himself or herself.

Shaping   a general procedure designed to induce the performance of new behavior by the initial reinforcement of behaviors in the individual's repertoire that have some similarity to the target behavior. It further involves the reinforcement of successive improvements in the target behavior.

Social reinforcement   reinforcement that occurs solely in the interaction of two or more persons. If used contingently, it refers, for example, to praise, attention, and approval. In groups it may be delivered by the group leader or members.

Standard deviation   a statistical term used to indicate the range of a given set of data. For example, standard deviation of rates of participation among members at a given meeting is used to indicate the distribution of participation at a given group meeting. The higher the standard deviation, the more uneven the participation among members.

Stimulus control   a stimulus which exerts control over behavior whenever rates or probabilities of responding vary as a function of the presence or absence of that stimulus in the environment (White, 1971, p. 167). For example, a client in a weight loss group reported that he used chopsticks to eat with to lower the speed of eating. The chopsticks served as stimulus control of his speed of eating.

Stop-the-world   a procedure of stopping all activity related to a given child when that child fails to respond to time-out or fails to meet an agreed-upon expectation.

Systematic desensitization (see **desensitization, systematic**).

Subjective units of disturbance (SUDS)   the level of internal discomfort experienced by the client and reported on a scale of zero for no discomfort to 100 for highest discomfort (panic) (see also Wolpe, 1969, pp. 116-17). It is used by the group leader to help the client assess potential problem situations. Often clients will rate situations occurring outside the group or role play situations in the group as to their SUDS level.

Target behavior   a behavior which becomes a focus for planned behavior change. It may be a behavior the client wishes to increase in frequency, decrease in frequency, maintain, use in more appropriate circumstances, eliminate, learn for the first time, or relearn.

Thinning   the process of gradually eliminating specific conditions of the reinforcement until it is eventually eliminated. In children's groups, for example, tokens and social reinforcement are gradually replaced by social reinforcement only.

Thought stopping   a procedure designed to help a client control his or her thoughts (see Wolpe, 1969, p. 110). In this technique, the client is instructed to concentrate on the given persistent thoughts. After several seconds, the therapist suddenly yells "Stop!" After several repetitions, the client is told to stop his or her own thoughts in the same way. And finally, the client thinks "stop!" subvocally in response to the persistent thoughts.

Time out   a technique in assertiveness training designed to obtain time to think about an unclear situation (Booraem and Flowers, 1975). It involves postponing a response to the antagonist until either the antagonist or protagonist has calmed down or had time to think about the issue clearly: e.g., "That's heavy, I need some time to think about that one."

Time-out from reinforcement   the process of eliminating rewarding consequences typically contingent upon a behavior, as well as the removal of all other potentially rewarding stimuli that are present (Rimm and Masters, 1974, p. 163). In a group, if a child is highly disruptive, he or she might be given time-out from reinforcement by being removed to another room or a quiet location within the same room for a period of 30 seconds to two minutes. Although it is not commonly used in groups; in parent-training groups, the parents are often taught the appropriate use of this procedure with their children.

Time series design   a particular research design in which successive observations are made throughout treatments. Variations of this design make possible the determination of whether relevant changes occur following the onset of intervention. (For details of different types of designs used in small group research, see Rose, 1977.)

Token economy   a system or reinforcement in which tokens are administered as the immediate reinforcer and "backed up" later by allowing the tokens to be exchanged for more substantial reinforcers (White, 1971, p. 184). In children's groups, the token economy involves the children earning tokens for successful completion of homework assignments and performance of desirable in-group behavior. These tokens may purchase food, activities, or small toys from a "group store."

Transfer of learning (Training, Behavior)   all the various effects that the acquisition of one response may have on responses that must be acquired or emitted later (Goldstein, Heller, Sechrist, 1966, p. 215). In groups, it refers to the degree to which newly learned patterns of behaviors learned in the group are manifested in settings outside of the group. (See **Generalization**.)

REFERENCES

Alberti, R. E. and M. L. Emmons. *Stand Up, Speak Out, Talk Back!* New York: Pocket Books, 1975.

Bandura, A. *Principles of Behavior Modification.* New York: Holt, 1969.

Booraem, C. D. and J. V. Flowers. A Procedural Model for the Training of Assertive Behavior. University of California-Irvine, unpublished manuscript, 1975.

D'Zurilla, T. and M. Goldfried. "Problem Solving and Behavior Modification." *Journal of Abnormal Psychology,* 1971, *78,* 107-26.

Ellis, A. *The Essence of Rational Psychotherapy.* New York: Institute for Rational Living, 1970.

Foreyt, J. P. and D. P. Rathjen (eds.). *Cognitive Behavior Therapy: Research and Application.* New York: Plenum Press, 1978.

Franks, C. M. *Behavior Therapy, Appraisal and Status.* New York: McGraw-Hill Book Co., 1969.

Gambrill, E. D. *Behavior Modification.* San Francisco: Jossey-Bass, 1977.

_____ and C. A. Richey. "An Assertive Inventory for Use in Assessment and Research." *Behavior Therapy* 1975, *6,* 550-61.

Goldstein, A. P., K. Heller and L. B. Sechrist. *Psychotherapy and the Psychology of Behavior Change.* New York: John Wiley, 1966.

McDowell, C. F. Leisure Counseling: Selected Lifestyle Processes. Eugene, Oregon: University of Oregon, Center for Leisure Studies, 1976.

Rimm, D. C. and J. C. Masters. *Behavior Therapy: Techniques and Empirical Findings.* New York: Academic Press, 1974.

Rose, S. D. *Group Therapy: A Behavior Approach.* Englewood Cliffs, N.J.: Prentice-Hall, Inc., 1977.

_____. *Treating Children in Groups.* San Francisco: Jossey-Bass, 1972.

_____ and J. A. Hall. *Categories for Observation of Assertion Training Group.* University of Wisconsin-Madison, 1978.

Whaley, D. L. and R. W. Malott. *Elementary Principles of Behavior.* Englewood Cliffs, N.J.: Prentice-Hall, Inc., 1971.

White, O. R. *A Glossary of Behavioral Terminology.* Champaign, Ill.: Research Press, 1971.

Wolpe, J. *The Practice of Behavior Therapy.* New York, N.Y.: Pargamon Press, 1969.

index